# Miyazakiworld

# Miyazakiworld

## A LIFE IN ART

Susan Napier

Yale UNIVERSITY PRESS

NEW HAVEN AND LONDON

Yale University Press books may be purchased in quantity for educational, business, or promotional use. For information, please e-mail sales.press@yale.edu (U.S. office) or sales@yaleup.co.uk (U.K. office).

Designed by Sonia L. Shannon.

Set in The Sans type by Integrated Publishing Solutions.

Printed in the United States of America.

Library of Congress Control Number: 2017958122

ISBN 978-0-300-22685-0 (hardcover : alk. paper)

A catalogue record for this book is available from the British Library.

This paper meets the requirements of ANSI/NISO Z39.48-1992 (Permanence of Paper).

10 9 8 7 6 5 4 3 2 1

For Steve: *In memory of a snow-splashed angel*

# CONTENTS

Prologue: In Search of Miyazakiworld  ix

1. *Hametsu*  1

2. Constructing an Animator  16

3. The Joy of Movement  33

4. Ups and Downs: *Castle of Cagliostro*  55

5. *Nausicaä* and "the Feminine Principle"  70

6. Orphans of the Sky: *Laputa: Castle in the Sky*  86

7. Umbrellas in the Haunted Forest: Transcending National and Personal Trauma in *My Neighbor Totoro*  101

8. The Witch and the City: Time, Space, and Gender in *Kiki's Delivery Service*  122

9. *Porco Rosso* Lands in Casablanca  140

10. From Messiah to Shaman: The *Nausicaä* Manga Seeks Light in the Darkness  158

11. The Faces of Others: Boundary Crossing in *Princess Mononoke*  176

12. The Intimate Apocalypse of *Spirited Away*  195

13. The Castle, the Curse, and the Collectivity: *Howl's Moving Castle*  212

**14.** Rich and Strange: The Apocalypse of the Innocents in *Ponyo*  229

**15.** "A Terrible Wind": *The Wind Rises*  246

**16.** Conclusion  260

Notes  265

Bibliography  281

Acknowledgments  289

Index  291

*Color illustrations follow page 124*

# PROLOGUE

*In Search of Miyazakiworld*

On a gray Sunday in February 2014 I drag a little suitcase through rolling woodland paths outside Nagoya, Japan, to visit the sole remnant of the 2005 Aichi World Expo. The twenty-first century's first world's fair (121 nations exhibiting on the theme of humans' harmonious coexistence with nature) drew twenty-two million visitors over six months, but its greatest attraction, and the goal of my journey, wasn't a 3D ride or a woolly mammoth. Rather, it was a replica of a modest country house from the 1988 Japanese animated film *My Neighbor Totoro* (Tonari no Totoro). The house is known as Satsuki and Mei's House in honor of the two young sisters who live in the house with their father while their mother lies ill in a nearby sanatorium. Although the girls do encounter natural wonders around their woodland home, it is less their coexistence with nature that draws so many visitors than their discovery of a large, furry magical being who can fly with the aid of a spinning top and an umbrella, make plants grow exponentially fast, and find lost children. This creature, whom the sisters call Totoro, becomes a quiet, benign presence lending enchantment to their lives.

And, over the years, the lives of tens of millions of animated-film viewers. Totoro, Mei, and Satsuki are characters in one of eleven feature-length animated films directed by Hayao Miyazaki since 1978. Miyazaki officially retired in 2013, at the age of seventy-two, but came out of retirement in 2017 and is now superintending the development of another film, to be released perhaps as early as 2020. Over his tenure, anime, especially Miyazaki's work, has gone from drawing a chiefly Japanese audience to being truly international, touching the lives of so many that, twelve years after the Expo's conclusion, the local prefectural authorities keep Satsuki and Mei's House open. It remains eerily vacant except for prearranged thirty-minute tours, such as the one I'm joining. I'm quite conscious of a strange admixture of the real and the unreal as I plod on through occasional rain showers in the largely abandoned fairgrounds. At the fair's entrance there was nowhere to check my suitcase (full of books and articles in Japanese on Miyazaki), so it gets heavier and heavier until I am finally able to leave it behind an umbrella stand at the house.

What inspires me to visit Satsuki and Mei's House is what has inspired millions in Japan and around the globe, a love of what I call Miyazakiworld, the immersive animated realm that varies delightfully from film to film but is always marked by the director's unique imagination. At my home university in America I teach a seminar on Miyazaki in which I explain to my students that Miyazaki is an auteur—a director whose personal and artistic vision is so strong that each film consistently contains trademarks that make his or her entire work a distinctive cinematic experience. Even some of my students are skeptical at first: "Can an animation director really be an auteur?" they ask.

Yes, he can, as I hope to show in this book. If anything, animators have even more control over their aesthetic product than live-action directors do, and Miyazaki is someone whose detailed artistry extends to the way his characters' hair blows in the wind. This controlling master vision enables Satsuki and Mei's House to be a perfect replica of the one in the movie, based, as it is, on Miyazaki's painstakingly realized drawings. As the tour moves slowly through the house, everyone seems united by a pleasing familiarity. We have all "been here before": in the study of the sisters' archaeologist father, packed with books and artifacts pertaining to Japan's prehistoric Jomon period; in the fully equipped 1950s-style kitchen, where ten-year-old Satsuki proudly makes bento boxes for her father and little sister; in the old-fashioned bath with two tubs—one for rinsing and the other for soaking. It is while taking a family bath that the girls learn a valuable lesson from their father—to laugh and be resilient in the face of darkness—and that almost mystical combination of courage, acceptance, and joy is the emotional core of Miyazaki-world. While Miyazaki's vision has darkened over time, Miyazakiworld is still a realm where hope triumphs over despair.

I FIRST ENCOUNTERED Miyazaki's work more than a quarter-century ago, when I saw *Nausicaä of the Valley of the Wind* (Kaze no tani no Naushika, 1984). A postapocalyptic science fiction fantasy, the film intrigued me partly because of its surreal beauty and its surprisingly nuanced vision of technology, humanity, and nature. Most compelling, however, was the moral complexity of its young female protagonist, Nausicaä, and her interactions with the denizens of her postapocalyptic Earth—human, animal, insect, and plant. They not only showed a thinking person with a subtle, compassionate mind but also evoked a world that was far more multifaceted than a conventional science fiction movie's—or most movies', for that matter.

Nausicaä, named for Miyazaki's favorite heroine in *The Odyssey,* is Miyazaki's alter ego: passionate, angry, judgmental, sentimental, and ultimately apocalyptic, as evidenced in the startling ending of the manga version of *Nausicaä,* a thousand-page epic comic that Miyazaki completed twelve years after the movie. It is hardly surprising that Miyazaki, born into war-torn Japan, should be sensitive to technological and environmental catastrophe, and there is a side of him that imagines world-ending events as cathartic, even purgative. "I want to see the sea rise over Tokyo and the NTV tower become like an island," Miyazaki once told an American journalist. "Money and desire—all that is going to collapse and wild green grasses are going to take over."[1]

Apocalyptic imagery is a staple of much of Japanese animation, but in Miyazakiworld it is often females who lead us through the endtimes. At a time when female characters still tended to be sidekicks or romantic interests in Japanese cinema, Miyazaki conjured up a battery of unforgettable young women: Lana, Nausicaä, Sheeta, San, Chihiro, Ponyo. Often they are associated with nature and the supernatural, expressing the animistic vision that underlies much of Miyazakiworld. And these are only the preteen or teenage heroines: Miyazaki is also one of the few directors in the world who consistently created roles for older women: Dola, Eboshi, Gina, Sophie, and Toki.

Children also constitute a major focus. The director has stated, "The child is proof that the world is beautiful," and in Miyazakiworld, childhood becomes a utopian site, reminding us of what we could be if somehow that innocence were recaptured.[2] Miyazaki's ability to create an entire story through a child's viewpoint in a film such as *Totoro* is a revelation. Remarkably, few animated films (including those of Disney and Pixar), actually have child protagonists. *Totoro* was the second movie I saw by Miyazaki, and Mei and Satsuki, in their believable brightness and brattiness and in their openness to the wonder of both nature and magic, delighted and moved me, ushering me back to my own childhood.

Nostalgia—not only for childhood but in themes of yearning for a lost past, both national and global—also plays out across Miyazaki's films. We discover a ruined Roman city in the director's first feature, *Castle of Cagliostro* (Rupan Sansei Kariostro no Shiro, 1979), while his most recent film, *The Wind Rises* (Kaze tachinu, 2013), ushers us into an exquisitely detailed re-creation of prewar Japan in which technology itself becomes an object of yearning. With nostalgia come darker themes of exile, loss, and trauma that the director also explores. Although they may yearn for home, not all his characters are able to find it, and sometimes home itself is threatened or even annihilated.

But Miyazakiworld adds up to more than apocalypse, empowered female protagonists, believable children, and elegiac or utopian visions. His interweaving of all these elements in an emotionally resonant tapestry makes him an exceptional world builder. Miyazaki deserves his place among the great fantasy world builders, from Lewis Carroll and Jules Verne in the nineteenth century to Tolkien, Rowling, and Disney in the twentieth. Using such animation hallmarks as metamorphosis and surreal or dreamlike imagery, Miyazaki creates imagined empires, sometimes uplifting, sometimes heart-breaking, realms we can walk into, inhabit, and mourn when we have to leave. From scenes of flight through translucent blue skies or underwater glimpses of a surreal sea domain to a far future toxic jungle or a fourteenth-century forest inhabited by gods, his detailed fantasy creations offer alternatives to what he deems an increasingly oppressive reality.

Miyazaki uses his skills as artist and animator to encompass intimate moments and create soaring epics. "We are returning to you something you have forgotten": With this tagline *Totoro* recaptures childhood innocence through precisely observed instances of wonder and delight. In a three-second sequence in *Totoro* an insect climbs up a plant on a spring afternoon, creating a "pillow shot," tiny visual interludes that anime critic Dani Cavallaro notes "invest [the moment] with a sense of thoughtfulness."[3]

On the epic front Miyazaki's blockbuster hit *Princess Mononoke* (Mononokehime, 1997) tackled history, humanity, and environmental apocalypse in a work running longer than two hours and built from tens of thousands of drawings that Miyazaki had done by hand. The film introduced Miyazaki's oeuvre to the West, revealing that animated movies can be much more than simply children's entertainment. *Princess Mononoke*'s violent vision of a world on the brink of ecological disaster resonates all the more in the twenty-first century.

The director's passion extends to a strong antiwar stance. In 2013 I came across a recent publication of *Neppū*, the house journal of Studio Ghibli, the studio that Miyazaki and the director Isao Takahata founded in 1985. Having previously confronted issues such as environmental waste and nuclear damage (especially after an earthquake and the resultant meltdown of a Fukushima nuclear power plant in March 2011), the journal now took aim at a controversy roiling Japanese politics, the question of whether to amend the Japanese constitution to allow for an aggressive military. In a Japan that had been proudly pacifist since World War II, this measure stirred strong emotions across the country, roughly equivalent to the passions stirred by gun control in the United States. But it is difficult to imagine a major Hollywood studio issuing a twelve-page polemic on gun control. The essays in *Neppū* were written by Miyazaki, Takahata, and other colleagues, including Toshio Suzuki, Ghibli's main producer, and Rieko Nakagawa, a children's fantasy writer. Miyazaki in particular took on the difficult issues of war guilt and responsibility to argue against the "stupidity" of war, earning him the fury of some of Japan's right-wing nationalists.

Clearly, Miyazaki is a complicated and passionate man. The Japanese-language books and articles on him and Studio Ghibli would fill a room. They range from discussions of his love of Celtic archetypes, to what Japanese critics call his "mother complex," to his role as a national icon. Overseas, critics and fans are catching up, issuing a rising tide of books and articles about various aspects of his movies, from studies of their religious elements, to analyses of the director's fondness for *Beauty and the Beast*–type stories, to discussions of him as a public intellectual. In particular, Helen McCarthy's 1999 book on Miyazaki has been an inspiration to me.

Missing from the flood of commentary on him, however, is much discussion of Miyazaki's own history. I have been able to find only one biography of Miyazaki, written by the popular-culture specialist Mitsunari Ōizumi. Published in 2002, Ōizumi's book concentrates on Miyazaki's youth and early career, with little emphasis on his personal life. Japan is a society that to some extent still guards the privacy of major public figures. Furthermore, Miyazaki is an animator, not a movie star. It would be remarkably easy to write a book about him repeating ad nauseam: "Miyazaki went to his studio and worked really, really hard."

But Miyazaki's life, work, and world are much richer than such an assessment, accurate though it might be. In many ways he is his own best spokesman through his work and through his words. As anime specialist Kumi Kaoru says, Miyazaki "is a person of frightening talent and energy and we the audience can only be overwhelmed by [his] works.... We struggle for adequate words to critique him. Therefore the creator himself must speak."[4] Fortunately, Miyazaki does indeed speak; he is eloquent and wide-ranging on many subjects in both essays and interviews. Two enlightening volumes of his interviews and essays are available in English, *Starting Point* and *Turning Point*. Japanese materials are extensive. In particular, a two-volume set of interviews with Yōichi Shibuya, editor of a popular music journal and one of the few interviewers who seems unintimidated by Miyazaki's status, offered fascinating glimpses into Miyazaki's work, and his political and artistic passions. Another invaluable reference was the film researcher Seiji Kano's in-depth history of Miyazaki's films. Recollections from some of his closest colleagues, notably several books by his formidable producer Toshio Suzuki and the reminiscences of the veteran animator Yasuo Ōtsuka, also provided intimate glimpses into Miyazaki's working life. Recently, younger critics, such as the anime specialist Toshio Okada and the educator Shunsuke Sugita, have offered unsentimental views of the director's work.

And of course there are the films themselves, the imaginary empire he has so arduously created. In this book I explore Miyazakiworld principally through his eleven films and his major manga. While usually fantasy or science fiction, his art shows the director's sensitivity to the "real world" around him, not simply in response to political or social events but also in expressing his own personal and professional interactions.

As is obvious from his attention to detail, prolific production schedule, and extraordinary success, Miyazaki is the very model of a workaholic, inspiring and sometimes overwhelming his exceptional group of animators, many of whom toiled alongside him for decades. Even after announcing his "retirement," he immediately started laboring on short films for the Ghibli Museum, the inviting jewel box near his studio that he and his son Goro worked to create.

In his occasional free time, the director seems to enjoy simple pleasures, all of which in one way or another have contributed to the development of Miyazakiworld. He loves to travel, often with colleagues on location or on company outings, especially at home or in Europe. His two trips to the Eden-like island of Yakushima in the southernmost part of Japan inspired two major movies, *Nausicaä* and *Princess Mononoke*. His European journeys are reflected in everything from *Nausicaä*'s windmills and *Cagliostro*'s castles to the sparkling city of Koriko in *Kiki's Delivery Service* (Majo no takkyūbin, 1989) and the dark German towns of *The Wind Rises*. Ironically, for a man who loves to draw airplanes, Miyazaki is not particularly fond of flying.

When not working or traveling, Miyazaki splits his time between the modest Tokyo suburb of Tokorozawa and his beloved mountain cabin in Shinshū in Nagano prefecture. There he welcomes guests, including children, who delight in the area's natural surroundings, ever more precious in an industrialized Japan. Famous animators have also visited, including the directors Mamoru Oshii, revered for his *Ghost in the Shell* (Kōkaku kidōtai) films, and Hideaki Anno, who worked with Miyazaki on *Nausicaä* and went on to become internationally known for his bleak apocalyptic television and film series *Neon Genesis Evangelion* (Shinseiki Ebuangerion, 1996).

For a major film director, Miyazaki does not spend a lot of time seeing movies, although in the past he admired not only Russian and European animation but also such Western art films as the Italian neorealistic *Bicycle Thieves* and Russian director Andrei Tarkovsky's mind-blowing *Stalker*. He also appreciates the great Japanese director Akira Kurosawa, whose epic masterpiece *Seven Samurai* was a touchstone when Miyazaki made *Princess Mononoke*. An avid reader of European (especially English) literature, as well as science fiction and fantasy, he came to Japanese literature relatively late. Tatsuo Hori's plaintive 1936 romance *The Wind Rises* (Kaze tachinu) inspired the director's eponymous final film. In the past decade he has increasingly turned to Natsume Sōseki, the greatest of all Japan's twentieth-century writers, whose works depict anguished individuals confronting the stresses and terrors of modernity.

Miyazaki is quick to explain that he is not "cultivated," perhaps in comparison to Studio Ghibli cofounder Takahata, who graduated with a degree in French literature from Japan's most prestigious university. In fact, however, his tastes are refined and extend across the cultural and political spectrum. I have met Miyazaki three times, first in 1992, when I was visiting Studio Ghibli to do research for a book on Japanese anime in general and the director happened to pass by. This meeting would inspire me a decade and a half later to devote a book entirely to Miyazaki and his work.

On that first visit I was impressed by the light and airy studio, by the many female staff members, and by the drawings that I was allowed to see. Most impressive of all was the idiosyncratic, clearly brilliant man who was at the heart of the studio. Dapper and debonair, Miyazaki resembled an old-fashioned Victorian scholar/inventor, although his vitality and enthusiasm were anything but staid. His conversation swept me into a verbal whirlwind peppered with interesting facts and colorful details. The town of Tokorozawa, the bucolic setting for *Totoro,* was in the news that winter, unfortunately because of toxic environmental damage. I had lived in Tokorozawa in the 1970s while studying at a Japanese language school in Tokyo and had enjoyed its lovely rice fields and relative peace and serenity. Miyazaki and I bonded a bit over the sad state of the environment, and he drew a picture of Totoro for me, his characteristic signature beneath. The simple but lively drawing expressed the youthful ebullience that is another of the director's characteristics.

This is not to say that Miyazaki is Santa Claus, as one of my Miyazaki seminar students once endearingly suggested. You do not become the world's greatest animator, the head of a major studio, and the progenitor of a string of hit movies by being cozy and comfortable. His producer Suzuki refers to Ghibli as a "utopia," and certainly Miyazakiworld contains many utopian visions.[5] Other industry insiders have different opinions, however. This is clear in a surprisingly outspoken discussion between anime scholar Toshiya Ueno and the director Mamoru Oshii, who had worked with Miyazaki as early as *Nausicaä* and taken issue with the director's left-wing sympathies. Oshii called the atmosphere at Ghibli "Stalinist."[6] Ueno was even more colorful, mentioning the theory that Miyazaki's former colleague and acolyte Hideaki Anno created the dystopian organization NERV, led by the brilliant and forbidding Gendou Ikari, in his hit series *Evangelion,* as a satirical vision of Ghibli.[7] Undoubtedly, Oshii and Ueno were exaggerating a bit for humorous purposes.[8] But there is no denying that Ghibli was an intense environment, and Miyazaki remains an intense and complicated man. Miyazaki himself has described the frenetic realm of the bathhouse in his masterpiece *Spirited Away* as being modeled on Studio Ghibli, with the witch Yubaba, the bathhouse head, serving as a hybrid of himself and Suzuki.

The complex, sometimes conflicting, but always fascinating aspects of Miyazakiworld are a strong part of its appeal to me and have brought me all the way to Aichi's deserted fairground. Retrieving my suitcase from behind the umbrella stand, I start back on the long journey home to the United States, where I will try to pull together the many elements I have discovered that make up Miyazakiworld. I feel a sense of melancholy at leaving Mei and Satsuki's empty house, a house that is a testament to a unique imagination, one that itself contains melancholy attributes. Miyazaki is a man deeply sensitive to the world around him and, as this book will show, his life and times have been turbulent.

Over the eight years that I worked on this book I came to believe that Miyazaki projects aspects of himself and his world into many of his artistic creations. He remains an idiosyncratic genius, but he and his art are also an amalgam of the time and place he was born and raised, the extraordinary and sometimes excruciating cultural experience of twentieth-century and twenty-first-century Japan. In a *New Yorker* profile of Miyazaki the journalist Margaret Talbot suggests that "it was almost inevitable that the world's greatest animator should be Japanese," given Japan's popular culture of cuteness and its contribution to superior animation.[9] I would suggest rather that Japan's complex history, combined with its rich visual, literary, and spiritual culture and a cosmopolitanism perhaps surprising to Westerners, contributed to producing an unprecedented animator. This book is an examination of why and how Hayao Miyazaki came to be that animator: of the world he has created and of the worlds that created him.

# Miyazakiworld

# 1

## *Hametsu*

The country is ruined. Only the mountains and rivers remain.

—TU FU (712–770)

The world Hayao Miyazaki was born into on January 4, 1941, was on its way to destruction. In his most recent film, *The Wind Rises,* set before and after World War II, the director shows nightmare visions of shattered airplanes while a character intones the single word *hametsu:* ruin. Ruin shadowed Japan from the start of the military campaigns that ultimately became the country's World War II. By the end of 1945, millions of people would be dead and their countries devastated. Japan was hardly the only nation to suffer from ruin, and many would argue that it invited destruction through its brutal imperial expansion on the Asian continent and in Southeast Asia, and finally through its bombing of Pearl Harbor and the ensuing Pacific war. Historians endlessly debate the complexities of Japan's imperial project, but the fact remains that the country was in ashes by the end of World War II.

The atomic bombings of Hiroshima and Nagasaki came after myriad conventional air raids that swept Japan beginning in 1944. At the war's conclusion almost every one of the country's major cities—the single exception being the old capital of Kyoto—had been firebombed beyond recognition. Historian John Dower, in his book *War Without Mercy,* quotes an American commander who described the relentless American air raids of 1944 and

1945 as "one of the most ruthless and barbaric killings of non-combatants in all history."[1] The air raids blazed a scar in the memory of all who experienced them. Although only four years old when the war ended, Miyazaki says, "I remember the air raids. I see my street burning."[2]

Yet in the year of the director's birth, Japan seemed to be riding high. Sacrificing its traditional institutions and customs and replacing them with Western ones, from schools to steak dinners, Japan had become the first non-Western nation to successfully modernize. By the late 1930s Japan had developed an empire respected, even feared, around the globe. Finally, it seemed to have gained admission into what historian Roger Louis calls "the white man's club of imperial domination."[3] The last month of 1941 would begin with Japan's stunning military victory over the United States at Pearl Harbor, when its bombers, escorted by the superbly designed planes known as Mitsubishi Zeros, shocked America with a devastating attack.

The attack on Pearl Harbor and the planes that led it had a special connection to the Miyazaki family. As the director readily acknowledges, his father and uncle owned a factory that made fan belts for the Zeros. Throughout the war the family maintained a large house and was even able to obtain a precious and rare commodity, gasoline for transportation. Gas and a vehicle would help them escape the most destructive of the bombings.

Miyazaki clearly feels guilt for his family's wartime prosperity, but his attitude toward the plane that provided it and the period that produced it is an ambivalent one. The mixed blessings of technological progress would become major themes in Miyazakiworld. The director admires the Zero's state-of-the-art technology, evidence of a nation catching up with the West by quantum leaps. It is also clear that the director sees the 1920s and 1930s as a crucial era for the nation and for his family, a time of technological innovation and political ferment but also of rising militarism and natural disasters. In scenes of panicking crowds and shuddering buildings, *The Wind Rises* depicts the 1923 Tokyo earthquake, an event that directly affected Miyazaki's father and grandfather.

Notwithstanding the depredations to come, the prewar period was marked by excitement and mobility, as modernization continued and formerly feudal Japan began to try on different identities. The so-called modern boys and modern girls (*modan boi* and *modan garu*) carved out new paths of adulthood that veered sharply from the conservative traditions of the nineteenth century. Miyazaki would refer to his own father disparagingly as a "modern boy," suggesting irresponsibility and hedonism, but *The Wind Rises* also features a sympathetic portrait of Kaya, the protagonist's sister, whose determination to become a doctor is a distinctly modern touch.[4]

At war's end, the Japanese confronted not only the physical devastation of their cities and an unparalleled loss of life but also the Allied Occupation, the first time in its history the country had ever been occupied by a foreign power. Japan's prewar attempts to modernize and Westernize had already left psychic wounds, leading to what Natsume Sōseki had called a "national nervous breakdown."[5] This time the wounds were not only spiritual but painfully physical—visible in the flattened buildings and in the piles of rubble covering empty streets. Big American soldiers offered chewing gum to hungry children whose parents might never return.

Miyazaki and his colleagues at Studio Ghibli are keenly aware of the traumatic effect of World War II and are determined to remind their younger countrymen about it. The 2013 issue of Ghibli's house journal *Neppū* was conceived as a manifesto against the current conservative government's attempt to revise the constitution's Article Nine, which states that Japan renounces war "forever." More moving than the abstract antiwar polemics are Miyazaki's and his colleagues' reminiscences of their own childhoods during World War. II. Miyazaki's longtime partner Isao Takahata gives an account of his own war experience that is all the more memorable for its brevity:

> The American air raid in Okayama [a medium-sized coastal city] was the most significant event of my entire life. My sister and I were away from home when the American raids came so we experienced the full horror of the attack. My sister was hit by a bomb fragment and lost consciousness. I thought it likely

that we would both die. We went to the river and stayed there shivering until dawn, pelted by the black rain [the aftermath of bombing]. Half of Okayama was destroyed in the B-29 raid. The area around our home and our home itself were burned. We saw an incredible number of corpses. Many were baked and many had drowned in the nearby river.

He concludes simply, "I do not wish to ever experience such horror again."[6]

Equally searing are the war memories of children's book writer Rieko Nakagawa. In *Neppū* she describes fearing that her parents would be taken away as "spies" because the family had an extensive library of foreign books, and worrying that her own copy of Hans Christian Andersen stories would be confiscated. Rieko and her sister were eventually sent away to their grandparents' house on the northern island of Hokkaido. Even in this remote place, absence and sorrow predominated: "My grandfather, who had taught elementary and middle school, every day would receive letters about a student killed in action. I felt heartbroken for my grandfather, seeing him with his head hanging, his shoulders bent, wiping his glasses."[7]

The war that the Japanese had entered into with high hopes and militaristic zeal had come home to them. The nation collectively struggled for an appropriate reaction—mourning competed with despair, mixed with anger both toward the military leaders who had led them into this quagmire and toward the American invaders who underlined their powerlessness. Miyazaki remembers his father weeping when the Japanese emperor announced the country's defeat.

MIYAZAKI'S ART AROSE, in part, out of the ashes of World War II. Many elements must come together to create genius—family, childhood, education, culture. Surely another element may be trauma: psychic wounds that do not heal. C. S. Lewis endured his mother's death from cancer when he was ten years old and went on to create the luminous world of Narnia, in which the dead are reborn. Tolkien's brutal experiences and loss of good friends in the trenches of the Western Front in World War I undoubtedly contributed to his vision of the death-haunted realm of Mordor and the anticipation of a final apocalyptic battle. J. K. Rowling's uneasy relationship with her father probably contributed to the number of absent or problematic father figures who populate the *Harry Potter* series. If trauma becomes the catalyst for the artist to develop the art he or she needs to process and transcend pain, creating an alternate world takes that process one step further.

Miyazaki has described what he calls the "power of fantasy" in relation to his own life: "They tell you to face reality, but at least for me the power of fantasy was that it gave me a space to be a hero in. Even if it's not animation or manga, it can be old stories or legends. This is what humanity has developed to help us get by."[8]

It should be acknowledged that Miyazaki maintains that he does not see his art in terms of processing trauma. According to his biographer Mitsunari Ōizumi, the director is adamant that he bears no traumatic wounds: "I do not believe that I am the kind of person who was [emotionally] scarred and makes that the theme of the movies or manga that I create." Miyazaki instead suggests that trauma is universal, "the kind of thing that everyone has—whether you carry it along carefully or try to sublimate it into other forms."[9]

Rather than dwell on trauma, Miyazaki insists on the virtues of perseverance. "If you ask whether the scars can be healed, no, these are things that must be endured. There is no healing." He calls emotional scarring one of the "fundamentals of human existence," adding simply, "you just have to endure."[10]

There is no question that perseverance, endurance, and acceptance are major themes in Miyazakiworld, emphasized in the many invocations to "live" in works as early as the *Nausicaä* manga or as late as the final lines of *The Wind Rises*. Resilience, not suffering, is what Miyazaki repeatedly stresses. Nevertheless, trauma has a place in both his life and his works. Sometimes it is when we are closest to something that we have the most trouble seeing it.

Natsume Sōseki, who endured an unhappy childhood and who struggled with neurosis, is, as we have seen, one of the writers to whom Miyazaki returns. He has also made clear his admiration for Ryūnosuke Akutagawa, the brilliant young short story writer who, beset by family troubles and fearful that he had inherited his mother's schizophrenia, committed suicide in 1926. The works of both writers include fantastic and surreal creations that exert an uncanny power. Another Miyazaki literary hero is Kamo no Chōmei (1155–1216), a trenchant essayist who lived through earthquakes and military uprisings and ended up rejecting medieval court society to find comfort in an alternative world of nature and Buddhism.

Many of Miyazaki's male characters carry a curse of some sort, an expression of internal conflicts: Ashitaka's toxic arm in *Princess Mononoke*, Marco's pig face in *Porco Rosso* (Kurenai Buta, 1992), Haku's magic indenture to Yubaba in *Spirited Away* (Sen to Chihiro no kamikakushi, 2001), and Howl's imprisoned heart in *Howl's Moving Castle* (Haoru no ugoku shiro, 2004). These are the most obvious examples, but even the seemingly happy-go-lucky Lupin in *Castle of Cagliostro* (Rupan Sansei Kariosutoro no shiro, 1979) and the remarkably mature five-year-old Sōsuke in *Ponyo* (Gake no ue no Ponyo, 2008) bear traces of a gravity unusual for protagonists in movies aimed at a young audience. Although these choices make aesthetic sense in helping to create more intricate and compelling characters, they also suggest a view of the world that goes beyond simple family entertainment.

Curses in Miyazakiworld are not limited to human beings. In one of the more memorable speeches in the blockbuster ecofable *Princess Mononoke*, the cynical monk Jiko-bō states, "The whole world is under a curse!" The traumatic landscapes of the film support that statement as we see woodlands destroyed, skies shrouded, and the god of the forest brought down with a rifle shot. *Spirited Away* makes the curse on nature even more specific: the enigmatic character Haku is not actually a human but a river god, and it is his river that is "cursed." Another river in the film is so polluted that its god has been turned into a "stink spirit," signifying both spiritual and environmental pollution.

The director's visions of natural despoliation are often related to specific aspects of environmental damage wrought by postwar Japan's frantic drive to industrialize. Haku's polluted river is probably evocative of a river near Miyazaki's house that he and other community members have worked to clean up. But images of vast and ruined landscapes appear in Miyazaki from as early as his 1970s television series *Future Boy Conan* (Mirai shōnen Konan) and continue to his most recent film, suggesting a familiarity with destruction implanted early on. In this regard, Miyazaki goes beyond the great Chinese poet Tu Fu, who, in his vision of the "mountains and rivers" that remain, still views the sorrows of the world from a human perspective. Miyazaki says of the rivers in *Spirited Away*, "It is not only the people of Japan but the rivers themselves that are suffering."[11]

Miyazaki's vision of environmental and cultural disaster emerges out of a national consciousness. Western scholars frequently mention what might be called Miyazakiworld's "Shinto" aesthetic, a reference to the indigenous Japanese religion that sees the world as a realm of spirits (kami) who are not necessarily human. Indeed, kami can be found in rocks, waterfalls, mountains, and trees, as we see in the ancient camphor tree under which Totoro makes his home in *My Neighbor Totoro*. This animistic cultural consciousness has for centuries explicitly emphasized the deep connections among humans, other species, and even natural forces.

As they have celebrated an intense spiritual connection with nature, the Japanese have also been acutely aware of nature's overwhelming power. Throughout its history Japan has suffered a staggering number of volcanic eruptions, earthquakes, and tsunami, leading to what I have described as a Japanese "imagination of disaster."[12] Religious cultures including Zoroastrianism and Judeo-Christianity have entertained apocalyptic visions throughout the centuries, but the Japanese imagination of disaster, linked with a fundamentally pessimistic and at times tragic worldview, has long been part of Japanese aesthetic and popular culture. Miyazaki's near contemporary, the Nobel Prize–winning writer Kenzaburō Ōe, envisioned a final cleansing flood as early as the 1970s. On the popular culture front, a novel of all-out disaster with the revealing title *Japan Sinks* (Nippon chimbotsu) became a nationwide best seller in the 1980s and has since been made into two blockbuster movies. Japanese animation virtually assaults the viewer with apocalyptic images, beginning with the classic 1970s *Space Battleship Yamato* (Uchū senkan Yamato) series, continuing through Katsuhiro Ōtomo's apocalyptic masterpiece *Akira* (1988), and still prevalent in more recent works such as the dark fantasy series *Puella Magi Madoka Magica*.

More than the art of any other Japanese artist, however, Miyazaki's gives the most compelling substance and expression to this cultural vision by exploring and expressing the paradoxical beauty of disaster. In film after film Miyazakiworld offers us battles, ruins, widespread destruction and its aftermath—richly delineated visions of postapocalyptic realms—while giving us characters who transcend chaos and cataclysm. Ultimately, his works offer images of hope and resilience to viewers both in Japan and around the world.

Miyazaki's representations of apocalypse are linked to the nation's experience in World War II, but their intensity and beauty also connect with a centuries-old Japanese notion of life's fleetingness. One thinks in particular of the strangely peaceful and purifying tsunami in *Ponyo,* but even the engulfing flames of war in *Howl's Moving Castle* offer an eerie visual appeal. This notion is embodied in the poetic eleventh-century term *mono no aware,* which roughly translates to "the sadness of things" but also encompasses the notion that beauty itself is based on transience.

*Mono no aware* is expressed most beautifully in the cherry blossoms that scatter in the wind at the height of their beauty. Its most sinister embodiment is to be found in the idealization of the kamikaze pilots, young men who at the end of World War II flew suicide missions in a futile attempt to save their country from ruin. As Miyazaki is well aware, the planes these young men flew were the last remnants of the fleet of Mitsubishi Zeros. Made redundant by advances in Allied technology, the Zeros would become flying coffins, out-of-date emblems of a dead world.

But Miyazaki's imagination of disaster is manifested not only on a societal or cultural level. Some of his best films are works of intimate apocalypse in which a character confronts what one Japanese critic has called "world-ending events as seen from the point of view of a child.[13] This most intimate apocalypse was something experienced by Miyazaki himself at a young age when his mother became bedridden with tuberculosis. Now largely eradicated in the industrialized world thanks to antibiotics, tuberculosis in the prewar period was a rapacious killer disease, causing sufferers to cough up blood and waste away into emaciation and death.

Writers of the twentieth century and earlier found tuberculosis romantic. The German writer Thomas Mann set *The Magic Mountain* in a Swiss sanatorium for tubercular patients. Closer to home, the Japanese writer Tatsuo Hori wrote *The Wind Rises* about a doomed love affair between a young man and his tubercular sweetheart. Together these works would inspire Miyazaki's most recent film, whose female protagonist Naoko (named for the protagonist of another Hori novel) is afflicted with tuberculosis and waits, futilely, for a cure in a hospital in the Japanese Alps.

*The Wind Rises* is perhaps Miyazaki's most romantic movie. The reality of tuberculosis, however is hardly romantic. Miyazaki's mother, while allowed to come home, spent eight years largely immobilized, relying on her four sons to bring the world to her. Although she did eventually recover, she was bedridden throughout most of Miyazaki's childhood and adolescence. Not only did the young boy have to deal with his mother's illness, but he and his family also had to contend with the constant and omnipresent fear of her death. In fact, as Miyazaki would later discover, his father's first wife had died from tuberculosis at a young age within a year of their marriage.

A ruined country and a mother with a potentially fatal illness—surely these factors can be considered traumatic, especially when experienced in childhood. But childhood is a multilayered experience, and Miyazaki's early life was not wholly dark. His personality is characterized more by resilience and perseverance than by the depression or anxiety with which many artists contend. In public Miyazaki comes across as strong-minded and assertive, although one wonders whether the touch of melancholy and even self-doubt in some of his male characters is perhaps Miyazaki's projection of difficult emotions.

Born and raised in Tokyo, Miyazaki exemplifies aspects of what the Japanese term Edoko—child of Tokyo—a personality tending to the straightforward and the assertive, perhaps a bit mercantile. Even in childhood, Miyazaki was known for having an explosive temper, and as early as his college years he possessed strong opinions from which he seldom backed down. Critics rightly emphasize his artistry; he also seems financially canny, highly aware of budget constraints both for movies and for his studio. While he joined a children's literature study group in college, it should be remembered that he majored in politics and economics.

Miyazaki may have inherited his financial acuteness from his paternal grandfather. It was Miyazaki's grandfather who made the family fortune, becoming an apprentice at the age of eight and going on to build a factory that employed twenty-five workers by the time of the 1923 earthquake. Miyazaki clearly admires his grandfather's energy and praises his "cleverness." In one anecdote he recounts, his grandfather managed during the earthquake to rescue all his family and workers, telling them to "eat up everything you can and run in socks or barefoot if need be!"[14] He made use of the postearthquake chaos to help his family financially. Rather than carry household objects with him in the escape, he had taken as much money as possible in his pockets. He used it to buy lumber, reasoning correctly that the fires caused by the quake could lead to extensive rebuilding.

His grandfather's wealth provided the family a safe haven during the war. In a way that seems to presage the light and darkness interwoven in Miyazaki's art, the director spent 1944–1946, the most traumatic years in Japanese history, on the beautiful estate owned by his grandfather in Utsunomiya, a small city about sixty miles from Tokyo. His family had moved there partly to escape the increasing air raids and partly to be nearer the Nakajima Aircraft Factory, with which the Miyazaki family factory was affiliated. Thanks to its connection to the war industry, the family factory had grown much larger. Miyazaki's uncle was president and his father the manager. Although the numbers are uncertain—Miyazaki asserts that his father often exaggerated—family lore had the factory employing at least fifteen hundred workers by war's end. As Miyazaki says, "The more the war went on, the more money we made."[15]

Miyazaki, his older brother, Arata, his baby brother, and his parents resided in the guesthouse rather than the main villa, but the children had access to the estate's large and beautiful garden. Arata remembers the garden as "heaven," recalling how "there were waterfalls, a pond, all in all about two thousand to three thousand tsubo [one and a half to two and a half acres] of land." Rhinoceros beetles and cicadas added excitement and sound to the garden. "Every morning we would feed the carp in the pond, and it was okay not to go to school [presumably because of the air raids], and we could play all day long."[16]

Indeed, a Japanese private garden of more than an acre and a half must have seemed enormous, constituting a personal kingdom for the brothers to enjoy, even as the war raged closer and closer. It is not surprising that one of Miyazaki's favorites among the many English children's books he read is Philippa Pearce's classic fantasy *Tom's Midnight Garden,* about a boy who discovers a magic garden hidden in the past. Nor is it difficult to imagine that this "heavenly" garden might become the basis for some of Miyazaki's best-loved utopian landscapes. Most conspicuous is the benign and tranquil countryside of *Totoro,* but we can perhaps find other childhood traces in the several "secret" gardens depicted in later films.

None of these is a traditional Japanese garden, but Miyazaki lovingly re-creates not one but two traditional gardens in *The Wind Rises:* the garden of the house where his protagonist Jirō grows up and the exquisite landscape garden belonging to Jirō's professional mentor, Kurokawa, through which the young Jirō and his fiancée, Naoko, stroll on their seemingly fairy-tale wedding night. Not only does what was thought to be Miyazaki's final film describe destructive moments of prewar Japanese history, but it also offers the beauty of traditional Japan and aspects of Miyazaki's own life.

Just as tragedy and loss subtly enter the Kurokawas' garden in the form of Naoko's deepening illness, tragedy and chaos entered the Utsunomiya house, if in a far less subtle fashion. On July 19, 1945, in the last month of the war, Utsunomiya was firebombed with such devastation that half the city was destroyed and forty-nine thousand people rendered homeless. Fortunately, the Miyazakis escaped serious harm, but the memory of that night has remained with Miyazaki all his life.

Intriguingly, it is not the firebombing that seems to have particularly affected him. Instead, an incident occurred during the family's flight that would become, in the view of Ōizumi, Miyazaki's biographer, a kind of "starting point" (*genten*) for the director:

> When I was four and a half, Utsunomiya was bombed. . . . Even though it should have been the middle of the night, outside it was bright red or maybe pink as if it was sunset. Even the inside of the room was colored pink. . . . My uncle came by with a company truck, smaller than the vehicles that we have these days; the space for luggage was really tiny. . . . The streets that he passed along were burning, right down to the sides of the road. . . . We covered ourselves with a blanket—we had to somehow get through the place where the flames were burning.
>
> Just then at the guard rail a bunch of people arrived looking for shelter. My memory isn't totally clear on this, but I'm certain that I heard a woman's voice saying, "Please let us on." I'm not sure if it was my memory or if I heard it from my parents and felt like I had seen it, but, anyway it was a woman carrying a little girl, someone from the neighborhood running toward us saying, "Please let us on!" But the car just went on going. And the voice saying, "Please let us on" got farther away and it gradually took root in my head the way a traumatic event does.[17]

Reflecting on this event later, Miyazaki expresses a complicated set of emotions, including guilt about his family's relative affluence and resentment against his parents' unwillingness to help the woman and her child. His persistent awareness of his family's profiting from its connection to the war industry clearly deepens his sense of guilt and responsibility: "The fact that I had been raised comfortably in a family getting rich through munitions at a time when most people were suffering materially and that, in the very midst of people dying, our family was able to escape in a truck when there was almost no gasoline to be had, and that we ended up abandoning people who were begging us to let them on—this is a memory that became a firm part of my four-year-old self."[18]

He ceaselessly ruminates on how the situation might otherwise have concluded: "If I had been a parent and been told by my child to stop, I think I would have stopped. There are plenty of reasons why you couldn't do that . . . but I still think how much better it would have been if I had told them to stop. Or if my older brother had said it."[19]

Arata remembers the experience somewhat differently: the truck was tiny, he says, and fitting another person would have been impossible. More surprising is Arata's recollection that it was a male neighbor rather than a woman who asked for help that night. According to Arata, the man had a child at home. If his older brother's memory is more accurate, Miyazaki's recollection presumably not only made the situation one in which his family *could* have helped but conjured a mother carrying a baby—for Ōizumi an early example of the role that mother figures would play in Miyazakiworld.[20]

Mothers or mother figures are important in many Miyazaki films, but what is particularly thought-provoking in Miyazaki's recollection of the air raid is his assumption of responsibility for his four-year-old self. Having suggested first that he should have pleaded with his parents to stop, he goes on to offer alternative endings, in which he and his brother could have become the voice of responsibility: "I guess it doesn't seem realistic that a four-year-old child would tell his parents to stop the car, but I felt that if such a child were to exist, this would have been a good time to tell them to stop."[21]

In this early memory we already see children as the voices of conscience transforming thought into action: *If such a child were to exist.* In Miyazakiworld we repeatedly see such children—young people who take on surprisingly adult responsibilities: Satsuki, who cares for her motherless household in *My Neighbor Totoro;* the young adolescents Sheeta and Pazu in

*Laputa: Castle in the Sky* (Tenkū no shiro Rapyuta, 1987), who combine forces to save the world from destruction; *Ponyo*'s five-year-old Sōsuke, who not only nurtures his lonely mother but also copes with the aftermath of a gigantic tsunami.

In Miyazakiworld little children become dynamic, responsible individuals. These children shoulder burdens and serve as guides, not only to their fellow characters but to Miyazaki's global audience. His utopian impulses have as one of their main foundations the notion of childhood as a space of innocence, freedom, and connection. One of Miyazaki's most famous expressions is the invocation "to see with eyes unclouded." The words come from *Princess Mononoke,* one of his most adult-oriented works, but the idea of seeing without the accumulated detritus of bias and prejudice brought by experience suggests a child's viewpoint, one that is infinitely clearer than that of adults.

In the director's imagined re-creation of the air raid we find responsible children and a rescuing mother. In response to a world of mass destruction the director imagines his childhood self or another child telling the adults to "stop" in order to help a mother figure. Miyazaki does not minimize the chaos and loss of that terrible night in Utsunomiya. But he does offer an alternative vision of humane interaction in which responsibility, community, and courage play a part. That these elements appear as part of an uncertain or even false memory only underlines their centrality in Miyazaki's desire to create a more positive worldview.

Japan in 1945 was "ruined," but its people endured. Even as the director's art makes heroes out of nature and inanimate objects, it always acknowledges the human connection. Children in particular become the agents of change and reassurance in his work, experiencing and processing trauma but also transcending calamity by working to ameliorate it.

Even in Miyazakiworld's most apocalyptic expressions something always endures. In his animations of lost or unreal worlds the director presents catalysts for hope and action, not simply vehicles of escape. In this regard Miyazaki may be said to engage in what theorists David L. Eng and David

Kazanjian label "a politics of mourning"—neither passive nor resigned but activist, concentrating on "what remains" rather than "what is lost": loss motivates more than memorials; it also motivates art.[22] Along with Takahata, Toshio Suzuki, and the dedicated staff at Studio Ghibli, Miyazaki would go on to make films that inspire action when confronting loss, community when dealing with absence, and resuscitation in the face of ruin.

# 2
# Constructing an Animator

*What rushes forth inside you is the world you have already drawn inside yourself, the many landscapes you have stored up, the thoughts and feelings that seek expression.*

——HAYAO MIYAZAKI


How did Miyazaki discover the beauty of animation? And apart from the technical skill he was to bring to the art form, what suggested to him that this was his life path? To become a great animator requires more than exceptional drawing skills and extraordinary perseverance, although these were a fundamental part of Miyazaki's aesthetic toolkit. But he also possessed the psychological depth that would make him not only a great animator but also a great director. His recurring themes run a psychological and aesthetic gamut, incorporating radiance and darkness. Many elements of Miyazaki-world emanate from the director's childhood and adolescence. Growing up after an all-out war, the young Miyazaki loved to draw military planes, an obsession that would pay off in the stunning flying scenes in his movies. Deeply complicated relationships with his parents inform his depiction of many of his early adolescent and child protagonists. Finally, ideological and economic changes in Japan contribute to his developing political consciousness, which expressed itself in stories referencing the rise of Japanese capitalism, industrialization, and the environmental, political, and psychological sacrifices attending it.

In the twenty-first century many people want to become animators. While adults of my generation may still find the profession a bit rarefied, many of my students actively study animation and aspire to it as a career. Animation is an essential part of media culture, showing up not only in cartoon series but in commercials, live-action films, and across the internet. In the Japan of the 1950s and early 1960s, however, the notion of becoming a professional animator was virtually nonexistent. At best, one might aspire to become a manga artist, and this became the young Miyazaki's goal— not one that his family or high school classmates would sympathize with. Manga were for children. In respectable middle-class families sons were expected to go into white-collar careers and become "salarimen," part of the new army of hardworking executives sacrificing themselves for the good of an economically successful country.

Miyazaki showed no interest in sharing this fate: "I spent my high school years in the period right before Japan's economy entered its high-speed growth period. And during that time I was probably the only guy I knew in high school who actually read manga. If I'd told people then that I also drew comics, they would have treated me as though I were an idiot. I had an alibi ready, of course, so it was easy for me, because at the time I thought that anyone who didn't appreciate the potential of manga has to be an idiot."[1]

He saw that potential quite early, and he saw, too, his own path to becoming a manga artist. Much of his childhood and youth can be seen as preparation for his career—in terms of the skills he was developing but also on psychological and moral levels. A love of drawing and a visual awareness of his surroundings came with a strong sense of responsibility and an ability to work with others, if only his brothers at first. He also needed to get away, into the realm of imagination.

This need probably arose from the family crisis of his mother's ongoing illness and his consequent loneliness. As an adult Miyazaki speaks darkly of his childhood, describing it as "shamefully pathetic" and admitting that as he grew older, he had "locked [his childhood] away from himself."[2] Yet from his childhood and youth came the tools that would help make him a successful artist and animator.

A superior artistic ability was clear from early childhood. Japan has a centuries-old tradition of artistic creativity, as Miyazaki's partner Takahata makes clear in his discussion of the influence of Japanese scrolls on modern animation.[3] Early art education in Japan is widely considered superior to that in the West, with children developing sophisticated technique at much younger ages than in Europe or America.

Miyazaki's innate talent was enhanced by this schooling and culture. His brother Arata mentions an elementary school competition in which both brothers were to draw their garden as seen from the second floor of their house. Despite being two years older and good at art, Arata saw that Hayao already drew at a level he couldn't imitate, noting his younger brother's uncanny skill at "drawing everything correctly": "No matter how you looked at our pictures, Hayao's was better." Arata once saw two teachers pausing in front of Hayao's work. "That's just too good," one of them said, implying that his little brother must have had adult help. Arata ended up winning the competition.[4]

Miyazaki's ability to draw with such exactness and attention to detail would profoundly affect his career. Unlike many animated films, both in the West and in Japan, Studio Ghibli films are known for the depth and resonance of their backgrounds. Miyazakiworld especially offers what Eleanor Cameron describes as "particularity of place," the sense of a narrative anchored within a larger whole that has both texture and specificity.[5] This lends a sense of heightened reality to everything from the bucolic landscape in *Totoro* to the Adriatic coastline in *Porco Rosso*.

Miyazaki's first and enduring artistic love was for machines, starting with the red fire engines he drew as a young child and continuing to the planes that fascinated him after the war. Arata wonders whether the latter obsession dates from the fragments of planes that the boys found on the grounds of the shuttered family factory, which the brothers collected and showed off to envious children after the war.[6] It is also possible that Miyazaki inherited his fascination with machinery from his grandfather, who had held patents on several inventions.

While Miyazaki's father attempted to continue the factory after the war, manufacturing household items such as spoons, Miyazaki's family was no longer as affluent, though still better off than many of their countrymen. Many Japanese were stunned and starving. Miyazaki remembers the American soldiers of the Occupation and their practice of handing out sweets. For the Americans, putting something into the bellies of hungry children was a way of getting on better terms with the defeated enemy. For Miyazaki and for many other Japanese, these were humiliating acts. "After the war many Americans came and we would gather around. But I couldn't embarrass myself to the point of taking chocolate or chewing gum from them."[7] That complicated attitude toward the United States is reflected in *Porco Rosso,* in which the American flyer Curtis is depicted as an arrogant buffoon but the young girl Fio, "recently returned from America," is shown as enthusiastic and hardworking.

Miyazaki's generation could not avoid the new ideas and practices that the Occupation imposed. The young encountered them most directly in the new school system, based on an American model. Prewar education had emphasized sacrifice for the nation above all else; the novelist Kenzaburō Ōe remembers being asked by a teacher at the age of eight, "Would you cut open your belly and die for the emperor?" There was only one correct answer: "Yes."[8]

Occupation schooling emphasized democracy and democratic behavior, with debate clubs and a free exchange of ideas. A vision was also promoted of recent Japanese history as a succession of terrible, indeed evil, actions. The effect on Miyazaki's cultural identity was pronounced: he has said how much he "hated Japan" as a youth.[9]

Yet "if I had been born a little bit earlier, I would absolutely have been a zealous 'military youth,'" he has said, invoking the militarist and imperialist indoctrination of the 1930s and 1940s. "And if I had been born even earlier, I would have been the kind of person who volunteered and rushed to die on the battlefield."[10] The postwar period, when a shattered nation reassessed itself, offered little emotional excitement for a passionate young boy. Dealing with troubles at home and growing up in a still impoverished and constricting society, Miyazaki may have craved the all-embracing intensity of war.

Fortunately for animation, his date of birth meant that his passionate nature would ultimately play out in art rather than on the battlefield. Miyazaki came to love technology that no longer existed or that existed only in his mind. "I have a strong desire to be liberated from being tied down by reality," he once said, speaking of his love of drawing airships.[11]

But the planes also signified autonomy and power. "I grew up being very excited about war films and drawing military things all over the place," he recalls. "I was an overly self-conscious boy and I had a hard time holding my own in fights with others, but my classmates eventually accepted me because I was good at drawing. I expressed my desire for power by drawing airplanes with sleek and pointed noses and battleships with huge guns. And I found myself thrilled with the bravery of sailors who—even as their burning ships sank—continued to fire guns until the bitter end, [and] by the men who plunged into the hail of fire and flak spewed forth by an enemy formation's guns. It was only much later that I realized that in reality these men had desperately wanted to live and been forced to die in vain."[12]

Quick to speak of the horrors of war, Miyazaki also rendered dynamic battle scenes obsessively. The contradiction is most apparent in *The Wind Rises,* which simultaneously denounces war but lingers on the artful design of military technology, taking pains to show its destructive power.

Miyazaki's earliest years at school were defined by periods of loneliness and a sense of powerlessness. By the time he was in fifth grade, he had changed schools three times. His family had left his grandfather's beautiful estate and moved back to Tokyo, to a house in Eifuku, in the Suginami-ku Ward. According to Ōizumi, the house in Eifuku would become the model for the house in *Totoro.* Unlike the Totoro house, however, which is set in the countryside, Suginami-ku is very much part of Tokyo, a pleasant suburban area with green spaces and good schools. The Miyazaki brothers attended a "good school where you studied hard but they didn't make you suffer."[13]

But each move made Miyazaki more and more uneasy, and being uprooted to Eifuku "shook the depths of my being. It was like mist—I would look at the textbook and not understand it . . . [and] if I can't understand this, what am I going to do?"[14]

Miyazaki credits his brother Arata with protecting him from some of the harder aspects of the changes. Physically impressive, good at sports (and fighting), Arata was a born leader, whereas Hayao tended to stay in the shadows reading and drawing: "an introvert," as Arata recalled, "delicate, not good at sports. What he liked to do was read books and draw pictures. I spent my allowance on things to eat. Hayao spent his on books!"[15]

"More than manga," says the director, "I read books": *The Count of Monte Cristo, The Three Musketeers, The Prisoner of Zenda* (which would influence his first feature film, *The Castle of Cagliostro*).[16] He loved both the book *Gulliver's Travels* and the movie by Max and Dave Fleischer, whose studio Miyazaki has compared approvingly to Walt Disney Studios. In the thrilling stories told in these works, the young boy found inspiration for the fast-paced adventures that would become a hallmark of Miyazakiworld.

The young Miyazaki also appreciated more intimate small-scale dramas about children, often girls, such as *The Secret Garden,* and *Heidi,* a novel about a young girl in the Swiss Alps that he and Takahata would re-create as a successful television series. Immersion in these works was to contribute to Miyazaki's preternatural ability to populate the screen with likable, believable child protagonists.

More visual stimulation and other forms of fantastic adventure came from manga, fast becoming a staple Japanese entertainment medium. Like most Japanese children at the time, Miyazaki adored the manga of Tezuka Osamu, the artist and animator whose impact on popular culture would be superseded only by his own, and then only after he could transcend the master's overwhelming early influence. Although he never lost his love of literature, by high school Miyazaki was fully immersed in reading and drawing manga.

His fondness for reading, art, and fantasy adventure was abetted by a growing need to escape his home life. His mother's tuberculosis, hospitalization, and subsequent confinement to her bed effectively ended the boys' childhood. With their mother incapacitated, the boys—eventually four in all—had to shift for themselves. Miyazaki remembers with a strong degree of resentment the need to be a "good kid," and being forced to take over the cooking and washing.[17]

Reading and drawing provided a creative outlet and helped allay the terror of coming home to a house that felt increasingly empty. One household maid after the next left, and those who stayed for any length of time had no sympathy for Miyazaki, who remembers being "at war with" the help.[18] "I always felt that I had to apologize for my existence," he told an interviewer years later. "I have no enjoyable memories from childhood—until I entered university I felt only humiliation . . . and I worked to forget everything and I have almost forgotten it."[19]

Miyazaki's profound connection with a lost childhood is one of his greatest strengths as a storyteller and underlies the rich evocations of children in Miyazakiworld. While his early works conjure marvelous fantasy worlds and remarkably realistic characterizations of young people, it is his third feature film, the beloved *My Neighbor Totoro,* that manages most expertly and sympathetically to combine the escapist fantasies and the painful realities of his childhood.

We will discuss *Totoro* in more depth later, but for now it is useful to note the critic Hikaru Hosoe's suggestion that in making the movie Miyazaki projects himself onto both of the sisters, the film's leading characters.[20] Miyazaki's relationship to Arata can be seen in the younger Mei's heartfelt emotions and dependence on her older sister, Satsuki. It is Mei who first encounters the woodland spirit Totoro, who serves as comfort and helper to both. While the outgoing and active Satsuki may correspond in some sense to Arata, she is also an example of the "good kid," Miyazaki's description of himself, the ten-year-old who takes over the family responsibilities when their mother is sick. In speaking of *Totoro,* Miyazaki explicitly compares himself to Satsuki: "A ten-year-old can do kitchen chores. I did. I also cleaned house, fired up the bath, and cooked." Satsuki, says Miyazaki, tried "too hard to be good."[21]

For a director who made his name with family-oriented movies, Miyazaki has conveyed a surprisingly vehement sense of resentment, even rage, toward child-adult relationships, once warning children "not to be devoured by their parents."[22] The injunction suggests an anger and hostility toward parents that deserves further exploration.

The roots of this resentment probably stem at least partially from his relationship with his father. Miyazaki displays an almost total lack of respect for his father, and what appears at times to be genuine hostility. This seems initially surprising, as so many of the fathers depicted in Miyazaki's work are remarkably decent people, from the kind and playful father in *Totoro* through *Ponyo*'s hardworking sea captain father, Kōichi. But not one of these father figures is masculine in any overtly traditional way; for instance, we see Kōichi bossed around by his wife, Lisa. This overall lack of paternal authority is particularly intriguing in that in the patriarchal prewar Japan into which Miyazaki was born, the father was absolute head of the household. In Japanese tradition, there were "four things to be feared: thunder, fire, earthquakes and father."

Miyazaki's father, Katsuji, was born in 1914 in Ryōgoku, a traditional part of Tokyo still known for its "shitamachi" (old downtown) flavor. Ryōgoku is close to Asakusa, now a popular district for tourists thronging to its red-gated Sensoji Temple. During Katsuji's youth, however, it was known mainly as an amusement area whose entertainment ranged from the refined (Western theater and opera) to the dissipated ("teahouses" that were actually houses of prostitution). According to Miyazaki, his father went to Asakusa "all the time" when he was younger and would constantly tell his sons how "great" it was.[23]

The area is bounded by the Sumida River, a major artery that ran cleanly through Tokyo at the time of Katsuji's birth and which Miyazaki would nostalgically evoke in *The Wind Rises*. In fact, around the time of making *The Wind Rises* Miyazaki seems to have been reaching toward a deeper interest in, if not a deeper understanding of, his father, or at least of his life and times. In both his *Neppū* article and an interview with the historian Handō Kazutoshi, he goes on at some length about a movie made by the great director Yasujirō Ozu. Entitled *Where Now Are the Dreams of Youth?* (Seishun no yume imaizuko, 1932), the movie follows a young man's progress through college and early adulthood as he inherits his father's company. Miyazaki recounts with amazement how he found the film's protagonist to be exactly like his father. He describes the protagonist as a quintessential *modan boi* (modern boy).

Ozu's handsome young protagonist, Horino, is "pleasure-seeking" and "anarchistic," and he "resists authority"—words also used by Miyazaki to describe his father.[24] He is given to such hijinks as helping his friends cheat on exams, not only at the prestigious Waseda University (which Miyazaki's father attended) but also later on when these same dissolute friends apply for jobs at Horino's own company. At the film's end, however, Horino straightens up—relinquishing the girl he loves to one of his friends and seemingly reaching a certain level of maturity in his understanding of human relationships.

This does not seem to have been the case with Katsuji, at least not in Miyazaki's eyes. The director has made no secret of his father's boastfulness and lack of responsibility, or of his other "dissolute" qualities, which include, by Miyazaki's admission, questionable business ethics: the director has accused his father of selling substandard airplane parts to the military. In a 1995 interview, Miyazaki revealed that as early as his time in high school, his father would say to him, "When I was your age I was already paying for geisha girls." In the same interview he states baldly that, at his father's funeral, "Those of us gathered together agreed that he had never once said anything particularly lofty or inspiring."[25]

Japan's prewar patriarchal society tacitly encouraged men, especially those with money, to have sexual relationships outside marriage, and the heady atmosphere of the 1920s and early 1930s encouraged experimentation of all kinds. It should also be noted that Miyazaki's father had to survive an unprecedentedly savage war while managing both a household and a factory, and had to make a living while caring for a seriously ill wife after the war.

Arata remembers that "our father really cared a lot about our mother."[26] He would come home from work and tell her about what was happening in the company, and on Sunday would take over the cooking. Miyazaki has said that his father got out of the army by telling his commander that he had a wife and child at home and should not be sent to the front. While the director seems disparaging of his father for not having served in the military, he also wryly notes that without this attitude, he himself would not have been born: "I am grateful on that score."[27]

Miyazaki also acknowledges his father's "realism" in "making money off the war," even if it came to bribery and the sale of defective parts. Katsuji's attitude toward war—that it was "something that only idiots engage in"—is one side of Miyazaki's own complex and ambivalent attitude toward war. He ruminates: "After all, I am like him. I have inherited my old man's anarchistic feelings and his lack of concern about embracing contradictions."[28]

That latter tendency is particularly clear in Miyazaki's films and manga of military adventure. We also see a bit of his father in the "playboy" characters of Lupin in *Castle of Cagliostro* and Marco in *Porco Rosso*. The subtle gloom that pervades both, however, may be a trait shared with the director himself.

With the important exceptions of *Porco Rosso* and *The Wind Rises,* we see little of adult sexuality in Miyazaki's films. While that restraint is entirely understandable, given Miyazaki's initial target audience of families with children, it also raises the question of whether his father's behavior made the director more likely to deemphasize sexuality in his art. A father boasting of his exploits with women must surely have created complex feelings in Miyazaki, and it is hardly astonishing that so many of his characters are young girls and children, and that the director emphasizes their "purity" and "innocence."

It is also likely that his father's behavior helped engender strong bonds between mother and son. Arata relates that during the time his mother was bedridden, "the person who most fully reported on school activities was probably Hayao." His biographer Ōizumi speculates that "despite being introverted, the fact is that during elementary school and middle school, the young boy was exposed to all sorts of 'cultures.'" Ōizumi goes on to wonder what kind of conversations "the bedridden mother would have had with her son whose world was widening spiritually around him."[29]

One wonders whether Miyazaki's warning to children not to be "devoured by one's parents" is at some level also related to his intense relationship with his mother, especially since at one point he pictures a mother who "swallows up [a young boy] in her womb and strips him of his strength."[30] Belying her physical frailty, Yoshiko Miyazaki was by all accounts a woman of great strength of character. Her tuberculosis cured by antibiotics, she lived to the age of seventy-two. It is ultimately less her frailty that Miyazaki seems to remember than her tough-mindedness. She was not much inclined to praise her children or the rest of humanity. Miyazaki loves to quote his mother's favorite saying—"Ningen wa shikata ga nai mono" (Human beings are hopeless)—although he has also insisted that his own attitude is less "nihilistic."

Their relationship lacked what the Japanese call "skinship." "I didn't have a close relationship with my mother like Satsuki. I was overly self-conscious, and my mother was that way too. When I went to see her in the hospital, I couldn't rush to hug her."[31] This lack of overt intimacy likely has to do with the traditional culture Yoshiko was raised in. Born in 1910, she left her native province, the beautiful, mountainous prefecture of Yamanashi, to seek her fortune in Tokyo, as did so many young adults in the early twentieth century. She studied clothing design and helped out at a friend's coffee shop, where she met Miyazaki's father.

Miyazaki came to disagree sharply with his mother about politics, the two engaging often in active debates. Miyazaki leaned toward the left even at a young age, while his mother espoused conservative views. She was an avid reader of *Bungei Shunjū,* a news and analysis magazine that at the time would have been targeted at an elite male audience.

Arata describes their mother as "meddlesome, strong-willed, kind to others, strictly brought up, and *hade*"—a word that can mean "loud" but also flashy or showy, as in Yoshiko's fondness for shoes, of which she owned many pairs.[32] Film critics and family members alike have suggested that Dola, the impressive (and strong-willed, meddlesome, and loud) matriarch of the family of air pirates in *Laputa: Castle in the Sky,* is based on her. It is an affectionate if clear-eyed portrait of a woman who inspires and organizes her rather feckless group of tall, bearded sons. The red-haired, full-bodied Dola is a far cry from Yoshiko, however, who, in the only photograph I could find of her, seems petite and delicate.

By now, it is virtually a cliché to talk about Miyazaki's many strong female protagonists, but often such discussion is reserved for the many depictions of *shōjo,* or young girls. These shōjo were probably inspired by Yoshiko's femininity, although they also owe a debt to Miyazaki's favorite animated movie heroine, the protagonist Bai Nyang of *Panda and the Magic Serpent.* The fortitude, intellectual curiosity, and upbeat spirit of heroines such as Nausicaä, Kiki, and *Laputa*'s Sheeta undoubtedly owe much to his mother's memorable presence as well.

An even more unusual and appealing aspect of Miyazaki's work, however, is the number of powerful older female figures. A favorite moment in my three meetings with Miyazaki came at our first encounter, after I had seen *Princess Mononoke* and read some critiques. When I suggested that the film's older female character, Lady Eboshi, was rather negatively portrayed, Miyazaki seemed genuinely surprised, insisting, "Eboshi is my favorite character in the movie!" Whether very young (Mei and Ponyo) or very old (Sophie in *Howl's Moving Castle* or the women at the nursing home in *Ponyo*), female characters are almost entirely distinctive, passionate, inquisitive, and, crucially, three-dimensional in ways that few female characters in cartoons or, for that matter, live action ever are.

Miyazaki's deep bond with his mother is borne out in these remarkable women and by many personal anecdotes. Both mother and son were profoundly interested in the world around them. Arata remembers how similar they were in personality, each refusing to revise an opinion when challenged. It is highly likely that his mother's interest in politics became an important factor in Miyazaki's lifelong concern with politics and world events, even if their specific views were often opposed.

A fight between them over the political incident known as the Matsukawa incident—a fatal train accident—emphasizes Miyazaki's evolving political views and his intense dynamic with his mother. Ōizumi begins his account of Miyazaki's life with this argument, very much a product of the new ideological strains in Japanese society as the country grew away from the highs and lows of Occupation.

In the heady initial postwar days, Occupation authorities seemed to be pushing Japan in a surprisingly left-wing direction. The cavalcade of reform abruptly came to an end with the rise of the Cold War and the incipient Korean War. In a "Reverse Course" policy, Occupation authorities decided that stability was more important than radicalism; they even brought back leaders who only a few years before had been labeled war criminals. The negotiating power of unions was drastically cut, and to many impressionable Japanese citizens this wholesale cutback of early Occupation policies seemed a betrayal of the bright hopes of democracy and Western ideals.

In the eyes of many left-wing Japanese citizens, the so-called Matsukawa incident was one in a string of events that amounted to a covert government war on the unions. A flash point between Miyazaki and his mother, it involved a derailment on a railway line that caused the deaths of three train crewmembers. The incident was blamed on the Japanese Communist Party and members of the national railway union, perhaps in revenge for the government's antiunion measures. Miyazaki was too young to have been much aware of the 1949 derailment, but the case became a cause célèbre, with the guilt or innocence of the accused unresolved to this day. Miyazaki supported the union members, believing them to be scapegoats of the government, while his mother fervently believed in the government's case. The family remembers one occasion when the argument between mother and son escalated until Miyazaki ended up leaving the room in tears.

The argument is significant for a number of reasons. It shows the intensity of the mother-son bond and, arguably, the genuine respect Miyazaki had for his mother. His passionate attempt to win her over demonstrates both how deeply each felt and the deep concern Miyazaki had for his mother's opinions.

But it also shows the increasing strength of Miyazaki's political convictions in general. At the time of the argument in question, he was twenty-two and had just graduated from Gakushūin University, with a degree in politics and economics. Many members of the imperial family attended Gakushūin, and the controversial right-wing writer Yukio Mishima attended high school there. It was hardly a place likely to engender strong left-wing sympathies, but by the time Miyazaki was in college, a Marxist approach was an important part of the economics curriculum in most Japanese universities.

Marxism was particularly appealing in postwar Japan. Intellectuals, disillusioned first by the war and then by the Occupation's Reverse Course, searched for an alternative ideology and sought to rehabilitate the few leftists of the prewar period who had taken stands against militarism and imperialism. Marxism was also linked to Europe, both in its nineteenth-century roots and in the massive socialist experiment being carried out in Eastern Europe under the Cold War hegemony of the Soviets. For many at the time, Europe was glamorous, a perspective that shapes Miyazaki's depictions of an exotic and attractive European world as early as *Castle of Cagliostro*.

Miyazaki's leftist leanings are an important part of the political underpinnings of Miyazakiworld, showing up as early as his version of a communal agricultural utopia in *Future Boy Conan,* in his depictions of starving Welsh miners in *Laputa: Castle in the Sky*, and, most obviously, in his characterization of *Porco Rosso*'s world-weary hero, who would "rather be a pig than a fascist." But other features of his high school and college life played more directly into his development as an animator, the most prominent a deepening immersion in art.

In middle school, Miyazaki began taking oil painting lessons with a teacher named Satō, who seems to have become not just an art teacher to

Miyazaki but a mentor, with whom the young man had wide-ranging conversations. Although not always giving the boy the emotional sustenance he might have wished for, Satō can perhaps be seen as one of the first in a series of older-brother figures in the director's life. Beginning with Arata, these were men who inspired and guided him personally and professionally, if at times irritating and frustrating him—as elder brothers do. Satō served as the go-between for Miyazaki's wedding, an important symbolic role indicative of someone who has been influential in a couple's life. Miyazaki's most important older "brother" has been his fellow Ghibli director, the cerebral and politically committed Isao Takahata. Later, the ebullient and energetic producer Toshio Suzuki, although actually younger, played a dominant role in Miyazaki's work and life.

Though his long conversations with Satō helped Miyazaki sort through the trials of adolescence, his high school years remained challenging, particularly the misery of what the Japanese call "examination hell" (the nationwide college entrance exams). Preparation for the exams is grueling if one wants to get into a first-rate university, to this day the ticket to a respectable middle-class life in Japan.

Miyazaki, however, seems already to have decided such an existence was not for him. He states that he spent most of his time in high school drawing manga, in particular a kind of manga known as *gekiga*. Realistic, often bleak and more socially committed than children's manga, gekiga flourished in the activist politics of the 1960s, but even as early as Miyazaki's late high school and early university years the genre had emerged as an alternative to the lighthearted entertainment of more mainstream manga. Miyazaki discovered gekiga "during my dark days of studying for university entrance exams. . . . In the gekiga there were no happy endings. The artists made every effort to provide cynical endings. For a student in examination hell this disillusioned perspective was totally refreshing."[33]

He eventually grew away from the violence and bitterness in gekiga. "I thought it might be better to express in an honest way that what is good is good," he recalls.[34] But violent class-based strife is explicit in *Future Boy Conan,* and is implied in *Princess Mononoke,* with its brutal battles and extreme social hierarchies.

While remaining a sharp leftist observer of social issues, Miyazaki also fought hard against easy cynicism or cheap nihilism. The children's literature study group in which he participated in college offered a more positive experience. Study groups are an important part of Japanese colleges even today, often revolving around the cultural and pop cultural: music, manga, science fiction. With universities forbidding manga and sci-fi study groups in Miyazaki's time, he turned back toward children's literature, particularly the English literature of his childhood.

He speaks highly of such Japanese fantasy masterpieces as *Night Train to the Stars* (Ginga tetsudo no yoru) and the Chinese classic *Journey to the West,* but many of the stories he read were European, especially English. English children's literature at the time was hopeful and upbeat. Whether the protagonists were setting up camp by themselves on a lake (as in an early favorite, *Swallows and Amazons*) or exploring the magic of *Tom's Midnight Garden,* they were enthusiastic participants in a world that ultimately held more light than shadow. We can see influences of English literature in much of Miyazaki's art, from echoes of *Winnie-the-Pooh* in *Panda! Go Panda* (Panda kopanda, 1972) to the 2012 film *Howl's Moving Castle,* directly based on the English young adult novel by Diana Wynne Jones.

Yet the major cultural influence in Miyazaki's own young adult years turns out to be a hybrid of Japan and China, the animated movie *Panda and the Magic Serpent* (Hakujaden), released in 1958, when the director was seventeen. Lore of Miyazaki's encounter with this film, the first full-color animated movie produced in Japan, has reached almost mythic proportions. He went to see it at a "third-run theater in a seedy part of town" while in the midst of "examination hell." He remembers his first viewing in terms more commonly used for describing the beginnings of romantic love: "I was moved to the depths of my soul and—with snow starting to fall on the street—staggered home. After seeing the dedication and earnestness of the heroine, I felt awkward and pathetic, and I spent the entire evening hunched over the heated *kotatsu* table weeping."[35]

Based on an ancient Chinese ghost story about a white snake who falls in love with a human young man, the movie is sweetly conventional, with a villain (a disreputable monk) and a couple of adorable animals who seem straight out of Disney. It was neither these animals nor the appealing animation that bowled Miyazaki over, but the movie's lovely young heroine, particularly her "purity of emotion."[36] We can see those exact aspects of the heroine in many of Miyazaki's own protagonists, from the self-sacrificing Lana in *Future Boy Conan* to the earnest young Fio in *Porco Rosso*.

While still acknowledging the film's impact, Miyazaki now seems to regard *Panda and the Magic Serpent* with some ambivalence. He describes it as a "cheap melodrama" while still acknowledging the strong effect of its "pure earnest world."[37] At the time, though, it helped lead him away from the "bitter" world of the gekiga manga of high school toward not only a more "earnest and pure" worldview but an appreciation of the animated medium itself, an appreciation augmented by a 1963 viewing of the Russian animated film *The Snow Queen*.

Miyazaki's intense reaction to the film suggests that he was at an emotional turning point. Buffeted by family issues, immersed in examination hell, he found in *Panda and the Magic Serpent* a vision of an alternative world, one whose cartoon purity, innocence, and beauty would set him on the path to become an animator.

# 3
# The Joy of Movement

My real schooling was at Tōei Animation.

— MIYAZAKI

Miyazaki became an animator in 1963 at the age of twenty-two, still unsure about animation and believing that his real talent lay in drawing manga. Tōei Animation had produced *Panda and the Magic Serpent,* the film that first generated Miyazaki's interest in animation. At Tōei he learned the joy of movement, how to give life to his inanimate creations so that they would speak to audiences even more eloquently than do the still pictures in a manga.

Miyazaki embodied movement during that formative time and for the next decade as well. Years later two of his fellow animators from that period, the husband and wife Yōichi Kotabe and Reiko Okuyama, describe his eight-year whirlwind progress up the company ranks in an interview revealingly entitled, "He Was a Man Who Could Not Be Satisfied Unless He Was Running Like the Wind."[1] Miyazaki remained on the move, even after leaving Tōei, not only from studio to studio but on several location trips to Europe and America that would open up a new visual world for him.

With Studio Ghibli and Tezuka Osamu's Mushi Productions, Tōei ranks among Japan's most influential animation studios. After *Panda and the Magic Serpent,* Tōei went on for another fifty years giving Japan and the world such hits as *Galaxy Express 999, Dragonball Z,* and *Sailor Moon.* One wonders whether the psychologically believable young heroines of the 1990s megahit *Sailor Moon* were influenced by Miyazaki's many empowered female protagonists. By the time of *Sailor Moon,* however, Miyazaki was long gone from Tōei.

His eight years at the studio had an enormous impact. In addition to his swift mastery of animation techniques, which became something of a legend in the company, his leftist political leanings became solidified in a dispute with Tōei authorities. And perhaps most important, at Tōei he met two men who became his "elder brother figures": the master animator Yasuo Ōtsuka, a happy-go-lucky artist famous for his grayish cap and love of model planes, who ended up becoming a vital colleague on Miyazaki's *Future Boy Conan* and *Castle of Cagliostro,* and Isao Takahata, the visionary, intellectually inclined director who became his partner in founding Studio Ghibli.

The studio was housed in a wooden building (concrete was too expensive), in Nerima Ward, an area that became home to other major animation studios, most important Mushi Pro. An outgrowth of a live action movie studio that specialized in *jidaigeki* (historical samurai drama), Tōei Animation was established in 1956 by the financier Hiroshi Okawa. In the decades after *Panda and the Magic Serpent,* Japanese animation took exciting new directions, still inspired by Disney and other Western studios but increasingly treading its own distinctive path.

The animated works that remain from the prewar period already show both technical skill and imagination in producing entertaining, sometimes almost surreal, fantasy works. During the war, the government exploited these qualities to produce two memorable propaganda films, *Momotaro's Divine Sea Eagles* (Momotaro no umiwashi) and *Momotaro's Divine Sea Warriors* (Momotaro no umi no shinpei). At more than two hours long the latter was Japan's first feature-length animated film. Both films featured cute fairy-tale characters and attack scenes depicting, respectively, the attack on Pearl Harbor and the invasion of Singapore. Truly incongruous combinations of the cute and the deadly, the films do not seem to have made any impression on Miyazaki. I find no mention of them in his interviews. Yet in certain scenes, we can see a similar thematic merging of darkness and beauty that animates both Miyazaki's and Takahata's work, most notably a strangely lyrical episode in which bombs float across a bucolic landscape like fireflies.

One finds surprisingly rich emotional depths in the Tōei features that the young Miyazaki became involved with. Yasuo Ōtsuka suggests that even at that period Japanese animation emphasized "story and characters" rather than the "gag-based cartoons" coming out of American animation studios. Ōtsuka believes that Japanese audiences care more about *fun'iki,* a word that means atmosphere but also has a strong emotional resonance. He also insists that American audiences are more "utilitarian" in their attitudes, implying that Japanese animation was more willing to go in different directions, with unexpected twists and turns.[2]

This is certainly the case with two of the Tōei works that Miyazaki is most prominently associated with, *Gulliver's Travels beyond the Moon* (Garibā no uchū ryokō, 1965) and *The Great Adventure of Horus, Prince of the Sun* (Taiyō no ōji Horusu no daibōken, 1968). While Tōei advertised that it was bringing "pleasant and bright entertainment" to the children of the world, these two movies contain surprisingly dark, complex themes. That they include cute characters and adorable animals, in sync with Tōei's stated ambition to become the "Disney of the East," makes for sometimes strange juxtapositions. In a scene from *Gulliver,* for example, a group of travelers from Earth attempt to explain to alien robots what their planet is like. They sing a song whose tune and accompanying images initially evoke bright clichés of the seasons and nature. But the images sometimes turn grotesque, as when a school of silvery fish instantaneously become skeletons while the characters sing about a "bomb dropping." Needless to say, such a sequence would be inconceivable in a Disney film.

The animation itself is quite good, an impressive accomplishment considering the constraints of budgets, resources, and staff members that Tōei had to contend with. In his memoirs Ōtsuka proudly remarks that, as early as *Panda and the Magic Serpent,* Tōei was able to create a film that was worthy of Disney with far fewer animators and financial resources.

The actual techniques of animation did not vary greatly among different countries. In Japan or the United States the work was inordinately time consuming and the animators largely underpaid and often overworked—although they managed to include time for play as well, for example, taking off to study animals at the zoo and not returning to the studio for hours. To animators today Tōei Animation of the late 1950s and 1960s might seem as quaint and quirky as a contemporary engineer would find the Wright Brothers' workshop. In a world without computers animation was hand drawn on sheets of celluloid known as cels. A "key animator" made the original drawing, after which "inbetweeners" would draw numerous versions of it to fill out the sequence until the next key drawing in the series. At the end a colorist would provide the finishing touches. This arrangement required not only excellent drawing skills but an ability to produce pictures at a maximum speed.

According to Ōtsuka, "Right from the beginning, Miyazaki was someone who could produce sketches at an incredibly fast rate." This talent had clearly helped get him hired at Tōei. Ōtsuka recalls that the studio's entrance exam emphasized "showing through movement."[3]

Initially, Tōei assigned Miyazaki to be an inbetweener, one of the most arduous jobs in animation. It is also a job that teaches the most basic nuts and bolts, the importance of paying constant attention to detail and how to create movement through a series of drawings. The new employee showed a strong work ethic, but it was not only his work ethic that made an impression. Within a year the newest hire was beginning to build a legend for himself.

The original building block of the Miyazaki legend was his contribution to Tōei's first space opera, *Gulliver's Travels beyond the Moon*. Part of an incipient trend toward science fiction anime, the film is very, *very* loosely based on Jonathan Swift's *Gulliver's Travels*. Tōei made Gulliver, the English adventurer, into an elderly scientist, and sent him off on an adventure to the planet of Blue Hope. The movie is quite entertaining and animated with the fluidity and brightness of a Disney film. The backgrounds are particularly impressive, ranging from a Parisian-looking European city to a nightmare technopolis on the alien planet.

The story itself is considerably more disconcerting and challenging than typical Disney fare, however, with dark themes and unexpected images bordering on the surreal. In addition to the song explaining life on Earth to robots that devolves into a vision of transience and decay, another scene employs discordant, sinister music to evoke a sophisticated sense of technological threat.

What Tōei employees remember most about the movie is a totally unexpected ending twist suggested by a young animator, Miyazaki. In retrospect, that twist points the way toward key aspects in the director's life and vision that would become Miyazakiworld.

*Gulliver*'s initial premise was that the explorers land on a world in which one group of robots is fighting another, more vicious, group of robots. The latter have taken over the Planet of Blue Hope and made it into a "demonic" realm. In another of the movie's surreal song (and dance) numbers, the "good" robots sing regretfully about their arrogance and stupidity in creating a dominant robot race. The song mingles a mechanistic beauty with dystopian rhythms and imagery to create a compelling warning about the dangers of hubris and technology.

Less interesting was the movie's original conclusion, in which Gulliver and his sidekicks foiled the "evil" robots and rescued the "good" robot princess, who, in another surreal touch, has been carried off by the evil robots inside a giant chess piece shaped like a horse. This scene was retained but with a simple but fundamental change that Miyazaki suggested to the writers: when the heroes open the chess piece, the princess robot splits apart to reveal a human girl.

Ōtsuka vividly remembers the impact this suggestion had: "The change was only a single cut but from the point of view of the work as a whole it was an enormous departure." Commenting on how this change reflects Miyazaki's fundamental worldview, Ōtsuka adds, "From that time on Miyazaki pursued the core of animation in terms of strongly advocating the evocation of human beings within the overall theme of the work."[4]

A revelation, *Gulliver's Travels beyond the Moon,* Toei Studio, 1965

Kotabe and Okuyama, who worked with Miyazaki during that period, also remember the incident vividly. They explain how incongruous it was for a newbie to push himself forward in that way. "It's a famous story . . . his changing the final storyboard," Okuyama recalled. "He was an inbetweener, you know. So there was the producer and the director and there were other inbetweeners above him. . . . And yet, by pushing his opinion to change a single section of the story, he completely changed the meaning of the movie." "I was shocked when I saw how he had changed the scene," said Kotabe. "The difference was amazing. From something inorganic emerges a real human being, and for an instant the wind flutters her hair. That was really something never done before. We thought 'Wow!' when it turned out that it was Hayao Miyazaki who had thought it up."[5]

This episode prefigures a central tenet of Miyazakiworld: the director puts human beings inside a larger cultural matrix, one that includes robots, and many other "others" as well. Simple changes such as the wind fluttering a princess's hair can make a scene truly memorable. Throughout his work Miyazaki has used both wind and hair as visual shortcuts to express his characters' psychology and, again, to place humans within a larger cultural and natural context.

The story also demonstrates how far Miyazaki had traveled psychologically from his "timid" childhood and adolescence. The seventeen-year-old who had wept all night in the kotatsu seems to have disappeared. Although it is likely that his old insecurities and anxieties still bedeviled him on occasion, the face the young animator showed his fellow animators was a confident one, even a touch arrogant.

This attitude did not always play well with his colleagues. Ōtsuka describes Miyazaki as "rolling forward like a heavy tank," noting that the newcomer's "fiercely keen insistence" was a bewildering shock to some of the old-style animators, and even to his peers. Senior colleagues "displayed undisguised opposition" to the young upstart.[6] It is unusual for new employees to push themselves forward in any organization and in the hierarchical Japanese society of 1965 such behavior was truly surprising.

What had changed in Miyazaki to give him this kind of self-confidence? Simply growing up and going out in the world may have had something to do with it. By the time he entered Tōei he was no longer living at home. Instead, he had rented a four and a half–mat tatami room in Nerima, where the studio was located. Four and a half mats—about eighty square feet—is truly tiny by American standards, but it was all his own and helped Miyazaki develop an identity as a young man away from his family.

It is also likely that Miyazaki was beginning to discover something important about himself—that he was an exceptionally talented artist. His colleagues may have been shocked or irritated by him, but they were already acknowledging his genius. The long intense hours of working at Tōei were bringing out Miyazaki's skills on many fronts, not only in art but as a storyteller.

This is not to say that he always loved his work or, more specifically, the working conditions at Tōei, which were marked by a charged atmosphere of conflict between the animators and Tōei management. Miyazaki was in the thick of the conflict. Again belying his newcomer status, Miyazaki became secretary of the company union and played a significant role in coordinating union activities as the tension between management and workers steadily increased through the 1960s.

Union tensions were strongly influenced by the increasingly fractious political atmosphere in Japan in that turbulent decade. The political climate in Japan, as in much of the world, was suffused with anger, stirred by the decade's social and cultural changes and by youthful resistance to government authority. Some of this unrest was exciting and fun. One of Miyazaki's female colleagues fondly remembers the youthful, collaborative spirit and the miniskirts of the era.[7]

But the 1960s had a deeply serious side as well. By the decade's end student and worker dissatisfaction with the government and corporations had flamed into violence and tumult, leading to massive strikes, widespread university closings, and the formation of terrorist groups like the Red Army. But in the early sixties, dissatisfaction centered around what the Japanese referred to as Anpo, the Japan-American Security Treaty, under which the Japanese government agreed to continue its policy of providing bases for the American military. In 1960 hundreds of thousands of Japanese students and workers had marched against renewal of the treaty, clashing with police and government troops.

By his own account, Miyazaki was largely a bystander during the most intense antigovernment agitation. The initial anti-Anpo movement had faded by the time he entered Tōei, and he took part in only a couple of small demonstrations. It was inside Tōei rather than on the streets that Miyazaki began to establish his new sense of himself, as an animator and as a politically aware and concerned young citizen. When Miyazaki said, "My real schooling was at Tōei animation," he was referring, at least in part, to his union involvement.[8]

The political and ideological struggles between the union and management were important bases for the antiauthoritarian outlook that the director still feels intensely. But it is also likely that simply becoming part of a group of committed and passionate people left a large impression on his future work habits. Kotabe and Okayama speculate that while someone like Miyazaki might have a tendency to be a lone wolf, the union gave him an opportunity to learn about being part of a team.[9] Associating with a variety of people in the union while creating works of art as a group taught the young man the value of harnessing other people's talents, which would be of enormous importance to him as head of his own studio.

Ultimately, disputes over wages and a growing distrust toward management led to an increased sense of solidarity and a renewed energy among the animators. The young men and women involved with the union believed that they could create a democratic workforce, with neither superiors nor inferiors, just a team of talented individuals working together to create good animation.

The product of this new sense of commitment would be *The Great Adventure of Horus, Prince of the Sun,* the first movie directed by Takahata. While that distinction alone makes the movie a landmark in Japanese animation history, *Horus* is memorable for other reasons. It may have been the first movie ever made in Japan by a team of supposed equals. Wanting to smash what he and his fellow union leaders saw as arbitrary distinctions and hierarchies, Takahata leveled the playing field, pulling in directors, artists, and finishers, who had been on different floors, and collecting them in one place. For Michiyo Yasuda, a colorist who would go on to become one of Miyazaki's most important collaborators, this change was liberating: "We felt as if we had gone from being workers in a factory to being members of a team," she remembers. According to Yasuda, the unofficial slogan of the *Horus* team was "Let's do this together!"[10]

The result of these genuinely exciting changes is a mixed bag of a movie. At the risk of being permanently drummed out of Ghibli fandom, I find it to be one of the more uneven works in Takahata's oeuvre. Part of the problem is the unevenness of the animation itself. Though the film went frighteningly over budget, there are moments when the animation looks surprisingly uninspired.

Horus pulls a sword out of the Rock Man in *Horus: Prince of the Sun,* Toei Studio, 1968.

The story, although innovative in its time, is clumsier than anything either director would do in the future. Set in a vaguely European-looking village during the Stone Age, the narrative is a coming-of-age tale. It features an energetic and courageous young boy, Horus, who, graciously pulls a "thorn" out of the shoulder of a gigantic creature known as the Rock Man. Upon extraction, he discovers that the "thorn" is actually a sacred sword. Horus soon learns that he needs both his sword and his wits in order to battle an evil ice monster, Grunwald, who had killed Horus's father and is now threatening to destroy an innocent village. This being, technically at least, a children's film, all ends happily, with Grunwald defeated and Horus becoming the leader of the village, companioned by the beautiful and enigmatic young woman Hilda, who is Grunwald's younger sister.

Beyond the adventure story clichés, there are some genuinely fresh and interesting elements to *Horus*. The backgrounds, largely drawn by Miyazaki, are beautifully realized, giving a detailed sense of the rustic village environment. Takahata, who himself was not an animator, created visceral action scenes, such as Horus being attacked by silver wolves or a tour de force sequence in which Horus battles a giant pike. In these scenes the figures' dynamic movements compensate for the simpler depictions of faces and hair. Grunwald himself is a clichéd evildoer, but the rock man at the beginning of the movie is more intriguing. Rising up out of the earth, he suggests a connection with a wider and older natural world that the film otherwise largely ignores. It is perhaps not surprising the Miyazaki was responsible for this figure. Nor is it surprising that Japanese critics find traces of the rock man in the primordial figure of the *shishigami,* the godlike creature who dominates the forest in *Princess Mononoke.*[11]

Hilda, Grunwald's conflicted sister, has supernatural powers and a combination of strength and distance that makes her a genuinely memorable character. The team created two animal sidekicks to express Hilda's inner conflicts, an evil owl and a kindly squirrel, employing the powers of fantasy to provide psychological realism at a surprisingly sophisticated level for the time. Hilda's complexity makes her both interesting and appealing.

It was Takahata's idea to bestow on Hilda her most memorable characteristic, her spellbinding singing voice. Music is also important in other scenes, and here too Takahata makes unusual choices. Influenced by his notion of the Eastern bloc countries under the Soviets as places of friendly group effort, the director created scenes in which the villagers work and play while euphorically singing Eastern European folksongs.

Okuyama recalls Miyazaki singing "Russian songs" while working at his desk, wearing a dirty mountain climber's cap and sporting a "really filthy" hand towel at his waist.[12] Clearly the young animator was getting into the spirit of the team. In an interview about *Horus* Miyazaki later recalled, "I can't count the number of things I learned from *Horus,*" saying the movie provided him with the "ABC's" of animation. He particularly credits Ōtsuka for giving responsibility to him, the "lowest inbetweener in the company."[13]

The veteran members of the team were soon taking the lowly inbe-tweener seriously. Ōtsuka remembers the dynamic back and forth between Takahata and Miyazaki. Ōtsuka describes the concept of snowballing, which he says came from American animation: "As you roll one idea along it gradu-ally gets bigger. . . . Takahata would take a look at a little sketch by Miyazaki, for example the village background, and he would ask, 'So if the village is like this, what kind of house would they have, what would be inside the house, what would be in the position of the village in relation to the river?' . . . He'd ask all kinds of things like that. . . . And Miyazaki would return to his desk and start drawing in response to Takahata's questions." In another interview Ōtsuka uses a baseball metaphor to describe Takahata as "pitcher" and Mi-yazaki as "catcher," saying that it was Takahata who "pulled out" Miyazaki's talent.[14]

"It was Miyazaki who remained till the end the audience for Taka-hata's anxieties," Ōtsuka states. Yet Miyazaki himself is surprisingly vague about his working relationship with Takahata on *Horus,* mentioning only that he considered Takahata "quite orthodox" as a director and that he took a "justifiable amount of time and space in making the movie." His comments about Takahata and *Horus* are somewhat less measured a few years later, pointing toward his impatience at Takahata's slow work pace, an element that would become an increasing bone of contention after the founding of Ghibli. While he praised Takahata for "proving that animation has the power to depict the inner mind of humans in depth," he also referred to the man who was by now his closest colleague as a "giant sloth." Takahata's slow pace would eventually drive a wedge between the two. Reminiscing about *Horus,* Miyazaki (perhaps humorously, perhaps not) asserts that Takahata's performance as director "showed how risky and scary it was for a corpora-tion to make him the director of a feature-length film."[15]

If anything, Miyazaki understates the depth of Tōei management's hostility toward Takahata. Hugely over budget and three years in the mak-ing at a time when most films took less than a year, *Horus* would prove to be Takahata's swan song at the company. Occupying a gray area between child and adult audiences and never catching on with either, the film was pulled from release a mere twelve days after it opened.

Tōei workers felt that the company's negativity toward *Horus* had to do with the film's close relationship with the union. No doubt they had a point. Yasuda still remembers that the *Horus* team "burned with idealism," and that the "real theme of the movie is the ideal of the labor union."[16]

However, even the compilers of a laudatory 1984 book on *Horusu* admit that the schedule and budget overruns were "an order of magnitude higher" than on any other Tōei features. While acknowledging that this was due to the commitment to excellence of staffers who "suffered" for their art, the compilers also acknowledge, "It must also have been really tough from the point of view of the company." The book includes a copy of a memo from management to the *Horus* team that reads like any studio's nightmare. Enumerating the many overruns and problems throughout all aspects of the work, the memo concludes rather pathetically that the studio "hopes that [the staff] will recognize and take responsibility for this serious mission."[17]

Fortunately, Takahata went on to achieve aesthetic and professional vindication through his partnership with Miyazaki. That vindication was not immediate, however. Takahata and Miyazaki left the studio in 1971, but it took them some years to achieve success. Joining A Production Studio, the two were excited to develop an animated version of the immensely popular *Pippi Longstocking* stories. The *Pippi* stories are set in Sweden, and A Production sent a team there to ask Astrid Lindgren, their author, for permission to film the work. The trip to Sweden was Miyazaki's first time abroad. Kotabe, who along with Miyazaki and Takahata had quit Tōei, recalls Miyazaki's nervously wandering the airport.[18]

The mission ended unsuccessfully. Lindgren rejected the proposal point-blank. Kotabe speculates that she "didn't want Japanese people" to make a movie of her book.[19] It is also possible that she simply hesitated to turn her beloved heroine over to an unknown group of animators. The rejection must have been deeply painful, especially for Miyazaki, who had made dozens of sketches in preparation. Years later Ghibli published these sketches in a book with the nostalgic title of *The Pippi Longstocking That Never Was* (Maboroshi no nagakutsu no Pippi), and the hundred or so drawings, full of charming details, attest to the effort Miyazaki had put into them.

All that preparation and travel was not entirely wasted, however. The sunny European childhood world of *Pippi*, not to mention the beauty of European cityscapes and nature, found its way into other works of Miyazaki and Takahata. The most famous example is the city of Koriko, where Miyazaki's 1989 movie *Kiki's Delivery Service* takes place, and which is modeled partly on the Swedish cities of Visby and Stockholm that the team had visited en route to meeting Lindgren. A love of Europe had been instilled in Miyazaki, and European settings and characters would go on to play an important role in Miyazakiworld.

But *Pippi*'s influence was not only visual. The red-haired, assertive Pippi in Lindgren's books was a highly memorable character. Adventurous and autonomous, she was a fresh kind of heroine at a time when women's roles were beginning to change. Pippi is undoubtedly another inspiration for the parade of resilient and adventurous young girls that would become one of Miyazaki's calling cards, from at least as early as Nausicaä to Ponyo in his second-to-last movie. Both are redheads.

A plucky red-haired heroine appeared only a year after the trip to Sweden. This is Mimiko, the very young girl who is the protagonist of one of Takahata's and Miyazaki's first major hits, the film *Panda Go Panda* (Panda kopanda, 1972) and its sequel *Panda Go Panda! Rainy Day Circus* (Amefuri sākasu no maki, 1973). While Takahata directed the first *Panda*, Miyazaki still played an important role in its creation, a role that expanded when he took over most of the direction of the second film.

The movies were an obvious attempt to pander to the panda frenzy that swept Japan after China had sent two of the cuddly creatures to a Tokyo zoo. It is not surprising that the two films were hits, but their genuinely idiosyncratic elements are indeed startling. The narratives seem to combine *Pippi Longstocking* with doses of *Winnie-the-Pooh* and anticipate the American live action *Home Alone* series.

The story begins with Mimiko's grandmother going to visit Nagasaki, leaving her granddaughter on her own. One might expect the tiny six-year-old Mimiko to be nervous about her grandmother's absence, but she seems unfazed, even when she encounters a baby panda and, soon after that, his very large panda father. The pandas have escaped from a nearby zoo, and Mimiko offers them shelter. They become a family, although the relationships are a bit complex, since Papa Panda becomes the "father" of both Mimiko and Panny, the baby panda, while Mimiko becomes Panny's mother.

The trio soon engage in a variety of adventures involving the townspeople, the police, and, in *Rainy Day Circus,* a visiting zoo, where they encounter another escaped wild animal, this time a cute baby tiger. Mimiko remains her plucky and adventurous self throughout both films, even standing up to an understandably puzzled policeman and zoo officials who are trying to recapture the pandas and, later, a whole troupe of circus animals.

The energetic little girl and a large cuddly creature prefigured Miyazaki's future masterpiece *Totoro.* In fact, one scene of Mimiko jumping onto Papa Panda's stomach clearly anticipates the famous shot of Mei jumping onto Totoro's furry chest, followed by her older sister, Satsuki. Yet it must be noted how very far *Totoro* is from the *Panda* movies. These are lighthearted and simple works that do little to suggest *Totoro*'s multilayered and subtle qualities. The silent, furry Totoro, who resembles no specific living creature, is a far more memorable and interesting creation than the chatty Papa Panda, and is capable of stirring the imagination in ways that the more prosaic Papa Panda cannot. Mimiko is also a fundamentally one-note creation, relentlessly enthusiastic and upbeat in a way that does not suggest the behavior of the average small child.

But *Panda Go Panda* can still be appreciated for its antic storytelling as well as for its links to other Miyazaki films, the most interesting being an episode in *Rainy Day Circus* of a flood caused by a rainstorm. Mimiko and the pandas venture out into the flood to rescue the little tiger. The self-sufficient child in a flooded world on his or her way to rescue appears again in Miyazaki's postapocalyptic adventure series *Future Boy Conan* and becomes the major theme of *Ponyo.*

While the *Panda* movies took place in a recognizably Japanese world, much of Miyazaki's work in the 1970s revolved around Europe. Again changing studios, Miyazaki, Kotabe, and Takahata moved to Zuiyo Eizō Studios, where they began work on an animated version of *Heidi,* the popular children's story about a young girl growing up in the Swiss Alps.

The *Panda* films, with their clearly Japanese domestic setting, and the European-based *Heidi* can be seen as two sides of what would become fundamental building blocks of Miyazakiworld. Johanna Spyri's *Heidi* is a lovely and inspiring book, which was adapted into a lovely and inspiring animation series. The mountain backgrounds are ravishing, based on a research trip to Switzerland undertaken by Miyazaki and Takahata before beginning production on the series. The characters are also appealing and believable, and the animation in general is of high quality. The narrative largely respects the original and, over fifty-two episodes, achieves some genuine psychological complexity as it explores the complicated and sometimes painful relationships of Heidi and her friends and family.

Given its beauty and charm, it is not surprising that the series was an enormous hit in Japan, where forty years later, a television special announced that *Heidi* was the "number one favorite anime" among Japanese female viewers.[20] But it was also a global hit, becoming popular in thirty-five countries around the world. Surprisingly, the series was never translated into English and never reached the United States.

Miyazaki's and Takahata's next project was *Anne of Green Gables* (Akage no An, 1979), a delicate coming-of-age story about a young orphan. Set on Canada's Prince Edward Island, its green beauty nonetheless evokes the lush scenery of *Heidi.* As with *Heidi, Anne* benefited from the talents of both directors and also became an enormous hit, especially among Japanese girls, to the extent that even today Prince Edward Island owes much of its tourist industry to the legions of nostalgic Japanese women who visit there.

As with *Heidi,* very little critical attention has been paid to *Anne,* perhaps because both are faithful renditions of their sources, and because it is hard to delineate Miyazaki's contribution from that of Takahata. In fact,

Miyazaki left the series after fifteen episodes, but Anne remains another example of the two directors' fondness for strong-willed young heroines.

Miyazaki's other work from the same period, the 1978 *Future Boy Conan* (Mirai shōnen Conan), was his first in a long time to prominently feature a boy as protagonist. The first work to have Miyazaki as its sole director, and unfortunately not available in the United States, *Conan* is significant for many reasons. The only television series ever directed by Miyazaki, its twenty-six episodes provide an invaluable glimpse into the development of Miyazakiworld.

Looking over Miyazaki's career at this point we can see two general trends in his work and in works he was associated with. Broadly speaking, we can see aspects of *Gulliver* and *Horus* as the dark side of Miyazaki's worldview. This is particularly true of *Horus,* although *Gulliver*'s dystopian technological vision would appear in more complex form in many future Miyazaki movies. Although much indebted to Takahata's directing, *Horus*'s strong political message and expression of a violent, sometimes ruthless universe is also deeply rooted in Miyazaki's own ideology. Authoritarian entities try to dominate and destroy their fellows. Corrupt leaders must be fought against. And nature itself is not always benign. Floods and earthquakes intrude, leaving the viewer with a sense of human vulnerability to larger outside forces. Ruins and remnants of human civilization cast long shadows over the characters' lives.

These being the works of Takahata and Miyazaki, human nature at its best always reasserts itself, usually in memorably lively, even rambunctious form. *Horus,* for example, highlights the importance of collective effort with utopian scenes of the villagers fishing, planting, and celebrating. Other positive elements include strong female characters who are in many cases the central characters. Often these females are connected with nature, and the appreciation of the beauty and power of the natural world runs through all of the works so far discussed. Water plays a major role in the *Panda* series and in *Horus,* anticipating its enormous significance in later Miyazaki films such as *Conan, Cagliostro,* and *Ponyo.* Sentient animals are major characters in *Horus* and *Panda Go Panda,* and family or at least pseudofamilies are hallmarks of *Heidi, Anne,* and the *Panda* series.

*Conan* unites the dark and the light. The series is a multithreaded twenty-six-episode tapestry that combines moments of apocalyptic despair with visions of exultation and humor, in the process becoming a blueprint for the many Miyazaki masterpieces that follow. Highly entertaining, even sometimes gripping in itself, as the seedbed of so much of the director's later work, it remains an essential text for anyone interested in the development of Miyazakiworld.

Like *Anne* and *Heidi, Conan* is based on a children's book, in this case the American young adult novel *The Incredible Tide,* by Alexander Key. Unlike *Anne* and *Heidi,* however, *Conan* deviates considerably from the novel. A postapocalyptic science fiction work with an overtly Cold War context, *The Incredible Tide* describes a world in which warfare and accompanying earthquakes and giant tsunamis have devastated the human race, leaving only a few islands in a largely ocean-covered Earth. Only two major civilizations remain, the New Order and High Harbor. The New Order and its main city, Industria, as their pompous names suggest, evoke the former Soviet Union with its rigid hierarchies, militarism, and emphasis on factory work. High Harbor, while hosting some sinister inhabitants, prizes nature and community.

The novel's protagonist, Conan, belongs to neither place but at the beginning is shipped off to Industria essentially as a slave in a factory. Uniting with Lana, a girl who can communicate with birds, and with her grandfather, Conan escapes from the New Order and arrives in High Harbor. Another giant earthquake has been predicted, and Conan and his friends appear just in time to save the inhabitants from another tsunami. And there the novel ends, or rather peters out, though with a suggestion that the remaining humans will finally resolve their differences and work together in the future.

Miyazaki took the basic elements of *The Incredible Tide*—the postapocalyptic setting, the diverse group of main characters, and the two conflicting civilizations—and transformed them into a completely original vision. Many of these changes were necessitated by the fact that a twenty-six-episode series was being spun out of a short novel, but it is also evident that the young animator was putting his intellectual and artistic stamp on the source material in a richly assertive fashion. Or as Ōtsuka, who worked with Miyazaki on *Conan,* puts it succinctly, "The fundamental element of Miyazaki's work is destruction and re-creation."[21] It is a predilection that would inform many of Miyazaki's future aesthetic choices.

The young director's willingness to perform extensive surgery on another's source material attests to his burgeoning self-assurance and is also evidence of his enormous commitment to the series. With some help from Takahata, Miyazaki took on all the main jobs, establishing the story's premise, doing all the storyboards and layout, and finishing the entire series in six months. Hard workers themselves, the rest of the staff were still amazed at his extraordinary work ethic. Ōtsuka admiringly compares Miyazaki during this period to the Incredible Hulk, as he transformed himself into a cauldron of focused energy. The veteran animator sees *Conan* as the first building block in what he himself calls "Miyazaki's world" (Miyazaki no sekai), and points to how "Miyazaki looked at his characters as real beings."[22]

Certainly in *Conan* the characters seem to leap off the screen, especially the "future boy" himself. Takahata has admiringly described Miyazaki's "exuberant energy," and this same description holds true for Conan, who, as many critics point out, always seems to be in motion. A parentless child, Conan is basically a force of nature. He runs, swims, somersaults, climbs, hunts, fights. He also rescues—usually Lana, the girl whose arrival sets the story in motion and inspires Conan in his many acts of bravery and sacrifice. In a discussion of Miyazaki's work, Takahata uses the memorable term "escort heroes" to describe Miyazaki's male protagonists.[23] Although Conan is actually more assertively masculine than most of Miyazaki's later male heroes, his utter devotion to Lana is one of the many distinctive aspects of the series.

Lana is the consistent feminine principle to Conan's over-the-top masculinity. Graceful but strong willed, courageous but loving, and gifted with telepathic talents, especially in her ability to communicate with birds, she can be seen as the true ancestress of Miyazaki's future shōjo heroines. In the deep bond Conan forges with Lana we can see a certain amount of wish fulfillment on the director's part, stemming from his own relationship with his mother. The omni-competent Conan "escorts" the loving and protective female out of danger time and time again, achieving in fantasy what Miyazaki could not do for his ailing mother.

Lana and Conan's bond is a major theme of the series, but there are other memorable elements as well, some specific to the series, and others that anticipate later Miyazaki works. The most interesting of the former are the comic male characters, Conan's friend Jimshi and his sometime nemesis the feckless sea captain Dyce. The laid-back, carefree Ōtsuka speculates that he may have been the model for both of them, but buddy/buffoon characters vanish from later Miyazaki works, perhaps because feature films often do not have enough space for more than one major pairing.[24] Other character types in *Conan* possess more staying power, most notably the evil Industria leader Lepka and his temporary henchwoman Monsley. The irredeemably evil Lepka provides the foil for Conan to exercise his resistance to adult authority, as the villain grimly pursues him across their watery world. In general Miyazaki is known for creating nuanced characters rather than two-dimensional villains, but Lepka's lineage is evident in the corrupt Count Cagliostro and the power hungry Muska of *Laputa*.

More intriguing is the character of Monsley, a female doctor in the novel whom Miyazaki makes far more important and interesting. Key should be credited with creating her, but it is Miyazaki who effected her gradual transformation from Soviet-style apparatchik into an immeasurably more complicated figure, both empathetic and endearing.

As Ōtsuka comments, "Miyazaki had already come to understand the kind of movies he wanted to make, and these were thrilling tales separated from the everyday world."[25] Yet not completely separated. What makes the series most memorably Miyazaki-esque are its occasional dark notes and a degree of political consciousness revealed in the depiction of the shadowy totalitarian realm of Industria and the utopian pastoral community of High

Harbor. Both are considerably more richly described than in the novel. Perhaps inspired by Takahata, Miyazaki's Marxist leanings come through both in his addition of a heroic community of resistance activists in Industria and in the collaborative farming that the inhabitants of High Harbor engage in.

The opening theme song balances celebration with catastrophe. Under the opening credits a beautiful landscape of sea and sky unfurls. While children frolic in the waves and among flowers and forests, an upbeat chorus sings about loving a "reborn Earth" and welcoming the "awakening morning." Abruptly, however, music and scenery shift into darker tones, and we see a vast glowing cityscape against the night. A voiceover reveals that a terrible nuclear war has destroyed most of humanity, and the viewer sees fires and earthquakes crumble the tall skyscrapers.

*Conan* thus begins with loss and a vision of humanity in exile from itself. The tour de force opening gives way to an equally active first episode that again combines melancholy and joy. Ruins and remnants pervade the setting. We meet Conan and his grandfather, the last survivors of a rocket ship that went down on a small island that the two of them call Remnant Island. In typical Miyazaki fashion, however, the two survivors are resilient, especially the young Conan, whom we see using his incredible strength to hunt and capture an enormous shark. We learn that Conan has trained himself not to breathe for long periods under water, and the camera follows him deep below the waves as he weaves among the ruins of modern civilization. At one point Miyazaki includes a quick cut of the boy hiding from the shark in a submerged bathroom complete with toilet, a tiny reminder of humanity's lost daily life.

Among original episodes Miyazaki adds to Key's story is a clearly Marxist-inspired revolt of prisoners inured in the bowels of Industria, aided, of course, by Conan. But the most affecting adventure Miyazaki invents is an earlier episode in which Conan and Lana escape Monsley and her minions and find themselves in what at first seems an empty desert. It turns out to be populated—by ancient and abandoned aircraft, their fuselages and wings barely peeping up from the sand. Aside from the apocalyptic opening credits, this is the only overt reference to the war in the series. The essentially elegiac vision, a graveyard of airplanes, is typical of Miyazakiworld, bringing to mind his youthful appreciation of the "young men who had fought and died and wanted to live."

Lana and Conan discover that the buffoonish Captain Dyce has also been abandoned and shackled in the desert as punishment by Monsley. The two children unshackle him, but when Lana's grandfather suddenly appears with a rescue plane, they realize that Dyce will not fit in it. "No room," says the grandfather brusquely. Yet they save him. The children and grandfather rig up a rope that allows them to tow an uncomfortable Dyce out of danger.

Ōizumi points out that this episode is clearly based on Miyazaki's traumatic experience of 1945, when his family "didn't have room" for the neighbor and his child in their escape from the air raids. As Ōizumi sums it up, "What he [Miyazaki] was unable to do, he entrusted to his characters."[26]

Ultimately Conan and Lana's adventures lead them to a new rebirth of humanity. The last episode features a wedding, fireworks, and a ship under full sail heading back to Remnant Island. As the voyagers approach the island, they see that the earthquakes and tsunami have resurrected it as a continent. But on its highest mountain still sits the rocket ship that Conan and his fellows arrived in, now covered in vines. "'I'm home," Conan tell Lana. But for Miyazaki, *Conan* would be just the beginning of a long journey.

# 4
# Ups and Downs
## Castle of Cagliostro

Honestly, that generation was all crazy about Europe!

—TOSHIO SUZUKI

A man in a jacket and tie carries a young woman in white through a stone archway. The two stand silently for a moment, looking out at a serene vista of temples, statues, and fountains. The man helps the woman jump across a fallen stone column. Is it a destination wedding? Are they elaborately dressed tourists on a European vacation?

Neither. The man is Lupin, a notorious "gentleman thief," wanted by Interpol and by fat cats around the world. The girl is Clarisse, an adolescent noblewoman, recently graduated from a convent school. The vista that absorbs the two is Clarisse's newly discovered inheritance, a ruined Roman city hitherto covered by a lake before a series of extraordinary events revealed the sunken realm beneath it.

But this is not Clarisse's inheritance alone. As Lupin points out, this is a "treasure" that no thief, not even he, can carry off in his pocket. The ruined city belongs to all humanity, a beacon of beauty, grace, and civilization in a corrupt and violent world.

In Miyazaki's first feature film, *The Castle of Cagliostro,* the director creates a work as idiosyncratic as it is charming. *Cagliostro* is a caper film in which the "thief" winds up empty-handed. But along the way the audience enjoys picaresque escapades and picturesque architecture, including a magnificent castle whose dizzying walls, secret pathways, sinister dungeons, and stratospheric clock tower mark the beginning of what we might call Miyazaki's "castlephilia."

Even more typical of future Miyazaki works is *Cagliostro*'s finale. A lighthearted James Bond–style action film for most of its length, the movie metamorphoses at the end into the indelible vision of those uncovered Roman ruins. In what we will see become a hallmark of Miyazakiworld, it is a vision of humans engaging with nature and history to create a scene that includes not only transcendent beauty but also a fleeting touch of loss. As Svetlana Boym reminds us in her essay "Ruinophilia," "Ruin literally means collapse but actually ruins are more about remainders and reminders. . . . Ruins make us think about the past that could have been and the future that never took place—tantalizing us with Utopian dreams of escaping the irreversibility of time." In an eerie echo of Boym's words, Miyazaki reminisces about a childhood discovery of the ruins of a country villa destroyed during the war and comments, "The scene I saw amid the grasses as a child . . . was the remains of the cultured life that prewar people had sought . . . now rusted, leaning, decayed, and full of holes."[1] The inexorability of time and fate, embodied in Cagliostro castle's clock tower, may have particularly spoken to the introspective director who was making his first feature-length movie at the relatively late age of thirty-eight.

In some ways the film is Miyazaki's most escapist work, not quite fantasy but playing on our desires for an alternative reality in which the laws of physics and time, both cultural and personal, can be transcended. "I began by drawing a bird's eye picture . . . the lake and castle of a small country."[2] From this specific sense of place grows a world that draws us in. Targeted at an audience older than those of his previous features, the movie also reaches out to male viewers. Beneath its surface sparkle, *Cagliostro* explores issues of masculinity and middle age and leaves a bittersweet impression of its hero as a man of action in search of an elusive male identity that combined honor with pleasure, desire with self-respect, and righteousness with generosity. When Lupin tells Clarisse at the end of the movie that the "treasure" they have discovered is something that must be shared, he is also anticipating his own renunciation of one last "treasure," Clarisse's heart.

*Cagliostro* is a far cry from the original source, the popular manga and anime series *Lupin III,* about a European gentleman thief. The Lupin of the series was a playboy adventurer inspired by Ian Fleming's famous James Bond. *Lupin*'s creator, Kazuhiko Kato (otherwise known as Monkey Punch), understood that his largely male Japanese audience wanted something similar to Bond's combination of sex and sophistication in graphic novel form. The series remains immensely popular and has spawned live-action films and video games.

*Lupin* was based on the detective stories of the early-twentieth-century French writer Maurice Leblanc. Kato, however, mixed in elements of modern action movies, especially the Bond films, to create an adult-oriented series with spectacular and violent adventures and strong sexual themes. Kato's Lupin is a master of disguise and a clever strategist but also the kind of overtly sexist man who might be booed off the screen these days, a man ruled largely by lust—for money, women, and the thrill of the chase.

Miyazaki had different ideas. Unintimidated by the prospect of taking on a popular series with a well-established fan base, Miyazaki altered Kato's template considerably. His longtime collaborator Yasuo Ōtsuka saw *Cagliostro* as Miyazaki's "springboard," the film that made him a full-fledged director for the first time. Others, such as the critic Shunsuke Sugita, see the movie and the central character's "incompleteness" more equivocally. I believe, however, that the very "incompleteness" and the "strange sense of melancholy" that Sugita identifies point to Miyazaki's maturing vision.[3] *Cagliostro* not only announces the beginning of Miyazaki's sumptuous visual and action style but also serves as a surprisingly deep expression of the director's life and worldview as he approached middle age.

Ōtsuka was responsible for choosing Miyazaki to direct. As Ōtsuka recalls, "I had started to work on *Cagliostro* when Miyazaki phoned me one day and suggested that he take on the work of directing. 'YES,' I thought, thanking heaven. If Miyazaki came on board this couldn't fail to be an entertaining anime." In an early interview after the film's premier, Miyazaki downplays his desire to become a director, insisting that it was simply his "turn to shoulder the burden."[4]

As with *Conan,* however, Miyazaki immediately centralized his authority. Although another writer was brought in to help add typical Lupin-esque features to the second part of the movie, Miyazaki dominated the production, taking over the art, layout, animation, and characters. The work pace was incredible. "It is possible to say that among great Japanese animation *Cagliostro* was the feature that took the shortest time," Ōtsuka declared. For four months the team worked day and night. They virtually went without sleep at the end, fueled by thirty-six hundred cups of ramen, according to Ghibli chronicler Seiji Kano.[5]

The result was a highly entertaining film full of extraordinary action sequences powerful enough to be remembered thirty-five years later by Pixar's John Lasseter in a moving tribute on Miyazaki's supposed retirement. Recalling how he had been shown a clip from *Cagliostro* when Miyazaki and Ōtsuka had visited the Disney studios in 1988, Lasseter described being "completely blown away" by its kinetic energy. According to Ōtsuka, the Cagliostro clip went on to become an "object of study" at the Disney Studio.[6]

As with *Conan,* however, the movie plumbs deeper levels than pure entertainment, in keeping with the evolving vision of Miyazakiworld. While not as clearly ideological as *Conan,* it delves (gently) into international politics and into the complexities of romantic longing, which *Conan* had dealt with more lightheartedly. A moral seriousness that would have amazed *Lupin*'s literary creator culminates in a bittersweet finale that once again touches on Miyazaki's obsession with destruction and re-creation.

Ōtsuka by this time was fully aware of the younger director's tendency to shape material to his own purposes, interests, and aesthetics. However, even Ōtsuka might have been uneasy had he read an open letter that Miyazaki published in the *Lupin* fan club newsletter that made clear that his Lupin was going to be a very different character from the manga's flamboyant playboy hero. The fledgling director explained, "Lupin's actions are not really motivated by superficial things such as money, jewels or women." In fact, Miyazaki suggested, "At the base of Lupin's soul swirls a rage toward the machinery of society that suffocates humanity, and he tries to bury the falseness of his heart through spurring himself to action. He is fighting to give his life meaning and is yearning for someone who can lead him to that fight."[7]

Perhaps this newly nuanced, thoughtful Lupin is another version of Miyazaki's "redoing" of childhood conflicts, in this case a makeover of his "playboy" father. If so, the movie's more obvious and clearly evil father figure, the Count of Cagliostro, suggests some interesting psychic dynamics as Lupin relentlessly squares off against the villainous count, ultimately forcing his impalement on the castle clock tower. Whether we choose to see Oedipal implications, Lupin's complexity makes him a far more interesting character than the original manga hero, positioning him as the progenitor of a long line of nuanced and complicated male Miyazaki heroes, from Marco in *Porco Rosso* to Howl in *Howl's Moving Castle*.

Miyazaki adds a more multilayered moral vision to the movie itself. Sugita points out that Miyazaki's characterization of Lupin was particularly directed toward those who came of age in the 1970s.[8] A generation characterized by their elders as apathetic and materialistic, lacking in ideological commitment or willingness to sacrifice, they were particularly disappointing to Miyazaki, a believer in sixties activism. The original Lupin character belonged to this apathetic generation, with Kato portraying him as the son of a rich family who performed burglaries to stave off his own ennui.

While still scruffily glamorous, Miyazaki's Lupin is older, possibly wiser, and impoverished. He and his sidekick Jigen fight over the last portion of spaghetti and meatballs in a seedy tavern and drive a Fiat (based on Ōtsuka's own car), not the manga hero's sporty Mercedes. Yoshiki Sumikura sees them as anarchists rather than aristocrats, their escapades "rejections of private ownership," whether a "private" possession is money, a young girl, or a Roman ruin.[9]

Miyazaki clearly shares Lupin's righteous fury against a society that "suffocates humanity." Lupin's contempt for wealth and its trappings may also reflect Miyazaki's unease with his own privileged youth. The movie makes a point of playing up the decadence evident from the count's extravagant domicile in contrast to Lupin's ascetic lifestyle.

The gorgeous European settings underline Miyazaki's love of the European landscape cultivated during his location trips for *Heidi* and other works. As Helen McCarthy writes, "*Cagliostro* takes place in the never-never land that is the Japanese dream of Europe." Kano suggests that the many thrilling vertical movements in *Cagliostro* emanate from Miyazaki's fascination with the Italian hill towns the director had visited some time before, vertical communities perched precariously between sky and sea.[10]

For many Japanese people, traditional Europe was a kind of utopia of beauty and tradition, contrasting with the ever more frantically modernizing Japan. Miyazaki felt this as well, but he also saw Europe in a more ambivalent light. On an earlier trip to Switzerland the director recalled seeing a "short legged Asian" coming toward him only to realize that it was his own reflection in a passing window.[11] While this sense of uneasy cultural identity was shared by many Japanese citizens of his generation, as an artist Miyazaki was able to transcend this unease by projecting himself on the complex (and long-legged) character of Lupin. At thirty-eight he knew he would never be Lupin, but he still yearned for another, more glamorous, more assured persona. When Miyazaki in his open letter to the fans alludes to Lupin's desire to "give his life meaning," he might as well have been speaking about himself, the film's plethora of ascents and descents the visual manifestations of a deeper sense of unease. Miyazaki was on the cusp of middle age.

While thirty-eight may seem rather young by twenty-first-century standards, in interviews and discussions about the movie the director consistently referred to himself and his colleagues as "sullied" by middle age.[12] By *Cagliostro* Miyazaki had been a hardworking animator for sixteen intense years, moving from job to job and company to company. During that time he had married, moved to a new home, and become the father of two sons.

Miyazaki is extremely circumspect regarding his marriage and family. At the age of twenty-four (young, even by the standards at the time), he married Akemi Ota, a fellow animator at Tōei. Initially, according to Miyazaki, the plan was for Akemi to keep working. She was slightly older than her husband, and making more money than he did. Akemi was clearly a good animator with a mind of her own. In a lighthearted but informative cartoon depicting Miyazaki's work style, one of the couple's coworkers shows the director redrawing storyboards according to his wife's advice.

The couple's plans changed with the birth of their two sons. In one of the few interviews in which he discusses his marriage, the director recounts that he and Akemi initially continued working while their sons entered preschool. One day, however, he found himself walking beside a half-asleep child, suggesting that the children were not getting adequate rest.

It seemed clear that someone had to stay at home, and by this point Miyazaki's creativity and talent heralded a bright future as an animator. Furthermore, Japan's highly patriarchal family and employment system did not encourage a woman to work while her husband stayed home. While many animation industry employees were female, they usually had to give up any thought of marriage or family if they wanted to stay in the industry. One of Studio Ghibli's key female employees, Hitomi Tateno, joked about titling her reminiscences of her long years at the studio as *Thanks to Miyazaki and Suzuki, I Wasn't Able to Get Married.*[13]

Miyazaki admits that he was not an ideal family man. Although he says he "feels contrite about breaking my promise," he immediately adds, "but since [the time Akemi agreed to stay home] I have been able to focus on my work."[14]

The same cartoon that depicts Miyazaki asking his wife's advice also shows the director referring to his lunch box as a "magic lunch box" because "someone" fills it for him during the nighttime, a typical task for a traditional Japanese wife. But Akemi went beyond this conventional role to become a father surrogate for their children. Miyazaki has said, "My wife would finish up the housework and often do the things that fathers normally do, such as teach our boys kite-flying and top-spinning. On holidays [she and the boys] would sometimes go hiking."[15]

Miyazaki's wife has never publicly discussed their marriage, but interviews with their children, especially with the elder son Goro, indicate that they felt shortchanged by their father's lack of attention. Even by the extreme standards of the 1960s and 1970s Japanese workplace, Miyazaki worked an extraordinary number of hours. Goro remembers him coming home after they were asleep and spending his few days off in bed.[16] It is obvious that the director's heart was in his work and not his home.

Lupin also enjoys his work. In our first glimpse of him, he and his friend Jigen smoothly descend a rope outside a Monte Carlo casino, hauling bags of banknotes that they have just stolen. This brief sequence establishes their profession and anticipates the numerous images of ascent and descent that pervade the movie. We next see them in their little Fiat heading down the highway, diving happily into a mountain of banknotes that threatens to overflow the car.

So far, the action is reminiscent of any standard bank robbery escapade.

Suddenly, however, Lupin's eyes widen—it turns out that the treasured banknotes are all counterfeit. Exasperated but somehow amused, the would-be robbers heave the counterfeits out the window. A whirlwind of notes trails the Fiat, and strangely, what should have been a scene of comic frustration—the robbers themselves robbed—becomes one of celebration, even liberation. Clearly, money is not the key to happiness in this movie.

Miyazaki continues to interweave scenes suggesting conventional caper films with imagery evoking something more reflective. Shortly after the money flies out of the car, the Fiat suffers a flat tire, and Jigen draws the short straw in deciding who has to fix it. Miyazaki uses this sequence as a chance to offer the audience a breathing space, a "pillow shot," in which Lupin climbs to the top of the car and gazes around at the pretty countryside, serenely indifferent to his friend's efforts.

The next action sequence disrupts this quiet moment, providing one of the most spectacular scenes in the movie. A car driven by a girl in a white dress and veil races by the Fiat, closely followed by another car full of thugs. Lupin immediately decides to rescue the girl. "Typical!" his friend Jigen points out.

The girl is Clarisse, and she is fleeing a forced marriage to her much older evil cousin the Count of Caglistro. The count is not in love with Clarisse (although Lupin will humorously call him a "pedophile") but wishes to gain her family ring, the twin of one that he possesses, and one thought to be connected with a secret treasure. The count had locked her in a tower of his castle, an ominous Gothic structure that looms over the tiny country of Cagliostro. The country's beautiful mountains and tourist-friendly appeal hide a dark secret: Caglistro's castle dungeon is the site of the printing presses that produce the counterfeit notes we have just seen Lupin and Jigen blithely throwing away.

Lupin, it transpires, had visited Cagliostro once before in a failed attempt to break into the counterfeit mint. Now he returns again, but not for the cash. Instead, he embarks on a mission to save Clarisse from the corrupt count. The effort will involve the ring the count hopes to possess, a botched cathedral wedding, a couple of quasi-romantic encounters, and an array of daring rescue sequences, each more memorable than the last.

The opening chase continues up dauntingly narrow cliff roads, the sea sparkling behind. A gigantic bus materializes ahead. No matter. The little car leaps over the bus and drives along the *side* of the cliff and through a forest where Jigen ably dispatches the villains' car with a specially constructed gun and Lupin leaps into the fleeing girl's vehicle. The car goes over the cliff and smashes into the ocean far below. Lupin, however, has thrown a rope around a tree trunk. In another vertical action sequence he safely lowers Clarisse and himself down to the shore as the waves waft over remnants of the smashed automobile.

Although the opening chase ends with Clarisse's recapture, it remains one of the most memorable in Miyazaki's work, the one that Lasseter felt compelled to honor in his tribute to Miyazaki. Indeed, the entire opening sequence of *Cagliostro* is a tour de force—fast-paced and crammed with surprise twists and turns that at moments are quite hilarious, as when Lupin attempts to reason with an emotional Clarisse while they dangle over the cliff. Overall, the sequence demonstrates one of Miyazaki's most important strengths as an animator—his ability to create indelible action scenes, characterized by almost vertigo-inspiring ups and downs. In the coming year he continued to use this talent, with the action moved largely to the sky, from the intense aerial combat through clouds in his next movie, *Nausicaä,* to the soaring flight scenes of *The Wind Rises.*

A number of *Cagliostro*'s action sequences are impressive not only for their dynamism but also for their surprising emotional appeal, as well as the moral and metaphysical ground they cover. One occurs underwater when Lupin and Jigen sneak into the castle via the Roman aqueduct that connects the count's domain to their hideout in a nearby ruin. At one point the two hurl themselves over an immense sluice gate, only to be caught up in the giant cogs of the aqueduct system. Lupin's battle to escape the underwater cogs echoes one of Miyazaki's favorite episodes, Charlie Chaplin's struggle as a laborer in *Modern Times* to avoid becoming ensnared by the literal "cogs" of industrial society. *Cagliostro*'s sequence offers a similar critique of technology's imprisoning qualities.

In the following episode, in which Lupin firsts visits Clarisse, locked away in her tower room, technology continues to be a hindrance. Ascending laboriously up the opposite tower, he finally makes it to the top and uncoils a length of line attached to a rocket, hoping to send it to Clarisse's turret so that it can serve as a suspension line that he can move across. The audience is primed for a display of technical virtuosity, but Lupin's lighter fails to ignite and the rocket falls out of his hands, clattering down the impossibly steep roof. He scurries down the roof but picks up too much momentum to stop. In an ebullient scene that ignores the laws of physics, he shoots across the night sky as if he were the rocket himself, leaping lightly from rooftop to rooftop until he reaches Clarisse's tower, where he is able to throw a safety line to the top.

This scene shows Lupin at his best—physically dexterous, innovative, and able to cope with myriad setbacks that would send another man to his downfall. As he transcends gravity to reach his goal, the animation captures Lupin's light spirit and phenomenal determination. The film's final action scene mixes visceral thrills with genuine emotional resonance. Having barely rescued Clarisse from her impending wedding in the castle's sumptuous Gothic cathedral, Lupin races with her across the aqueduct to the clock tower, followed by the count and his ninjalike minions. Inside the clock tower, however, the machinery starts to move, lifting the fugitives up and down. In another scene that harks back to *Modern Times,* giant mechanical devices threaten to crush the two in the teeth of relentlessly moving cogs. This is the "machinery of society" that Miyazaki, in his open letter to the manga fans, stresses that Lupin wages war against.

The whirling cogs with their steady up and down movement also evoke a much more traditional motif, the Wheel of Fortune that medieval European artists loved to depict. An allegory of fate, the wheel often carried lords and peasants, clergymen and artisans in its ever-moving orbit, reflecting the inevitable highs and lows that afflict all humanity. Ultimately the wheel suggests that our own fortunes are at the mercy of time and fate. Perhaps Miyazaki, at this watershed moment in his career, felt this particularly keenly.

Miyazaki underlines time's awesome power by having the gigantic clock serve as the other major mechanical symbol in *Cagliostro.* The clock tower is the setting for the movie's final climactic moments. Dragging Clarisse onto the clock's enormous face, the count attempts to throw her off. Lupin, clinging to the clock tower, bargains for her life, offering the count the twinned pair of Gothic rings. Lupin has figured out the riddle secreted in the rings for centuries, that the rings themselves are the key to unlocking the Cagliostro treasure. Evil to the end, the count grabs the rings but pushes Clarisse off the tower. In one more memorable vertical sequence, Lupin dives off the tower and embraces her as they both plummet into the lake below.

Back above, the count inserts the two rings into the eyes of a sculpture of a goat engraved on the clock tower and the clock's hands start to move . . .

From below, the Castle's minions stare up in horror as the metal hands come together, smashing the count into the face of the tower. The earth begins to rumble, the sluice gates open, and an immense wall of water pours out of the lake, while the clock tower collapses into rubble.

The next morning Lupin and Clarisse will discover the ruined city previously hidden by the lake, but for now the emphasis is on the count's downfall, brought about through the power of water and machinery. A surreal vision of destruction and beauty, the scene shows Miyazaki's mastery of the animated medium, in particular his skill at depicting catastrophe.

But it is in the interstitial moments between action sequences, or even after action has been carried out, that Miyazaki's unique creative talent is particularly impressive. We have already commented on the "pillow shot" of Lupin enjoying the pastoral landscape while Jigen changes the tire. The sequence includes another quiet moment after the car has crashed over the cliff and the director shows us the waves sweeping gently but relentlessly over scattered parts from the demolished vehicle, an image anticipating the unleashed waves that move implacably across the lake at the film's climax.

The director adds another quiet vision at the very end of this early sequence: Lupin, who has been knocked unconscious during the fall, awakens to find Clarisse gone. Only her damp glove is left, soothing his injured forehead. As Lupin gazes around he sees a last glimpse of Clarisse, a white figure vanishing through green trees.

This fleeting glimpse suggests, as did Miyazaki's use of the clock, the notion of ephemerality. The trope of a vanishing woman whose absence leaves a bittersweet void has long been a major element in Japanese literature, and it seems to speak to Miyazaki. In an earlier interview the director reminisced about the experience of "a kid, a bundle of complexes, who finds himself staring, amazed, at the sight of a girl wearing a white hat and long skirt zipping by on a bicycle right in front of him. . . . It's a feeling of extraordinary longing and frustration."[17] In *Cagliostro* he updates and globalizes this moment of poignant intensity with a twentieth-century European mise en scène, an action-packed narrative, and a variety of Gothic details.

The disappearing woman is a *shōjo* or young female, a character that would become an enduring and popular trademark of both Miyazaki and of anime in general. By the time he made *Cagliostro*, Miyazaki had offered other shōjo characters to the world, most notably the spunky young Mimi of *Panda Go Panda* and the supernaturally gifted Lana of *Future Boy Conan*.

Clarisse is, if possible, an even more perfect shōjo type. At sixteen she stands on the cusp of sexuality, but her white wedding dress and, at other times, her schoolgirl uniform, declare her purity and innocence. Less assertive than either Lana or Mimi or Miyazaki's many other shōjo heroines to come, she is still active enough to make the escape attempt that sets the film's action rolling. She is also passionate enough to ask Lupin to take her along with him at the movie's end. In a famous line that apparently pierced the hearts of many young Japanese boys, Clarisse looks up at the clearly smitten Lupin and whispers, "I'm not quite ready to become a thief, but I can work at it ..."

Miyazaki would invoke this pattern of a very young woman and an older, world-weary hero again in *Porco Rosso*. In *Cagliostro*, however, the paradigm appears in its purest and most conventional form. This is the Miyazaki film most straightforwardly structured on a heroic older adventurer rescuing an aristocratic young woman, in this case from a tower that would fit in a fairy tale.

Clarisse's youth, beauty, and relative powerlessness vis-à-vis older males has caused Japanese critics and audiences to link her to the specific Japanese erotic trope known as *roricon*. Deeply controversial, roricon is an abbreviated translation of "Lolita complex," a term derived from the Vladimir Nabokov novel *Lolita*, about a much older man's sexual obsession with a twelve-year-old girl. Clarisse is four years older, but her potential marriage to the much older count is suggestive enough for Lupin to refer to the count as "Pedophile Count" (literally, *rorikon* count). But of course the count is not the only older man enamored of Clarisse. Treading carefully in his depiction of desire, Miyazaki makes sure to have Lupin openly renounce Clarisse as a possible romantic partner.

Shocked by Clarisse's declaration that she wants to go with him, Lupin shows far more pain than he has in his encounters with physical obstacles. Clearly wanting to embrace the girl tightly, he instead holds her lightly, almost patting her on the back, and finally pulls away from her. When she presents her lips to him, he counters with a chaste kiss on her forehead, only the expression on his face betraying his yearning. Although he has allowed her to call him "Uncle" throughout the film, his true feelings are patently not avuncular.

Clarisse's popularity among the fans guaranteed that she would be a topic of intense interest whenever *Cagliostro* was discussed. In a question-and-answer session after the movie's release, fans repeatedly asked Miyazaki his opinion of Clarisse and his feelings about shōjo characters in general, discussions that show Miyazaki negotiating the complexities of having created a character with such powerful appeal. Asked whether Clarisse and Lana are his ideal women, he insisted that he employs shōjo characters because "having a girl makes the movie more glamorous. . . . It's sad if there isn't a girl."[18] He likened the strategy to the directive at Tōei to include cute animals in every feature.

Given the importance of female figures in Miyazaki's movies and life, this answer seems baldly disingenuous. In a 1982 question-and-answer session the director was far more forthcoming. Answering a question regarding whether such "pure and chaste" figures as Clarisse and Lana can really exist, Miyazaki insisted, "It's not the case that I have given up on real girls and am only pursuing a dream of a *shōjo* in animation."[19]

He went on to mention an example of a "real girl," a young woman who had worked with Takahata, Ōtsuka, and him while they were creating *Heidi*. Employed to do the finishing touches to their drawings, she ended up doing the final check on six thousand to seven thousand cels a week. She would not leave the office but slept at night on the couch with a blanket pulled over her. The men would tiptoe in in the morning, trying not to wake her. Almost immediately, however, she would slide off the blanket and "get up, all smiles, and make everyone tea. Then she would give a brief smile, say 'excuse me,' and go back to her desk."[20]

Acknowledging that her workload violated union rules, Miyazaki declared, "She never complained. She was cheerful, open-hearted, lively, a breath of fresh air.... You could rely on her."[21] In the end, not surprisingly, the young woman got sick, but even then she remained her cheerful self.

While Miyazaki apparently told her story to explain how much work went into making "good" animation, it is hard not to believe that this exceptional young woman is indeed his real "ideal girl," more than Clarisse or even the more assertive Lana. In some ways she is his alter ego—a workaholic who will persevere no matter what ups and downs life throws at her. But she is also clearly feminine—self-sacrificing, kindly, sensitive to others, almost motherly.

Miyazakiworld offers several fantasy versions of this young woman; Kiki in *Kiki's Delivery Service,* Chihiro in *Spirited Away,* and Sophie in *Howl's Moving Castle* are all iterations of this early ideal. But his first and still most memorable version was the protagonist of his next movie, the extraordinary Nausicaä of *Nausicaä of the Valley of the Wind.*

After *Cagliostro* Miyazaki occasionally played with the notion of having Clarisse and Lupin meet again. Ultimately, however, he preferred to stay true to the movie's wistful ending. Just as Lupin seems at the point of breaking down and gathering Clarisse in his arms, his old nemesis the policeman Zenigata appears with a fleet of Interpol cars flashing their lights. Lupin also catches a glimpse of his sometime lover/sometime collaborator/sometime enemy, the beautiful and sexy Fujiko, as she zooms by him on a motorcycle. The movie ends on a note of joy and the celebration of the chase. But the achingly wistful theme song that plays over the credits suggests the ephemerality of life and the persistence of yearning.

# 5
# *Nausicaä* and "the Feminine Principle"

And rest assured that, while most insects will survive, we are just a brief phase on this planet of bugs.

— SCOTT SHAW

*Nausicaä of the Valley of the Wind* (Kaze no tani no Naushika, 1984) was Miyazaki's toughest challenge to date. In 1982 the director had gone back to his artistic roots and begun writing a manga for the newly established magazine *Animage,* claiming that he had half hoped the magazine would fold quickly and relieve him of the responsibility. But it is clear that *Nausicaä* was a labor of love. Years later an interviewer would refer to the seven-volume manga, unfinished until 1992, as the director's "life work."[1] Miyazaki laughingly denies this, but his commitment verged on the superhuman. Frequently he worked on films during the day and drew the manga between midnight and 4:00 in the morning. He would continue to write manga off and on throughout his career (including the book on which *The Wind Rises* is based), and they constitute an important component of Miyazakiworld, but the *Nausicaä* manga is undoubtedly his most significant creation in that field.

Miyazaki had completed only two volumes when *Animage*'s editors, including Toshio Suzuki, who was to become Ghibli's main producer, suggested that the books provided ready-made material for a cinematic work. But *Nausicaä* was no ordinary manga. In its complexity, density, and length, it is comparable to an "epic poem," as Seiji Kano suggests.[2] Set in the thirtieth century, sweeping across civilizations, incorporating human and nonhuman, it confronts history and politics, envisioning utopias and apocalypses. An epic cast of characters, from its eponymous heroine to a tiny fox squirrel named Teto, are depicted amid a wide and imaginative range of settings, including the pastoral utopia of the Valley of the Wind, the ruined city of the Pejiteans, a crystalline cavern beneath the earth, and, above them all, the cloudy and cluttered realm of the sky, which dominates much of the action.

Miyazaki had to distill this intricately written, epically structured, and still far from finished, manga into a two-hour family entertainment, somehow tying up all the loose parts. The personality of Nausicaä, the manga's complex and multilayered heroine, had to be expressed by just the right voice actress (whom he found in Sumi Shimamoto, who had voiced Clarisse in *Cagliostro*), supported by an appropriately distinctive visual palette. Even more difficult was the finale, the implications of which were to haunt the director long after the movie was finished. The exhilarating climax, in which his heroine was clearly identified as a messiah figure, enabled him to end the movie on an upbeat note but created issues that he would have to address in the manga. Miyazaki later compared developing the movie to a *furoshiki*, a square piece of cloth that one ties neatly into a flexible carry-all for items ranging from food to toys to books.[3]

*Nausicaä* was not easy to tie together. Miyazaki had gone to a new company, Topcraft, and was dealing with new staff, not all of whom, he said later, were reliable.[4] Eventually he brought in trusted people he had worked with before and, even more important, persuaded Takahata to serve as the film's producer. Takahata's active participation, Miyazaki said, made him feel "safer." They brought in a new composer, Joe Hisaishi, who was destined to work with Miyazaki from then on. Although Miyazaki insists that he has no ear for music, the director and Hisaishi developed a strong and enduring collaboration, with Miyazaki working closely with the composer to find the appropriate melodies to express his vision. Hisaishi's music—sometimes swelling and symphonic, other times more minimalist and even experimental—would add a vital component to the overall success of Miyazaki's and Takahata's films.[5]

New techniques were used to animate clouds, gliders, and airborne gunships. In one unforgettable scene a new filtering process creates a surreal dreamlike flashback. The extensive labor needed for this feat of world building was commemorated in a tongue-in-cheek manga by Katsukawa, "A Record of the Battle to Make *Nausicaä*," subtitled "A Day in Miyazaki's Life: 'I'm Sorry I Yelled at You.'"

Comic and slapstick, the manga reveals a driven perfectionist obsessed with his work to the point that he runs to a nearby park to use the toilet rather than wait for someone to get out of the studio bathroom. He takes sudden quick naps in the middle of the room (rising exactly thirty minutes later without an alarm), plays the *Nausicaä* music over and over to his employees' distraction (and to Takahata's boredom), and talks so frenetically as to drive visiting interviewers into numbness. As the subtitle suggests, the quick-tempered director is also willing to apologize. Miyazaki also appears in the manga as generous and sincere, sharing *konbu* seaweed with his staff (although they suspect him of having earlier eaten all their chicken croquettes).

An especially revealing part of the manga is an "interview" with Miyazaki's youngest brother, Shirō, who at the time worked for Hakuhodo, an advertising agency involved in public relations for the film. Like Arata, Shirō, in Katsukawa's version at least, corroborates Miyazaki's own self-assessment as a young boy, describing him as "introverted and terrible at sports." Speaking of their mother's illness, he seems hesitant to recall his brother's intense yearning for their mother, using the term *mazacon,* "mother complex."[6]

A hybrid Japanese-English formulation, *mazacon* had become a cliché in Japan by the 1980s, signifying the intense relationship between mother and son typical of middle-class postwar households. In a culture where the father is expected to work long hours and socialize mainly with fellow employees, mothers tended to turn toward their sons for masculine companionship.

Because Miyazaki's mother was bedridden, the typical paradigm of the nurturing mother did not apply. Helping around the house with the chores and food preparation and entertaining his mother with stories, the young Miyazaki provided at least as much nurture as he received.

The manga invokes *mazacon* in the context of Nausicaä's maternally large bust, a theory the director himself humorously acknowledges, saying that her "bosom has to be large so she can embrace all those poor old men and women in the castle when they are dying."[7] Nausicaä is never paired romantically. She is all embracing, not only toward her fellow humans but toward animals, insects, and even the strange and prolific vegetation that grows in her thirtieth-century world. Hers is a rich and nuanced love, that of a grateful denizen of a large and multifaceted world, a stance that seems consonant to Miyazaki's own worldview.

This quality is manifest in a single, quiet scene early in the movie. Nausicaä stands alone in a wasteland confronting a gigantic insect. Rather than reach for her gun, she stares at the insect, which returns her stare, the two sharing a moment of wordless communication. Finally, the insect turns away and the young woman turns back to the task at hand, saving the postapocalyptic world in which she and the insect are both essential inhabitants.

The creature Nausicaä confronts is known as an Ohmu, a word based both on the Japanese pronunciation of the English word for "worm" (popularized by the sandworms of Frank Herbert's popular science fiction epic *Dune*) and on the Buddhist sacred word "Om." The Ohmu are majestic and mysterious entities, the first of many strange and memorable creations to come from Miyazaki's fertile mind, and of major significance in both film and manga. But Nausicaä occupies the heart of the film, and she remains to this day perhaps his most beloved heroine. She is also the heart of Miyazaki's own emotional world, a woman who is both real and idealized, embodying characteristics not only of Miyazaki's mother but also of the director himself. Although some of these aspects are clearer in the manga version of *Nausicaä*, the heroine remains the vital center in the churning world of the film.

To Miyazaki's disappointment, *Cagliostro* had not been a box-office hit, and in his appearances to promote the film, he felt distanced from his audience as well. Persistently, he described himself as "middle aged." *Nausicaä,* however, had an immediate emotional and aesthetic impact on a large and youthful audience, leading to what subculture analyst Shizuka Inoue describes as the "near deification" of the director by the growing ranks of anime fans.[8] The film's financial success helped to establish Miyazaki's and Takahata's Studio Ghibli, setting Miyazaki on the path to becoming Japan's most famous and treasured animator.

Given the beauty of its imagery, its compelling characters, and its upbeat ending, *Nausicaä* enjoyed an initial critical reception that was largely positive. The film did have detractors— one reviewer, for example, couldn't stand the film because she hated insects, which was unfortunate since insects (and very large insects at that) play a prominent role in the narrative. In general, however, audiences and critics appreciated *Nausicaä* as a remarkable piece of world building, evoking an alternative reality that eloquently buttressed the movie's strong message. One critic called it a "film that will appeal to adults with its clear message of anti-nuclear, anti-environmental destruction."[9]

*Nausicaä* appeared toward the end of a period in which anime had seized territory on the Japanese media map, as both film and television animation developed a strong fan base. Science fiction works were particularly popular, such as the trailblazing *Space Battleship Yamato* series, which in its romantic reworking of the space opera form became in some ways both the *Star Wars* and the *Star Trek* of Japan. The iconic *Gundam* series also became a lodestar to many young viewers, who responded to surprisingly nuanced characters dealing simultaneously with war and adolescent angst while wearing giant robot suits.

Though both the *Yamato* and *Gundam* series included female characters, their protagonists are all young males, typical of the science fiction and action anime at that time. Other manga and anime series, such as *Cutey Honey* and *Cats Eyes,* however, featured active female protagonists in dominant roles, leading Japanese critics of the period to talk of a blossoming of the "feminine principle" in Japanese popular culture.

Four decades after its premier, it is easy to forget just how ground-breaking a film *Nausicaä* was. In *Caglisotro* Miyazaki built on an existing manga, creating characters and situations reflecting his own personal preferences, but keeping the glamorous European setting and the thrilling adventures. With *Nausicaä,* however, some of the most distinctive elements of Miyazakiworld begin to form. He constructed an entire new world, offering a radical, even subversive vision of a future Earth premised on the beginnings of an animistic worldview.

Nausicaä, the agent of renewal and redemption, is named for a character in Homer's *Odyssey,* a young princess who nurses a shipwrecked Odysseus back to life. As a child Miyazaki had discovered the character of Nausicaä in a translation of Bernard Evslin's book on Greek myths. The story, both in Evslin and in Homer, is a sad one: Nausicaä falls in love with Odysseus, who leaves her to return to his wife. She ends her days wandering her island home singing, a brokenhearted former princess turned itinerant minstrel.

The wistful story deeply touched the young Miyazaki, who seemingly projected himself onto the character of Nausicaä while yearning for her as a maternal figure. Revealingly, Miyazaki calls Odysseus a "poor bloodstained man" in whom Nausicaä finds "something wonderful."[10] Her destiny to wander alone evokes the "vanishing woman" archetype mentioned in the previous chapter. But her fate also suggests a person inherently alone, a characteristic that Miyazaki may have identified with both as an introverted young boy lost in reading and art, and in his contemporary adult life as he increasingly shouldered the onerous responsibilities of being a director.

The film's Nausicaä has a harder task than simply saving a Greek hero, however. Her mission is to revive a stricken, war-torn world where life of any kind has become precarious. Set after catastrophes known as the Ceramic Wars and the Seven Days of Fire have laid waste to human civilization, *Nausicaä* introduces a world where a few pockets of humanity confront the Fukai, a toxic forest spreading across the Earth. While the Fukai is slowly wiping out humankind through a suffocating miasma that smothers the lungs and hardens the limbs, men prey on each other, inviting even further destruction.

The story's main thread concerns the discovery of a sinister humanoid machine known as a God Warrior by the country of Pejite, one of the last human communities bordering the Fukai. The Pejiteans hope to control the God Warrior and use it to destroy the Fukai and the gigantic and terrifying Ohmu that dwell there. But another group, the militaristic Torumekian empire, launches an attack on Pejite, largely wiping the community out in an assault whose aftermath is chillingly reminiscent of the effects of a bombing raid.

Through a tragic accident, the God Warrior comes to rest in the beautiful Valley of the Wind, a pastoral utopia of windmills and lush farmland. It falls to Nausicaä, the daughter of the valley's chieftain, to deal with the God Warrior and ultimately prevent the final destruction of humanity. In her tiny glider, navigating the brilliant blue skies above the miasma-covered Earth, Nausicaä assembles friends, confronts foes, and engages with the menacing natural world around her, searching for a way to prevent another apocalypse.

Nausicaä's powerful, charismatic, and genuinely loving leadership, combined with her telepathic ability to communicate with the Ohmu, lead her to a final sacrifice that barely saves humanity and the Earth as well. The cost is her own life. But in the movie's triumphant final scene, the Ohmu "open their hearts" (as one human character puts it) and resurrect her, leading to an unusually unambiguous Miyazaki ending.

Although both movie and manga are populated with memorable characters, perhaps the most unforgettable "character" after Nausicaä is the Fukai itself. One of the director's most impressive visual accomplishments, it is a diverse and fecund realm in which insects and plants play an increasingly significant role. While in the black-and-white pages of the manga the Fukai comes across as a dark and forbidding place, the movie's blue and purple palette, mixed with occasional flashes of red, turn the forest into a place of strangely beautiful Otherness.

The realm of the nonhuman, the Fukai asserts its power over the Earth through its intricate ecology and its many huge insect denizens, the inheritors of humanity's polluted history. It is not surprising that the Ohmu live there. Their size, power (both physical and mental), and emotional complexity suggest that they may well be the legitimate inheritors of this postapocalyptic realm, giving concrete expression to the entomologist Scott Shaw's assertion that "we are just a brief phase on this planet of bugs."[11]

Miyazaki's ability to create and animate insects and plants and set them in a multilayered ecosystem earned him accolades as an "environmentalist" director, an artist especially sensitive to environmental stresses and capable of expressing the connections between human and nonhuman. The impetus behind *Nausicaä* was a series of environmental crises that afflicted Japan in the 1950s and 1960s, including chemical poisoning both of humans and of the environment.

For many years Japanese industry had been given a pass to do what it wanted, as long as it provided jobs and the impetus for the economic growth that the Japanese government prized at all costs. As the country's skies and waters grew ever more polluted, and people and animals developed illnesses and physical defects, citizens began to protest, and environmental initiatives spread across the country. Many movements were led by women, usually mothers and grandmothers fearing for their children's health and safety.[12] In her assertive motherliness Miyazaki's heroine embodies the real-life female combatants in the environmental protests.

The chemical poisoning of Minamata Bay, caused by the dumping of industrial waste, was by far the most calamitous ecological crisis, resonating to this day in the term "Minamata disease." Initially known as "dancing cat disease" because cats that ate the polluted fish from the bay went mad and died in convulsions, the disease soon spread to humans. At least nine hundred people died, and both domestic animals and wildlife were stricken as well. The terrible illness caused physical defects in humans, especially children, and led to the wholesale destruction of marine life in the bay. Once dumping was banned in Minamata's waters, fish began to return.

Miyazaki's vison of nonhuman creatures that arise and heal themselves after being beset by human depredations comes from stories he read about the fish returning. He commented that the stories of fish "coming back in numbers otherwise never seen in Japan's other seas" had "sent a cold shiver down my spine."[13]

Increasingly environmental catastrophes occurred globally from the 1960s on, and film and literary works around the world engaged with them. Miyazaki acknowledges fictional inspirations as well. These included *Dune*, but another important fictional influence was Brian Aldiss's *The Long Afternoon of Earth*, in which a few stray human communities attempt to survive in a world that is overrun by plants and giant insects. The English writer's environmentally oriented book may have helped awaken Miyazaki's awareness of his own country's deep engagement with nature. For many years Miyazaki had felt alienated from his native country. Disgusted by its actions during the war, he stated that he "really hated Japan."[14]

Miyazaki's discovery of the ethnobotanist Sasuke Nakao's book *The Origins of Cultivated Plants and Agriculture* (Saibai shokubutsu to nōkō no kigen, 1966) offered him a new direction. Nakao's vision of Japan as part of a larger Asian cultural world of "broad leafed" forests had an almost visceral impact on Miyazaki, making him feel that a "fresh wind was blowing through my mind."[15] Miyazaki was to translate Nakao's theories more explicitly in *Princess Mononoke* and more subtly in *Totoro,* but the power dynamics and animistic elements in *Nausicaä* already suggest a major shift toward a more East Asian and environmentalist worldview.

Miyazaki, however, does not want to be known as "Mr. Ecology," stating, "Some people suffer from the misconception that Isao Takahata and I are both some sort of environmentalists, and that we will make a film out of anything as long as it has an environmental theme or message. Nothing could be further from the truth. Such a film would be like a fat dried-up log, propped upright. What we need is a living thing, with strong roots, a solid trunk and branches, so that we can be creative in the way we hang the ornaments."[16]

Exactly such a "living thing," *Nausicaä*'s imaginative range develops organically from the intimate engagement between its heroine and the natural world. This is clear from the very beginning of the film. The opening credits appear over what appears to be a medieval scroll, unrolling the catastrophic history of humanity over a thousand years. Wordless and enigmatic, the credit sequence immediately establishes the seriousness and strangeness of the film to come, something different from anything ever seen before in animation.

At the end of the scroll appears a winged figure, perhaps a messiah, promising salvation to the supplicant human figures kneeling below her. Another messiah figure will appear in a later scene, this time an androgynous young man who an old woman prophesies will appear to save humanity. The camera moves to our first glimpse of Nausicaä, piloting her little glider over a desert landscape. Dressed in blue, her face concealed by a breathing mask, she too seems an androgynous figure at first. A closeup reveals that she is female. Landing, she enters the teeming world of the Fukai, tall, masked, carrying a rifle, an intrepid investigator in an alien realm.

In an earlier book I have discussed Miyazaki's use of a female character to revitalize the hackneyed science fiction trope of the human explorer venturing into the alien wasteland.[17] In contemporary popular culture strong female characters are increasingly commonplace, but it is worth reemphasizing how unusual this was in 1984. Particularly refreshing is Nausicaä's combination of the conventional female attributes of compassion and nurturing with a steely and profound determination toward active involvement. In contrast to Miyazaki's earlier savior figure, the young boy Conan, whose overflowing masculine energy makes him an obvious leader of his much simpler postcatastrophe world, Nausicaä faces ideological and moral challenges with a matter-of-fact competence, intelligence, curiosity, and genuine love of life.

Miyazaki establishes these qualities, economically and memorably, early in this sequence. Upon entering the Fukai, Nausicaä immediately takes out a test tube and collects spores to analyze in the underground laboratory she maintains in her father's castle. She finds the tracks of an Ohmu that lead her to a gigantic discarded Ohmu carapace, which she knows can be used by the people of the Valley of the Wind to make tools. Nausicaä's initial engagement with the carapace is practical and straightforward. We see her using both a knife and gunpowder, not as weapons, but to chip out the Ohmu eyeshell so that she can carry it back to the valley.

Nausicaä's scientific curiosity and ease with natural surroundings seem to belong to our age, when a heroine such as Katniss Everdeen in *The Hunger Games* employs her inquisitiveness and practical abilities to become a leader. Nausicaä's lineage dates back a millennium, however, to the remarkably independent and free-thinking heroine of a tenth-century Japanese court tale, "The Lady Who Loved Insects," a story that had fascinated Miyazaki as a child. Nausicaä echoes the lady's unusual fondness, indeed empathy, for things that creep and crawl. Both protagonists are also unusually intellectually gifted. The lady adheres to the Buddhist principle one suspects Miyazaki's mother would have agreed with: "It is the person who wants the truth and inquires into the essence of things who has an interesting mind."[18] While investigating the "essence of things" in her underground laboratory, Nausicaä will come to understand the counterintuitive role that the Fukai plays in cleansing her toxic world.

Marveling in a gentle, girlish voice at the lightness of the Ohmu eyeshell, Nausicaä proceeds to whirl it around her head as if in a dance. Miyazaki makes the scene even more distinctive by having spores fall like snow over her while she does this. He then cuts to a scene of her lying pensively in a "snowbank" of fallen spores, a "pillow shot" allowing us time to reflect.

Moments of such sublime connection with nature make Nausicaä a unique messiah figure and the movie an unprecedentedly original work of art. We see Nausicaä's comfort and joy in a natural world that is both alien and uncannily beautiful. The wind that blows the spores over her is both her enemy and her agent. The spores are toxic and can destroy any human who does not wear a mask, but the wind is also her helper, since it will carry her in her glider back to the Valley of the Wind. It is the wind that keeps the valley clean, and its sudden disappearance and subsequent reappearance at the movie's end signals another kind of resurrection, that of nature itself.

Other scenes affirm Nausicaä's commitment to humanity. She risks her own safety, for example, by taking off her mask in order to encourage a group of elderly men from the valley while they are flying through the miasma above the Fukai. Previously, Nausicaä had shown immense courage by confronting a furious Pejitean pilot, Asbel, whose sister was killed by the Torumekians and who confuses the peaceful valley folk with the military from the brutal Torumekian empire. At one point during Asbel's fierce attack Nausicaä stands on the surface of her plane, arms outstretched in an almost Christlike pose, trying to stop the pilot's violent foray.

Nausicaä's combination of compassion and bravery appear again when she and the valley men crash-land at the bottom of the Fukai. The humans discover that their plane has landed on top of an Ohmu nest, and the giant Ohmu swarm up from the water toward them like creatures out of an aquatic horror movie.

In a more typical science fiction film such a landing would cue an immediate display of hostilities between human and insect, but these humans wait frozen in terror for an insect attack. In a tranquil, almost lyrical sequence, enveloped in a gentle music and suffused in a restful blue palette, the giant creatures surface slowly through the waters to investigate the human invaders, their enormous eyes a deep blue that seems to reflect both sky and water. Nausicaä knows that they are not angry, only "inspecting" them. But Kushana, the Torumekian commander who has forced her way onto the plane with the group from the valley, panics. She is about to draw her gun and shoot at the Ohmu when Nausicaä peremptorily stops her, then balances on the floating plane's wing to offer apologies for invading the insects' realm. The Ohmu surround her and, accompanied by lilting music, they extend their golden feelers around her, wrapping her body in what looks like a giant golden cocoon. She experiences a flashback to her younger self standing in a golden field, a magnificent tree behind her, its leaves sparkling in the sunlight.

The mysterious vision is disrupted by a sudden change in the Ohmu. Their eyes turn glowing red while a huge cloud of winged insects, also red-eyed, appears. Realizing (apparently through her communication with the insects) that Asbel is still alive and that he has somehow enraged the insects guarding the Fukai, Nausicaä takes off on her glider to find him. She leaves the men to take the pistol away from the stupefied Kushana, whose insistence on grasping it throughout the encounter with the Ohmu strongly underlines the difference between the two female leaders.

The insects now take center stage and bring action and excitement that contrasts with the previous surreally tranquil scene. Nausicaä, back in active hero form, rescues Asbel from the jaws of what appears to be a monstrous dragonfly. The two of them plunge even farther into the depths of the Fukai, Nausicaä losing consciousness as they do so.

In the subsequent sequence Miyazaki again slows the momentum, providing what is perhaps the film's most mystical episode. Nausicaä awakes to find herself beneath the Fukai, able to breathe without a mask. The setting has an almost cathedral-like beauty. Tall alabaster-colored trees extend their crown of branches to create a roof, and a vast blue river of pure water moves smoothly through the underground world. Sporadically, showers of golden sand come down in chutes from the dappled world above. If the Valley of the Wind might be considered a human vision of utopia, the land beneath the Fukai is a natural one, free of human intervention. Inspired by the aftermath of the Minamata Bay poisoning, Miyazaki brought his understanding of nature's self-purifying properties to bear, creating a vision of the Fukai removing the toxins from the air above to establish an uncontaminated space. Nausicaä's laboratory experiments had already led her to suspect this might happen, but now, witnessing it in person, she is overwhelmed by a bittersweet happiness that brings tears to her eyes.

Again Nausicaä experiences a flashback to her childhood, leading to the movie's most otherworldly episode. Shot through filters that create an eerie golden light, the scene is accompanied by an equally eerie child's song consisting only of the repeated syllables "la la la." Nausicaä appears in this dreamlike vision as a girl of about five or six playing in a golden field through which the wind blows. An adult male voice interrupts her quiet moment, and she recognizes her father and her mother at the head of a line of men

Nausicaä protects the Ohmu in *Nausicaä of the Valley of the Wind,* Topcraft Studio, 1984.

who look like warriors. The adults take the protesting Nausicaä to the giant tree briefly glimpsed in the earlier flashback, and we discover that the tree conceals a baby Ohmu. Nausicaä promptly tries to shelter the insect, but her father intones, "Humans and insects were not meant to live together." Adult hands reach down and rip it from her grasp as she cries, "Please don't hurt it." The camera pulls back to show the little girl kneeling among the grasses, her body curved over to the point where it almost takes on the shape of the insect she had just been sheltering.

We can see this uncanny episode as an origin scene that explains the mature Nausicaä's special connection with the Ohmu. But there are wider implications. Her childish sorrow for an insect that is, objectively speaking, quite grotesque projects a piercing grief that is even more stirring than the grown-up Nausicaä's compassionate acceptance of the insects. In contrast, the several shots of monstrous adult hands reaching down—toward either Nausicaä or the Ohmu—suggest the enormous difference between her world and the world of the adults who insist that "humans and insects cannot live together."

Miyazaki would go on to use the child's point of view frequently in such later films as *Totoro, Spirited Away,* and *Ponyo,* but this brief scene may be the single most poignant example in his work of the gap between adult and child. It may also explain the undercurrent of loneliness that Nausicaä's adult presence seems to express. Despite her consistent compassion and cheer, throughout the movie she seems happiest on her own, whether dancing with the Ohmu shell or walking quietly in the cathedral depths of the Fukai. In these brief respites Nausicaä seems to reflect the complex identity of her creator, who at times has wanted to be neither a leader nor a messiah but rather a quiet appreciator of natural beauty.

If the flashback sequence and the scenes in the Fukai are animistic or even Shintoistic in their insistence on humans' connection with nature, *Nausicaä*'s final scenes clearly have a Christian dimension. Nausicaä sacrifices herself to stop an invasion of Ohmu who are enraged that one of their offspring has been stolen and tortured. Offering her own body as recompense, Nausicaä is killed by the furious insects.

Her Christlike sacrifice leads to her miraculous resurrection. The Ohmu surround her body and raise her into the sky, where she revives to walk through a field of golden insect antennae. In her blue dress, surrounded by waving golden strands, she resembles the male savior figure whose coming was predicted by a blind prophetess early in the movie. This hint of androgyny recalls the androgynous aspect of the Buddhist Bodhisattva figure Kuan Yin. "It's a miracle, a miracle!" one of the valley's inhabitants intones.

But the final "miracle" of the movie is neither Christian nor Buddhist but animistic. As the valley people look up at Nausicaä in joy (a vision anticipated early in the movie in the opening scroll), they notice that the wind has returned. In the very last scenes of the movie we see the wind as an agent of life and a connector to the sublime as it lifts Nausicaä heavenward, once again on her glider.

Some critics were disappointed by the film's "miracle" ending. Over time *Nausicaä* has been criticized as being too upbeat, its ending pat, its heroine too perfect, and its moral vision too Manichean. In an essay years later about the film, a Japanese critic called the movie a kind of metaphysical "salon pass," a form of analgesic bandage that we paste upon our souls to take our psychic pain away.[19]

Miyazaki himself has admitted that he was "up to his neck in the religious zone that I had always wanted to avoid."[20] But he never really explains why he chose to enter the "religious zone." Perhaps his reason was that he simply needed to "tie up the furoshiki" and deliver a completed movie to an awaiting audience.

The director's vision of Nausicaä's resurrection is intriguing if we consider it in the context of his own life. Miyazaki's mother had died while he was working on *Nausicaä*. In a later discussion of his mother's death, Miyazaki spoke of cremation, widely practiced in Japan, and somewhat surprisingly said that he wished his mother could have been buried rather than cremated. He imagined the beauty of plants growing from her grave. "Then, if flowers bloomed above her grave plot I could think, 'Look my mother has turned into these flower blossoms.'"[21] Perhaps it is not a coincidence that the final image in *Nausicaä* links directly to this form of rebirth—a vision of a breathing mask (Nausicaä's?) next to a little plant springing out of the desert.

*Nausicaä* was the second anime that I ever saw. The first was Ōtomo Katsuhiro's *Akira*. The two movies emerge from the expansive decade of the 1980s, and both feature postapocalyptic visions of a world of out-of-control technology and human hubris. Both are masterpieces that taught the rest of the world to see Japanese animation in a new light. I teach *Akira* and *Nausicaä,* and each has stood the test of time. Yet to my mind, *Nausicaä* cuts deeper and lingers longer. This is due not only to the sheer beauty of the film and the unforgettable character of Nausicaä herself but also to its truly radical vision that a plant, a girl, and an insect all deserve to inherit the Earth.

# 6
# Orphans of the Sky
## Laputa: Castle in the Sky

[I saw] a city all floating in the air . . . measureless and splendid . . . adorned with magical buildings . . . on a base of a luminous crystal never beheld before . . .

—DOMENICO GIARDINA

After the challenges and intensity of *Nausicaä*, Miyazaki wanted to make a different kind of movie. With pressure mounting for a sequel, Miyazaki dabbled in possible *Nausicaä 2* scenarios, but his spirit did not rise to the challenge of animating his increasingly dark and complicated manga. He dreamed instead of creating an old-fashioned boy's adventure story that would be a "pleasure" to watch. He succeeded with *Laputa: Castle in the Sky*, "quite probably the most entertaining anime that Miyazaki ever made," according to the critic Manabu Murase.[1] At the same time the movie is a bittersweet vision of a lost utopia. That it is a utopia based on a terrifying weapon is a surprisingly sophisticated irony for a child-oriented film.

Featuring a goodhearted young boy and girl on a quest, *Laputa* bears resemblance to Miyazaki's first and only television series, *Future Boy Conan*. In fact, the original title for *Laputa* had been *Young Boy Pazu* (Shōnen Pazu). In a country whose landscape resembles that of Wales, a parentless boy,

Pazu, works in a mine and in his spare time builds an airship. He hopes it will allow him to reach Laputa, a mysterious flying island adorned with castle and gardens, which his pilot father had glimpsed through a rent in the clouds on a stormy flight. No one had believed his account, so Pazu dreams of vindicating his father's memory by finding the flying island himself. Of course his quest is successful, and in the movie's final third he and his fellow adventurer, the young orphan girl Sheeta, discover in Laputa a unique technological marvel that is both an adventurer's dreamworld and an elegiac commentary on humanity's complex relationship with technology and nature.

The movie's early scenes show Pazu living in a tiny house near a country village and helping his fellow miners search for coal in deep and increasingly depleted mineshafts. His main pleasure besides building his airship is playing his trumpet every morning as the sun rises, summoning a flock of white doves that wheel and spin around him before taking off for the mountains. Miyazaki's depiction of the young boy playing his trumpet as the sun turns the mountains momentarily gold is a scene of self-contained beauty that is barely plausible and at the same time profoundly magical, one of the classic gemlike moments that distinguish Miyazakiworld.

While Pazu is an ordinary young boy without special powers, *Laputa*'s young heroine, Sheeta, is an otherworldly shōjo heroine with links to *Conan*'s Lana, Nausicaä, and *Cagliostro*'s Clarisse. Like Nausicaä and Clarisse, she is of aristocratic birth, ultimately discovering that she descends from the nobility of Laputa. Like Nausicaä, she is connected to the sky, in this case through a magical pendant that allows her to transform a perilous fall into a gentle movement of floating through the air.

Sheeta also links outside of Miyazaki's own work to an increasingly popular genre of anime and manga that would come to be known as "magical girlfriend": young women with strange and magical powers such as Lum in the television series *Urusei Yatsura* (1978), who suddenly appear in the lives of ordinary young men. Invariably, the magical girlfriend unwittingly causes havoc with her powers.

At thirteen or so, Sheeta is a younger and unsexualized version of these magical girlfriends. Japanese critics point to an underlying "erotic" quality in her relationship with Pazu, as when he covers her with his jacket while she sleeps or puts his arm around her when they are flying in a tiny aircraft, but Miyazaki refused to make any romantic connection explicit. He grew impatient with an interviewer who kept harping on why the two didn't kiss at the joyous moment when they finally arrive on Laputa: "No, they wouldn't kiss. That's the bad influence of Hollywood. If they had it would have been a different relationship."[2]

Appropriately for a family movie, Sheeta's relationship with Pazu is very much that of a comrade in adventure. Her entrance into Pazu's world turns his life upside down. We first see Sheeta imprisoned in a gigantic dirigible, one of many distinctive aircraft the movie showcases. She has been kidnapped by military thugs led by an enigmatic man named Muska, but in this opening sequence she escapes both the military and a gang of air pirates. Protected by her pendant, she falls gently from the sky into the astonished Pazu's arms. The ensuing chase narrative mixes the magical with a sci-fi-inspired vision of apocalypse that, as in *Conan,* involves mysterious forces and an evil man attempting to wield unimaginable power.

Unlike the watery, postapocalyptic world of *Conan,* however, the world Sheeta and Pazu inhabit is a bustling alternative nineteenth-century Europe. *Laputa*'s cultural heritage is strikingly European. The visionary notion of a "castle in the air" is from medieval European descriptions of the so-called fata morgana, a meteorological mirage in which structures seem to be levitated above the horizon. As the epigraph of this chapter suggests, this phenomenon engendered both wonder and awe.

English literary antecedents also inspired Miyazaki. The image of a flying island in the sky powered by technology and called Laputa comes from Jonathan's Swift's satirical *Gulliver's Travels,* which Miyazaki had read as a child. While the director claims that he barely remembered the story and had to have his wife look it up in an encyclopedia, Swift's and Miyazaki's work share a mixed view of the technology that keeps their respective Laputas afloat.

Sheeta falls from the sky into Pazu's arms in *Laputa: Castle in the Sky,* Studio Ghibli, 1986.

Eschewing satire, however, Miyazaki's *Laputa* combines the thrills of such nineteenth-century adventure classics as his beloved *Treasure Island,* by the Scottish writer Robert Louis Stevenson, and the enthusiastic wonder typical of one of his favorite science fiction writers, the French visionary Jules Verne.[3] Like *Treasure Island, Laputa* appeals to its audience with a plucky orphan hero, breathtaking chase scenes, a gang of pirates, and, unusual for Miyazaki, a truly evil villain who remains unrepentant all the way to the movie's climax. The Verne-inspired elements were more idiosyncratic, expressing what we would now call a "steampunk" visual aesthetic, a retro–science fiction genre that imagines a time when, as the director put it, "machines were still fun."[4] The movie features a delightful array of eccentric flying machines. They included the ornithopter, a distinctive little aircraft that looks and sounds like a motorcycle mated with a hornet, on which Miyazaki lavished much love and labor, and the more sinister gigantic military aircraft called Goliath. Most impressive of all is the "flying machine" of Laputa itself, incorporating technology that is simultaneously magical and futuristic, with a dark secret at its heart, the fact that this superior technology makes it a devastating weapon.

Equally important to the film's look was the small country of Wales, whose landscape and people profoundly influenced the movie. Having successfully escaped doing *Nausicaä 2,* Miyazaki did location scouting for *Laputa* in Wales. With Takahata and Suzuki busy planning a new studio, he traveled alone, an experience that had a profound effect aesthetically and politically. Though part of Great Britain, Wales remains proud of its pre-Anglo-Saxon Celtic identity. Miyazaki had long been fascinated by the Celtic connection with nature, finding in it a European counterpart for Japan's Shinto tradition.

Arriving in Wales in the late spring of 1985, he was captivated by the eerie beauty of the Welsh countryside, studded with formidable medieval castles standing high above the sea. Immersing himself in mountainous landscapes, Miyazaki was also taken by the giant slag heaps, the grim but strangely evocative by-products of centuries of coal mining.

The miners' struggles particularly disturbed Miyazaki. Only two months had passed since the end of the most bitter and tumultuous strike in Britain's coal mining history. Enraged by Prime Minister Margaret Thatcher's plan to close the coal mines, miners across the United Kingdom had taken part in massive work stoppages and sometimes violent demonstrations. Some of the most savage took place in South Wales, where Miyazaki was traveling. The strikes' failure had left a bitter harvest in terms of empty buildings and shattered morale, and the director was deeply affected.

Seiji Kano speculates that the Welsh miners brought back memories of the union-management struggles during Miyazaki's time at Tōei, quoting his statement that he "felt a sense of solidarity with the miners."[5] That period seemed increasingly far away as 1980s Japan experienced its great era of economic growth and prosperity. Miyazaki's yearning for a simpler, non-materialistic way of life is clear in the depiction of the miners who make up the supporting cast of *Laputa* and, more metaphysically, in his insistence on creating a noncynical, nonnihilistic adventure story. The villagers who support and protect Sheeta and Pazu from both pirates and the military are rough-hewn and poor but enthusiastic in attempting to create a space of safety.

The movie was the first to be produced by Miyazaki and Takahata's new studio, Studio Ghibli. *Nausicaä*'s financial success had allowed the two directors to quit Topcraft; on June 15, 1985, roughly a year after *Nausicaä*'s premier, their new venture opened its doors in the first floor of a rental building in Kichijōji, a neighborhood in metropolitan Tokyo. Named after a warm wind from the Sahara that also became the name of an Italian military aircraft in the Second World War, Studio Ghibli's mission was to blow a "whirlwind" into a Japanese animation industry that the founders viewed as stagnant. Toshio Suzuki, the editor from *Animage* who had been a major supporter of *Nausicaä*, was also influential in establishing Ghibli. Suzuki's publishing company Tokuma served as a financial umbrella and has remained linked to the studio throughout its three decades.

That confidence and support were crucial. Most Japanese animation studios tend to rely on television series and the occasional movie spinoff. Miyazaki and Takahata were determined to offer original, high-quality, feature-length movies with dense and intricate imagery, and stories and characters with real psychological depth. Takahata insisted that they should spare no expense on *Laputa*. The film's fluid visuals, imaginative characters, and commitment to detailed, visually appealing settings established a new industry standard.

*Laputa* was a box-office disappointment, however, grossing only about two-thirds of *Nausicaä*'s take. Miyazaki was chagrined. He attributed the movie's relative failure to the fact that it was about "a boy with no special powers," rather than featuring the superhuman heroes of typical science fiction and fantasy anime. *Laputa* also suffered from the fact that it was not based on a popular anime or manga series. Though the film's originality and adherence to the director's unique vision stand among its strong points, the "Miyazaki brand" was not yet firmly established. Enticements like a tie-in with a juice company to produce "Laputa Light Fruits Soda" failed to convince general audiences to see a fresh work by a still relatively little-known director.[6]

Also at issue was the film's target audience—middle schoolers and their families, at a time when Japanese animators were increasingly aiming for males in their teens and twenties. A generation that would come to be known as *otaku* (or "geeks," as Americans would soon call them), they had "graduated" from heartfelt, even sentimental entertainment and sought edgier heroes and more adult situations.

Miyazaki hated this new direction. In an interview a couple of years before *Laputa,* he had defended his young hero Conan against criticism that the character was "too much of a goody two shoes." "So you want to see 'bad characters,' you fool?" Miyazaki asked. He went on to criticize the sort of "bad character" who talks back impudently to his elders. Miyazaki ended his critique with characteristic vehemence: "When I see that sort of thing, the characters seem so obnoxious I feel like knocking them down."[7]

The director believed in creating child characters who were believable and interesting but also fundamentally decent. Rather than presenting "obnoxious" little terrors, he carefully developed children who contend with calamity and even catastrophe while maintaining a resilient and upbeat attitude.

It is no accident that Miyazaki's children are usually orphans, or at least separated from their parents. In a discussion of sources of inspirations for *Laputa* he pointed out, "One of the essential elements of most classical children's literature is that the children in the stories actually fend for themselves."[8] The trope of the child on his or her own ranges from such nineteenth-century orphans as David Balfour in *Kidnapped* and Jane in *Jane Eyre* all the way to the young wizard in the *Harry Potter* series. The tradition allows for more freedom on the part of the child protagonist and adds more drama and poignancy to the work of art as a whole.

Miyazaki may have had deeper reasons for his insistence on children's independence and resilience. That they expressed his inner conflicts about his own parents becomes clear in an interview from 1982, significantly entitled "My Point of Origin," in which we see him return to the movie that had shaken his soul as a teenager, *Panda and the White Serpent*. "When I saw *Panda and the White Serpent* it was as if the scales fell from my eyes. I realized that I should depict the goodness and honesty of children in my work. But parents are apt to stamp out their children's purity and goodness."[9]

With no parents to "stamp" on them, Sheeta and Pazu are forced to become independent, living up to Miyazaki's ideal. Throughout the movie they learn to depend upon each other, and through their mutual respect and trust they end up rescuing not only each other but, at the film's climax, the world around them. They save the world from the apocalyptic machinations of Muska, who turns out to be Sheeta's evil older cousin. Muska resembles the villainous older male characters Repka in *Conan* and the count in *Cagliostro* but is even more dangerous since he intends to use Laputa's technological power to control the world.

Miyazaki does allow for older characters who are clearly "good" parental figures. Such is the case with Dola, the huge, red-haired woman who is not only the mother but also the chieftain of the air pirate family who early on chases Sheeta in an attempt to steal her magic pendant. Dola is a wonderful creation in her own right, a dynamic and flamboyant older woman. Aggressive and cunning, but also maternal, she refreshes the hackneyed nineteenth-century trope of pirate marauders. Miyazaki initially depicts her as a cantankerous enemy doing everything she can to get her hands on Laputa's treasure, seemingly ready to "stamp on the purity and goodness" of the two child heroes. In a major twist, however, she reveals a more nuanced personality, scolding Pazu for abandoning Sheeta at a tense moment, in a way that is more parental than piratelike. After Pazu rescues Sheeta, Dola effectively adopts them both. Putting them to work on board her family airship, she also gives them a little aircraft, the "ornithopter," that enables their voyage to Laputa.

Dola is widely considered to be an affectionate homage to Miyazaki's mother, Yoshiko, who had died during the making of *Nausicaä*. While the inquisitive, morally upright Nausicaä also shares elements of Yoshiko Miyazaki's personality, Dola's meddlesomeness and flamboyance clearly accord with the Miyazaki children's memory of their mother. Miyazaki's younger brother Shiro wonders whether at some level *Laputa* was an awkward but ardent farewell present to their recently deceased mother.[10] At the end of the movie we see Dola and her strapping sons perching on their fleet of flying machines, offering the children a family to return to if they ever need one.

With the advent of video and later the DVD format, *Laputa* eventually more than recouped its initial investment and is now regarded as a highly successful children's feature. But *Laputa* is something more than a children's film. In time, many critics came to hail it as an idiosyncratic masterpiece. In its final section the movie becomes a provocative ecofable, posing in unexpected ways the larger and profoundly contemporary questions about how humanity deals with technology and nature. *Laputa* seems to leave these questions open. It ends with a vision of the shining castle enmeshed in green roots but taking off into the open sky, the children and the pirate family left behind to fly in empty space.

*Nausicaä* ended with an affirmation of the interconnections of humans with the natural world. *Laputa*'s vision of the castle flying away blends science fiction and fantasy to ask whether humanity even deserves to be part of the world. It offers an unsettling view of humankind as orphans in exile from a potentially utopian home. As Kano puts it, "The movie's destiny was to be a fantasy that was backed by a bitter realism and a contemporary sensibility."[11]

How Miyazaki was able to weld exuberant fantasy, bittersweet realism, and apocalyptic science fiction into a seamless whole is worth examining more closely. One major tool he uses is the quest motif. The movie's obvious quest object is Laputa, but Laputa means different things to different characters. Muska and his military see Laputa as a potential source of a powerful energy, although Muska, a descendant of the original Laputans, also has a strong family connection. The air pirates see it as a target for looting and are also initially interested in Sheeta's magic pendant, whose power to help her float is a miniature version of the immense crystal that enables Laputa to fly. The two children have a deeper emotional attachment. To them Laputa is a connector to family and home. For Pazu it is a chance to vindicate his dead pilot father, who left a photograph of the island barely glimpsed through the clouds. For Sheeta, Laputa is the home of her ancestors, and she is physically linked to its energy source through her pendant.

The film does not disappoint when the quest object is finally found. In the gripping final third of the movie, Pazu and Sheeta fly through a storm to discover Laputa hovering before them. Landing their ornithopter in parkland outside the castle, they do cartwheels of joy at having completed their quest. Like Nausicaä visiting the Fukai, they are not intimidated by a world very different from what they had previously known, and they excitedly proceed to explore the emerald-green gardens around the castle and, ultimately, the castle's labyrinthine interior.

Accompanying them on their journey across the flying island is a rather whimsical-looking giant robot who first approaches them in a seemingly threatening manner. It turns out, however, that the robot is really concerned with some tiny eggs in a bird's nest that their flying machine had crashed on top of. The young people soon feel at ease with the robot. Later the robot takes them to a stark stone marker, perhaps a monument to Laputa itself, upon which he lays a small pink flower.

With its Edenic gardens, graceful architecture, and a kindly robot concerned with the minutiae of the natural world, Laputa comes across as an almost classic vision of a lost utopia, the friendly robot adding a charming touch to the conventional utopian element of advanced technology. As the young people explore the silent passageways of Laputa, the audience has reason to believe that the vanished people who built Laputa must have been a compassionate, sophisticated, and gentle race.

As the last sentient representative of Laputa, the robot itself seems the perfect embodiment of the best of the utopian impulse, perhaps even a new technocultural paradigm, as Thomas Lamarre suggests. With its quirky face and slightly deformed eye it is reminiscent of early cubist works, or the playful images of Chagall, an artist whom Miyazaki much admires. Even more overtly utopian is its kinship with animals. As Anthony Lioi points out, we often see it festooned with chattering animals, suggesting a kind of technological St. Francis of Assisi.[12]

The robot also suggests a grown-up and more powerful WALL-E, the little robot who is the eponymous star of Pixar Studio's 2008 postapocalyptic masterpiece. Since the staff of Pixar are known to be devotees of Miyazaki, it seems reasonable to suppose that WALL-E's love and protection of greenery left behind by human civilization may have its roots in *Laputa*'s nurturing robot.[13]

In the robot's devotion to both city and nature we find an ideal combination of the technological and the natural. Lioi describes this as "unprecedented: [Laputa] is a place where artificial intelligence has become the companion and guardian of the environment."[14] A disturbing element is the lack of humanity in this conception. Laputa is a dead place. At least initially, Sheeta and Pazu seem to inject a new human element, and their obvious rapport with the robot (which Japanese audiences raised on animation series devoted to giant robots would readily accept) implies a future where the technological, the human, and the natural can finally unite seamlessly and productively.

*Laputa* also gestures to the past and the notion of a lost home. Tom Moylan has described the utopian impulse as "focus[ing] on a quest for what has been repressed or denied, for *Heimat,* the sense of home which includes happiness and fulfillment."[15] In the film's case, the quest has been engendered by two Laputa-related artifacts. The first is the photograph of Laputa, taken by Pazu's father.

The second artifact is Sheeta's pendant. A token of the floating island and of her family, the pendant is made of a powerful mineral found only on Laputa. The pendant, passed down to her by her mother and her grand-mother, gives Sheeta extraordinary powers. Appropriately for an artifact of family and home, it both protects and serves as a connection with a lost past. Like Superman's kryptonite, except in reverse, the pendant's mineral increases her powers as she gets closer to its source.

Pazu and Sheeta are orphans and exiles who search for home and find adventure. Initially Laputa looks like a potential home for them, an en-chanted garden city where they can enjoy playing the role of a futuristic Adam and Eve. But Miyazaki does not allow either audience or the characters to remain long in this dream state. Shortly after the two young people arrive, Laputa is invaded by malevolent or at least greedy forces: the pirate family and the military led by the power-mad Muska.

In the film's climactic moments Sheeta and Pazu discover the secret of Laputa, that its core is actually a giant weapon, which Muska intends to use to conquer the Earth. Stealing Sheeta's pendant, Muska activates Laputa's war machine, destroying many of his soldiers in the process and unleashing hordes of no longer kindly giant robots. Finally, he produces a many-colored blast of energy that explodes on the Earth in the form of a rainbow-colored mushroom cloud. Calling on biblical examples of destruction such as Sodom and Gomorrah, and also invoking Indra's arrow, the ultimate weapon of the *Ramayana*, Muska seems unstoppable.

In the face of adult authority and insanity, Miyazaki brings his child heroes to the rescue. Sheeta and Pazu take adult responsibility. They decide that there is indeed one way to stop Muska, by invoking the "spell of de-struction" taught to Sheeta by her grandmother. The fact that this "spell of destruction" will almost certainly destroy the young people as well does not affect their decision. Holding hands, they recite the spell in unison. Muska is blinded, and Laputa disintegrates.[16]

As the children watch in amazement, the gigantic roots that hold Laputa together begin to rip the city apart. The castle's archways, towers, and building blocks hive off and fall into the sky to reveal the pure heart of Laputa, an enormous tree whose protective roots circle the castle's crystal and also allow Sheeta and Pazu to climb to safety and recover their little flying machine.[17] The movie ends with the two of them waving a friendly aerial goodbye to Dola and her family, who have also survived the destruction to loot another day. Together the children and the pirates watch in awe as the immense and beautiful tree-encased castle, now unencumbered by the fortress that had imprisoned it, rises high into the sky and vanishes from sight.

In his essay on *Laputa* Anthony Lioi points out that the flying island serves as a "critical ecotopia," an ecological utopia that also "contains an overtly dystopian element such that the implicit critique in utopian discourse becomes explicit."[18] By this Lioi seems to be pointing out the dangers inherent in utopian hopes, something that Miyazaki's generation, scarred by wartime mythmaking and the compromises of industrialization, might be expected to appreciate.

We could also describe Laputa as a deeply paradoxical utopia. Initially seeming to be a harbinger of an idyllic world, it also harks back to the destructive visions of past civilizations. The power that connects Sheeta to her past and allows her to float lightly into Pazu's arms becomes the same power that unleashes nuclear holocaust. Laputa is energy itself, and in the wrong hands, it can work only evil.

The notion of nuclear energy takes the film beyond the realm of child's adventure story. As Lioi suggests, the movie can also be interpreted not only as a "critique of American atomic power and its devastation of Japan but of the imperial Japanese use of nature and its spirits to justify empire."[19]

The loss of the war was a deeply embedded memory for Miyazaki's generation, but the film also suggests a more complicated and more universal sense of loss. The image of the alluring but literally deracinated Laputa sailing off into the sky, its roots trailing beneath it, evokes not only the loss of utopian hopes but the loss of home as well. For a brief moment earlier, as the children marveled at Laputa, modern technology could be seen as hopeful and sustaining, and the city welcoming to human visitors, offering the hope of a new and better life. Laputa's ultimate disappearance puts an end to that hope.

This sense of deracination and exile, while universal, might hold even more power for Japanese of Miyazaki's generation. All around them the green world they had grown up with had been demolished, first by war and later by the bulldozers, skyscrapers, and earth movers of the massive urban development that had overwhelmed postwar Japan. No longer firmly connected to their past, postwar Japanese have increasingly felt a sense of spiritual orphanhood, exiled from their own history.

It is easy to see *Laputa*'s many European influences, but the final image of the floating castle also evokes the Japanese spirit of *mono no aware*, the sadness inherent in the fleeting nature of life. More specifically it reminds me of a wistful poem from the thirteenth-century poetry collection the *Shinkokinshū*:

> The floating bridge of a spring night's dream
> Breaks off
> And from the mountain top a cloud
> Takes leave into the open sky

While the image of the "floating bridge" refers to romantic love, the overall vision of the poem sums up the image of an inherently fragile beauty that ultimately "takes leave into the open sky."

The film offers one last utopian possibility in the image of Pazu, Sheeta, and their air pirate friends bobbing in the sky. In an earlier scene we see Pazu being supported by his friends the miners, who, notwithstanding their own economic troubles, are there for him in his fight against outsiders. The pirates and the mine workers offer the possibility of a supportive collectivity, an image that becomes a staple of Miyazakiworld and an ideal that the director clearly hoped to establish in concrete form at Studio Ghibli. In his animations these utopian collectivities range from the pastoral communities of High Harbor in *Conan* or the Valley of the Wind in *Nausicaä* to the ill-assorted but endearing workers of Tatara in *Princess Mononoke*. Laputa, with its glorious gardens presided over by gentle artificial intelligence, also calls to Miyazaki but ultimately drifts out into the sky. The potential for genuine utopia remains with humans, if only they can manage to connect fruitfully with the nonhuman world and with one another. Miyazaki's next movie, *My Neighbor Totoro,* would show that even more explicitly, bringing him home from the transcendent but unsustainable heights of Laputa.

# 7
# Umbrellas in the Haunted Forest

*Transcending National and Personal Trauma*
*in* My Neighbor Totoro

Utopia is a place where time stops.

——HIKARU HOSOE

After three films set in either Europe or a postapocalyptic world, Miyazaki came home to Japan with his next and most beloved film, the 1988 *My Neighbor Totoro*. He also went home to his childhood and a time that had been shadowed by his mother's illness and his piercing loneliness and insecurities. In *Totoro* the director rewrites and reconstructs that boyhood, processing youthful dreams and nightmares to offer a magical world of protection, nurturing, and resilience.

Critics and audiences around the world loved the film's luscious pastoral imagery and its appealing characters. These range from a couple of remarkably believable little girls, the sisters Mei and Satsuki, to what many consider Miyazakiworld's greatest fantasy creation, the large, furry, and benevolent woodland spirit known as Totoro. Mixing fantasy and realism, the film balances supernatural images—whirling black soot sprites and a grinning "cat bus"—with seemingly artless moments of natural beauty, such as a vision of a snail languidly climbing a flower on a spring afternoon.

Despite excellent critical notices, the film was not an immediate blockbuster when first released. In an unusual move, the studio released *Totoro* as part of a double bill with *Grave of Fireflies* (Hotaru no haka, 1988), directed by Miyazaki's Ghibli colleague Isao Takahata. *Grave of Fireflies* is a shattering masterpiece about two children in wartime Japan, and perhaps the combination of the heartwarming *Totoro* and the heartbreaking *Grave* led to an uncertain audience response. It took a few years for *Totoro* to catch hold in Japan, but it became the kind of treasured film that is watched and rewatched time and time again to the present day. Indeed, the film eventually inspired a scholarly book about it with the memorable title *For Those Who Have Watched Totoro a Hundred Times and Are Still Not Tired of It*.[1]

What is it about the film that has drawn such fierce love and loyalty in Japan and abroad? Audiences can enjoy the movie as fantasy entertainment, but it also offers the clearest and perhaps most affecting vision of a pastoral utopia presented in any of Miyazaki's oeuvre. On a deeper level it explores traumatic issues of loss, grief, and the need for recovery or compensation. These issues stem both from Miyazaki's own childhood and temporary loss of his mother due to her struggle with tuberculosis and from the more universal losses that modernity had wreaked upon Japan, especially its countryside.

What makes *Totoro* so remarkable and affecting, however, is that Miyazaki resolves these issues through fantasy, allowing viewers to confront difficult emotions through a filter of enchantment that overlays the darkness with a sense of the possibility of joy and transcendence. This combination of darkness and light processed through a child's perspective is what strengthens the film's core message. While *Totoro* expresses far more joy than sadness, the director's ability to interweave challenging emotions throughout the film is what gives its overall optimistic message both nuance and substance.

*Totoro*'s time period is 1950s Japan, and the setting of forest and farmland is largely based on the director's neighborhood of Tokorozawa, a small city just outside of Tokyo. This is a world that is both place- and time-specific, conjuring deep memories for its Japanese audience.

In many ways the film seems to embody what Svetlana Boym describes as "glocal restorative nostalgia," which she explains as "at first glance ... a longing for place, but actually ... a yearning for a different time, the time of our childhood." She adds that "the nostalgic [person] desires to obliterate history and turn it into private or collective mythology."[2] But Miyazaki is not "obliterating" history in the movie; *Totoro*'s idealized landscapes and vision of childhood innocence represent an attempt to restore a "better" history on both a personal and a cultural level. While children adore the film's humor, subtle scariness, and fantasy creations, many older moviegoers, increasingly aware of the painful losses modernity has wrought on contemporary society, see the film through the lens of a bittersweet nostalgia. Indeed, the movie's promotional catchphrase on posters was "We are returning to you something you have forgotten."

It is no accident that the child's perspective is indeed a strong element in the film, evoking a "forgotten" utopia of lost innocence and freshness. But the film also offers to many Japanese viewers not only the "forgotten" realm of individual childhood but also a lost world of a past national culture. *Totoro* appeared in 1988, when Japan enjoyed a tremendous economic boom that would become known as the bubble period, a time when BMWs dotted the streets of downtown Tokyo, young people wore designer clothing while sipping champagne, and real estate prices reached dizzying heights. Beneath this splendid materialism, however, ran a countercurrent of unease at the environmental destruction and spiritual corrosion that were by-products of economic and industrial expansion.

Miyazaki was disgusted by the excesses of the bubble period. Although he had begun to embrace his traditional cultural identity, the director has little good to say about contemporary Japan. In typically provocative fashion, the director in a 1989 interview declared that he hated "the Japanese economy" and "the Japanese people." He continued ever more stridently, "Surely there can be no more superficial people than the Japanese. They were not able to transcend the demon of rapid economic development. And as a result, [we have] the corruption of the world, the loss of ideals, and the worship of material things."[3]

It seems reasonable to see *Totoro* as an alternative to this "corrupt world," but Miyazaki has declared that "*Totoro* is not a nostalgia piece."[4] Nonetheless, at least part of the movie's appeal is its ability to tap into an inchoate collective yearning for the opposite of the 1980s—a frugal, non-materialistic society distinguished by small rural communities in which neighbors supported each other and respected and appreciated the natural environment.

*Totoro* is the first of Miyazaki's major features to be set in Japan, an important change for the director. I have mentioned the director's encounter with the groundbreaking works of the ethnobotanist Sasuke Nakao, who posited that the early Japanese inhabitants of the prehistoric Jomon period had been part of a larger "green leaf culture" extending throughout East Asia. Liberated from what he saw as a narrow Japanese nationalism, Miyazaki felt that he could embrace the culture and beauty of his own country for the first time. It is consequently appropriate that the father in *Totoro* is an archaeologist who specializes in the Jomon, as the lovingly rendered books and pictures in his study attest. There is also an implied reference to the peaceful hunter-gatherer culture of the Jomon period. "Long ago, people and trees were friends," Mei and Satsuki's father tells them.

In his analysis of *Totoro* Philip Brophy warns of the colonialist patronizing that the term "lost Japan" suggests, implying that only Western critics see the film as nostalgic. In fact, however, the yearning for a past world is not an Orientalist projection but is very much alive and current in modern Japan. As Marilyn Ivy writes in *Discourses of the Vanishing,* about contemporary Japanese attempts to honor their culture, "What is striking is the extent to which essentialized images of Japan resonate in many self-descriptions."[5] These "essentialized images" include a vision of a still rural and harmonious Japan expressed in the terms *furusato* (literally "old town," but suggestive of yearning for one's childhood place) and *satoyama* (literally "mountain village").

*Satoyama* as an activist concept suggesting a more sustainable and beneficial approach to the natural environment has gone beyond popular culture to become a rallying point for governmental and environmental organizations. The notion of a creature such as Totoro, a spirit who lives in the woods near a village and interacts benignly with humanity, suggests the possibility of a revitalized relationship between humanity and nature. In fact, the movie inspired a real-life project near the director's home in Tokorozawa. The project, called Totoro's Forest, inspired enthusiastic support. Miyazaki was proud of the forest, although, characteristically, he commented that he appreciates the people who cooperated on the project because they were not "ecology fascists."[6]

While *Totoro* offers a distinctive vision of an alternative and more appealing way of life, this vision is built on an awareness of loss. The film's climax revolves around a lost child engaging with one of the most basic of human fears as it explores the larger theme of loss of innocence.

The American film critic Roger Ebert felt compelled to warn his readers that the film contains "no villains, no evil adults, no fight scenes . . . no scary monsters," but *Totoro* does present its young heroes with genuinely disturbing situations.[7] The film offers an intimate narrative about sisters Satsuki, ten, and Mei, four, who move to an old house in the countryside with their father while their mother is ill in a sanatorium. Although the film never explicitly states the nature of her illness, the book based on the movie and other sources reveal that it is tuberculosis, at that time a much feared and often fatal disease.

Adding darker shadows to the film's appealing pastoral world, Miyazaki incorporates an absent mother, the gloom of her possible death, and even the dramatic move from town to countryside. In the close-knit Japanese communities of the 1950s, such a move could be construed as potentially traumatic. This would be especially so for children, particularly those dealing with the ominous fears engendered by a mother's illness. We remember that Miyazaki himself moved several times as a child, with difficult emotional results. Initially, however, Mei and Satsuki's reactions to their new home are almost textbook examples of useful coping strategies toward potentially traumatic situations.

In contrast to most previous Miyazaki works, *Totoro* sees events entirely through the eyes of its children. The director uses low-angle shots to make sure the girls occupy a central place in the frame. Miyazaki also takes pains to highlight actions and movements that are particularly suited to a child's body. The critic Hikaru Hosoe suggests that this emphasis on the child is firmly linked to the work's utopian aspirations, especially its implicit call for a recovery of "innocence." In Hosoe's view, the movie is a call for the recovery of the best aspects of childhood and aims to inspire the curiosity, acceptance, and above all the openness to a "sense of wonder" that Miyazaki insists is a necessity in order to fully live in the world.[8]

Miyazaki's own frequent writing and pronouncements on childhood support Hosoe's analysis. In a memorable discussion of the four-year-old Mei, Miyazaki describes her willingness to open up to the supernatural without fear as something stemming from the fact that "she has not had her childhood violated by adult common sense."[9] "Violate" (*okasu*) is a strong term, suggesting Miyazaki's explicit privileging of the innocence and openness of childhood over the corrupting effect of growing older.

Like Satsuki, whom Hosoe describes as an "adult child," Miyazaki was a self-described "good kid" subsuming his own desires and taking on adult responsibility to avoid burdening his family during his mother's illness. Hosoe argues that Miyazaki in *Totoro* was attempting to "reclaim" his childhood by creating an image of an idealized family that interacts with the world in positive fashion—a microcosmic utopia in which home, society, the natural, and the supernatural combine in an enchanted realm where problems are overcome through kindness, mutual respect, and appreciation.[10]

As mentioned previously, Hosoe also suggests that the director projects two aspects of his personality onto his child heroes. The doughty young Mei, who wears her emotions on her sleeve and actively enters the world of the fantastic, is closer to Miyazaki's heart, untouched by the family responsibilities Miyazaki had to take on in boyhood. Satsuki, in contrast, gets up early to cook the family's breakfast and takes up the mothering role toward Mei. Understandably, given her older age and assumption of adult responsibilities, she is reluctant to believe in the fantasy world her sister wholeheartedly embraces. Ghibli's producer, Suzuki, recalls an angry discussion with Miyazaki in which Suzuki insisted that such a "good kid" as Satsuki couldn't possibly exist. Miyazaki furiously retorted, "She did exist. That was me!"[11]

Throughout the movie we see how a "good kid" can and should respond to traumatic situations. At the beginning of the film both children seem distinctly upbeat about their move to the countryside. High spirited and energetic, they dash about the lawn turning cartwheels and they enter their new house—a rather unusual residence for the period, incorporating both Western and Japanese architectural styles—with excitement and curiosity. The Japanese critic Shinichi Tanaka suggests that their almost excessively high spirits could be a kind of defense mechanism for dealing with the trauma of the move, "temporarily expelling their sense of loss."[12]

A more mysterious challenge occurs soon after they arrive: they find a shining acorn, one of several that drop enigmatically from the ceiling. The acorn (which reappears later in the film) signals more mysterious things to come. The sisters next encounter a phalanx of tiny whirling black spots. Nanny, an elderly village woman who has come to help them move in, explains that the black objects are "soot sprites," creatures that inhabit deserted houses and are visible only to the very young.

The soot sprites are an appealing explanation for the dust bunnies that take over old uninhabited houses. They deserve an honored place in the pantheon of original fantasy creatures that Miyazaki's imagination has given birth to, and in *Spirited Away* they reappear in quite a different iteration, one of the few Miyazaki's fantasy creations to cross from one movie to another. The soot sprites may also serve as visual emblems of the unease that swirls beneath the girls' or even their father's positive and upbeat attitude. Pitch black and insubstantial, they dart to and fro, collecting and then dissipating, just the way disturbing thoughts tug at and then vanish from the mind. In a scene that is both comic and a little frightening, Mei, the younger daughter, manages to "capture" a soot sprite in her hands. Opening her tightly clasped fingers, however, she discovers that it has escaped, leaving only black traces, much as a pesky thought eludes us but leaves its traces on our spirit.

The notion of the soot sprites as special entities visible to a select few seems to reassure the girls, suggesting not only the powers of the childish gaze but also hinting at their fortitude and agency in subsequent encounters with the supernatural. The girls also seem unfazed when Nanny's young grandson Kanta shouts at them that they live in "a haunted house." They are helped in this positive response by their father's enthusiastic declaration that his childhood dream had been to live in a haunted house, a cheerful embrace of the uncanny that provides a model for dealing with strange events.

This attitude is soon reinforced in one of the film's few genuinely frightening sequences, in which the father helps them deal with fears on their first night in their new home. As Tanaka describes it: "The return of this temporarily expelled sense of loss is beautifully illustrated in the scene where Satsuki goes out to gather firewood and the wind suddenly rises. The environment which, up till then, had seemed happy transforms as the wind blows through the dark depths of the night, as if the unease that they had gotten rid of has returned in amplified fashion."[13]

The wind then seems to take on a life of its own, blowing off roof tiles and shaking doors and light fixtures while the girls shudder and take refuge with their father in the bath. The gentle, dreamy father reacts to their fear in a way that is proactive and inspiring, an ideal example of coping with traumatic events. He laughs at the wind and noises, boasting that he is not afraid of ghosts, and teaches his daughters to follow his example. The atmosphere lightens considerably, and the image of the girls and their father in the womblike intimacy of the bath evolves from vulnerability to a comforting and intimate family scene. Our last glimpse of the soot sprites is an eerily beautiful one, as they glide up the side of the house and scatter against a gigantic camphor tree illuminated by the moonlit sky.

Psychiatrists have identified certain therapeutic responses to trauma relevant to *Totoro*'s narrative: providing a sense of safety, calm, and connectedness, teaching coping skills, and inspiring active rather than passive behavior in response to trauma. All appear in this early episode. That the sequence takes place largely in the bath is hugely evocative for Japanese audiences, as the household bath has for centuries been a place of family intimacy, relaxation, and purification. Atypically for the rest of the movie, the father towers above his daughters, suggesting a giant protector, an impression augmented by his large-scale laughter. The girls' imitation of his laughter shows that they are learning to protect themselves and will do so whenever darkness lurks outside.

In addition to such positive responses to trauma the film suggests one more: the solace provided by the spiritual and the sublime. Intriguingly, Miyazaki largely avoids explicit religious references throughout *Totoro,* even taking out some overt references to Shinto that had appeared in the original storyboards.[14] The film is nonetheless permeated with a sense of the numinous and the transcendent, both in its presentation of nature and in its evocation of the supernatural. Although the scene in the bath is cozy and domestic, our last glimpse of the soot sprites suggests another realm outside the family or even the human collectivity. The gigantic camphor tree that the soot sprites rise toward carries a clear religious connotation, the Shinto *shimenawa* or sacred rope that is wrapped around it. The moon illuminating the tree and the clouds shifting around it also evoke a vastness beyond the human realm.

Mei is the first to encounter the supernatural after the girls' quick brush with the soot sprites. With all the energy and inquisitiveness of a four-year-old, Mei is left alone in the ramshackle garden while Satsuki goes to school and their father busily grades papers in his study. Unable to capture her father's attention, and much like Alice of *Alice in Wonderland* as she copes with the peaceful boredom of a spring day, Mei is delighted to be distracted by a flicker of movement going past her in the grasses surrounding their house. She follows the movement and discovers two small fuzzy creatures (junior totoros, as we discover later), racing with a small bundle of acorns that keep dropping out onto the grass. Excited and curious, she follows the little creatures through a leafy tunnel, emerging at the bottom near a huge gray creature of unknown species lying peacefully asleep in a hole beneath the enormous old camphor tree.

Mei treats a clearly fantastic occurrence—the appearance of the totoros—with complete aplomb, happily climbing onto the large totoro's stomach and asking him his name. He grunts out a three syllable sound that she hears as "totoro," associating the word with the "trolls" (*tororu* in Japanese) she has read about in a European children's book. Having identified the creature to her own satisfaction, she promptly goes to sleep on his furry belly.

We can read this magical encounter as Mei's imagination conjuring up a benign "imaginary friend" out of her need for a safe protective figure. Perhaps she is also lonely. It is worth remembering, however, that Miyazaki is at pains to insist that the totoros are "real," at least within the confines of the narrative. Suzuki famously recounts that an early poster for the film featuring a large picture of Totoro was captioned, "This kind of strange creature doesn't live in Japan anymore. Probably." On seeing the poster Miyazaki was incensed, insisting that it should be changed to "This kind of strange creature is still living in Japan. Probably."[15]

The word "probably" leaves some room for doubt, of course. In many ways *Totoro* emblemizes a type of fantastic structure identified by the Russian scholar Tzvetan Todorov in his groundbreaking book *The Fantastic,* in which one is left "hesitating" between a supernatural and realistic explanations for a mysterious phenomenon.[16] That we never really know for sure adds to the pleasure of the encounter. Traditionally, East Asian philosophy and thought has been far more comfortable than the West with this sense of the betwixt and between. This is evident in the classic Taoist tale about the philosopher Chuang Tze falling asleep and dreaming that he is a butterfly, only to wake up and wonder whether he is now a butterfly dreaming that he is Chuang Tze. Content either way he has adopted a relaxed acceptance of the improbable quite alien to conventional Western rationality. From this vantage point what really matters in this and subsequent supernatural encounters in *Totoro* is not whether they actually happen but whether the girls believe they do.

Whether the totoros are "real" in a concrete sense seems less important than Mei's imaginative and positive response to their manifestation. This is clear in her decision to call the creature Totoro, based on her memory of European trolls. Since trolls are rarely furry, amiable creatures, Mei's naming of the creature as her own version of the word "troll" suggests an imaginative power to reconfigure something frightening (the conventional troll) into something reassuring, just as Miyazaki reconfigures his childhood darkness into something radiant.

Mei's actions in this scene can be viewed as a proactive response to what many children and adults would find to be a challenging and even frightening situation, a meeting with a very large and very mysterious Other. Mei not only accepts this supernatural Other but deals with it, not by anthropomorphizing (as Alice does with the White Rabbit and other Wonderland creatures) but by engaging with it as an autonomous entity she chooses to see as benign. Mei's relaxed interaction with otherness will become a fundamental feature of Miyazakiworld, evident later on in Ashitaka's relaxed acceptance of the kodama tree spirits in *Princess Mononoke* or Lisa's welcoming of the little fish-girl in *Ponyo*.

Totoro has a protective function as well. As many Japanese critics point out, Totoro's large stomach is evocative of the womb, as is his nest in a hole beneath the tree.[17] Thus, although English-speaking critics tend to identify Totoro as a male, it is certainly legitimate to see a maternal role here as well. Going down a tunnel to find a comforting round object suggests that Mei has temporarily found a substitute for her missing mother, something that Miyazaki as a child was never able to accomplish. The image of Mei lying on Totoro's stomach evokes peace and timelessness, an endless late spring day out of an idyllic childhood dream. This sense of sublimity and nurturing is heightened by a final high-angled shot, showing the forest's cathedral-like green roof extending protectively over the sleeping creatures far below.

The scene following Mei's first encounter with Totoro also supports the impression of Totoro as a benign creature with strong links to nature. Satsuki comes home to find that Mei is missing. Satsuki and her father find her asleep in the forest. Mei tries to show them Totoro, but he has disappeared, and her father and sister initially laugh at her frantic search. However, when she insists that she is not lying, her father takes her seriously, telling her that she has been lucky enough to meet the Master of the Forest. Even more supportively, he takes Mei and Satsuki to perform ritual greetings to the giant camphor tree, the very one that Mei recognizes as having been shielding Totoro's home. The father explains that the main reason he had chosen their house was that he loved the tree and hoped that their mother would love it too. Thus Totoro is linked to nature, the past, and, implicitly, to their mother, entities that both protect and need protection.

Further encounters with Totoro reinforce his protective and compensatory function. Waiting in the rain for their father's bus to arrive, the sisters grow increasingly tired and anxious. Mei falls asleep on Satsuki's back. Satsuki awkwardly adjusts her umbrella and peers uneasily into the rainy darkness and glimpses two large clawlike feet coming steadily toward her. Her eyes slowly travel up a large furry body to the face of what she recognizes must be Totoro. She asks the creature whether he is indeed Totoro, and he responds with his signature grunting sound.

The two stand for a while watching the rain come down. Satsuki decides to give Totoro the extra umbrella she had brought for her father. Pleased but puzzled, Totoro examines it and finally opens it above his head, appearing somewhat amused by the whole process. More than the protection from the rain it affords, he seems to particularly enjoy the sound of raindrops hitting the umbrella's top, eventually emitting a loud roar as he jumps powerfully enough to cause a cascade of raindrops to shower over him and the children. As if the roar were a summons, a set of headlights appears in the rain, racing toward the bus stop. What emerges from the rain is not, however, an ordinary bus but a gigantic grinning cat in the shape of a bus, complete with mouse tail lights and an inviting furry interior. Totoro boards the bus, and offers Satsuki a small plant-wrapped bundle as he ambles on.

Their father arrives shortly after the Catbus departs. He apologizes for being late and asks whether they were worried. The girls surprise him with their joy and excitement, dancing around him as they tell him about their marvelous encounter. They shout, "It was scary! It was cool!" With the girls hanging on to their father's arms, the three head home, the giant camphor tree looming above them.

In this quiet but emotionally intense scene, natural and supernatural forces interact with and augment the typical emotions of childhood. Boredom, loneliness, and frustration shift into sensations of surprise and joy. The girls' cries of "cool!" and "scary!" capture the mixture of terror and delight that children can feel when encountering something out of the ordinary. The rain and the darkness are beautifully realized and create a claustrophobic sensation of shivery suspense. Joe Hisaishi's soundtrack supports the atmosphere, evolving from clear tinkling notes evoking raindrops to a slightly ominous repetition of subdued low tones as Totoro draws near.

Miyazaki uses silence expertly to draw out the suspense, as when Satsuki and Totoro stand voicelessly together looking out at the rain, and to support the impression of a quietly developing bond between human and nonhuman that would be spoiled by too much vocal interaction. In this quiet rainy setting the suddenness of Totoro's roar and the noisy shower of raindrops operate as a cathartic relief from the slow buildup of intense emotions. In their own way the cascading raindrops are as wondrous and fantastical as Totoro's eerie roar or the frenetic Catbus.

The first storyboard that Miyazaki made for *Totoro* was an evocative, slightly surreal image: a young girl waits at a bus stop in the rain holding a red umbrella while a strange nonhuman creature (Totoro) stands beside her. This image would evolve into the film's iconic poster juxtaposing humanity, nature, and the supernatural, giving equal weight to all three. The tall trees in the rain suggest the mystery and power of nature while the large nonhuman form suggests another kind of mystery. Initially there was only one girl in the movie, and in this image she gazes calmly, taking both weather and the supernatural visitor in her stride. We are aware that she is protected by her umbrella, whose comforting bright color is a focal point.

Miyazaki derived inspiration from many sources, but a particularly interesting one is an old Japanese religious tale, the tale of Kasa Jizō, or Straw

Hat Jizōs: an old man sets off to sell protective straw hats on a snowy day. Passing by a group of Jizō Bodhisattva statues, he is stirred by their vulnerability to the snow. Bodhisattvas are beings who remain on Earth to help suffering humans rather than ascend to heaven. The Jizō Bodhisattva particularly protects children. In this tale the human protects the supernatural. The old man ends up giving away all his hats to the stone images. Of course he is amply rewarded, as the Jizō statues return his kindness the next day with food and drink or, depending on the variation, gold or silver.

In Miyazaki's contemporary reworking the hat has been replaced by an umbrella, the snow is rain, and the Bodhisattva is a large, furry unidentifiable creature. Totoro's small gift to the children echoes the Bodhisattvas' reciprocity. What was originally a didactic religious tale is now a story of spiritual interactions among humans, nature, and the supernatural.

Miyazaki's switching of the hats to umbrellas makes the story more contemporary and adds a charmingly realistic touch. The umbrella in the final poster protectively covers both Satsuki and Mei. When Satsuki lends her father's umbrella to Totoro, it is a demonstration of kindness and courage, as well as of a human proactively engaging with the nonhuman Other. Totoro's delighted play with the umbrella and the raindrops lends a comic air to the encounter and suggests the simple pleasures of childhood. Satsuki will later call on Totoro for help, but in this scene it is the other way around.

An umbrella also figures prominently in the next meeting between the two girls and Totoro, in which the small totoros and the sisters work together to transform Totoro's parting gift of seedlings into a luxuriant tree. In many ways this scene is the emotional high point of the movie, a gorgeously realized vision of natural, supernatural, and human community interacting to create growth and even life itself.

The girls awaken on a summer evening to sounds from the garden. They look out their window to see Totoro, holding the umbrella and accompanied by the smaller totoros, walking around the plot where Mei and Satsuki had previously planted the seeds. The girls had been waiting impatiently for the seeds to grow and had almost given hope, but now they leap excitedly from their beds to join the little group. Soon they are all bobbing up and down in what appears to be a plant-growing ritual led by Totoro, wielding his umbrella as if it were a homely version of a magic wand while the two junior totoros imitate him by waving large leaves up and down over their heads.

In fact, as Hosoe points out, the "magic" is a more subtle kind than a wand might suggest.[18] Totoro's umbrella does not simply transform the seedlings into a tree but helps the seedlings transform themselves. Nor is it an easy process. Everyone has to work together and they have to work hard. Even Totoro exudes beads of perspiration on his forehead as he continues with his labors. To soaring music, the seedlings become saplings that frantically intertwine to become an enormous leafy tree, dominating the moonlit landscape. The children shriek with delight, but the adventure is not over. Once again the umbrella comes into play, to help Totoro take flight above the trees. The girls and the small totoros clutch onto his stomach as he whirls and bobs above the rice paddies, lakes, and mountains of their rural domain.

With the help of Totoro, Mei and Satsuki have created growing things, an expression of newly found skills and their connection with the land itself. Their willingness to trust Totoro allows them to gain a new and nearly godlike perspective over their daily world; they transcend the vicissitudes of daily life in their flight above the countryside. Significantly, Satsuki hesitates before leaping onto Totoro's stomach, indicating the increased self-awareness of older childhood. Once airborne, however, both the girls delight in the merging of human, natural, and supernatural. At one point the girls are inspired by Totoro to roar along with him into the sky, symbolically finding their "voice." Toward the end of their flight they even exclaim, "We are the wind!"

Following the moonlit flight, the girls awaken the next morning to find that the seeds, while sprouting as tiny green shoots, have not actually developed into the lush shrubbery of the night before. Rather than being disappointed, they shout happily, "It was a dream! It wasn't a dream!" indicating that they, like the philosopher Chuang Tze long before, are now able to create their own form of imaginative reality without needing affirmation from external forces.

The children's final encounter with the supernatural, while exciting, is the least subtle one of the movie. This is the sequence in which Satsuki runs to Totoro to ask him to help find Mei, who has gone missing in an attempt to bring their sick mother a piece of corn from Nanny's garden. The search for Mei by Satsuki and the villagers is the action climax of the film, a genuinely traumatic situation that is resolved by recourse to the fantastic, aided by collective support and love. Miyazaki based this sequence partly on a recent incident in which a neighbor's child had been feared lost in a river, and on a childhood experience, when his younger brother went missing at a local festival.

Miyazaki combines this memory of temporary loss with the deeper loss of his mother's illness. Mei's disappearance is triggered by the news that their mother, who was supposed to be visiting them at home for the weekend, has taken a turn for the worse and must stay in the hospital. Both children are naturally disappointed and frightened about what their mother's relapse may foretell. Shockingly, Satsuki's carefully maintained adult composure finally cracks. She bursts into tears in front of Nanny and yells at Mei, accusing her of not caring whether their mother lives or dies.

Shocked, scared, and miserable, Mei sets out alone for their mother's hospital, a three-hour trip, and inevitably gets lost. Miyazaki brings to life the girls' fear and helplessness. In one scene, utterly overcome, Satsuki goes to sleep. Miyazaki has recalled that, shown no sympathy as a child by the family maid when his dog disappeared, he had fallen asleep in a paroxysm of grief, an admission of his powerlessness to alter terrible events.

In this final third of the film a variety of cinematic strategies heighten the inherent fear and tension arising from a child's disappearance. Particularly effective is a portrayal of the oncoming sunset, reminding us that time is running out. The landscape so inviting in the silvery blues and greens of the children's moonlight flight takes on an ominous quality as day darkens with Mei's whereabouts still unknown. Miyazaki effectively depicts Satsuki's panic and terror as, guilt ridden, she races wildly around the countryside calling for her sister.

As Hosoe points out, it is significant that Satsuki, whose father is at the hospital with her mother, does not ask for adult help either from the villagers or when she stops a young couple in a truck and asks whether they have seen Mei.[19] Not only does her lack of adult support make the sequence more suspenseful, but it also makes her final decision to rely on the supernatural more understandable.

This occurs after what is perhaps the most tense scene in the movie, when villagers find what they fear may be Mei's sandal floating in a pond. They show it to Satsuki. The camera rests on her face for several seconds as it registers fear, anguish, and then relief. Shaking her head, she says, "It's not Mei's," then sprints from the villagers back into the countryside. Passing by a Shinto shrine, she races toward the great camphor tree, calling on Totoro as she runs. The shrubbery opens into the tunnel that Mei had gone through and, like Mei, Satsuki discovers Totoro asleep in his nest.

In contrast to that sleepy spring day, the action is now fast-paced. Totoro quickly responds to Satsuki's request, leaping straight up from his grassy nest onto the top of a hillside with Satsuki held carefully in his claws. Letting out his trademark roar, he summons the Catbus, which arrives almost instantly, helpfully replacing its usual destination sign with the name Mei. Ushering Satsuki on board, Totoro waves goodbye as she and the Catbus race off into the distance on a breathless and exciting ride that echoes the girl's previous flight with Totoro. Soon Satsuki spots Mei crying alone next to a group of Jizō statues and the two are joyously reunited.

The final moments of the film play again on Todorov's notion of the fantastic as hesitation between natural and supernatural. It seems to end on the side of the supernatural. We see the girls and the Catbus on a tree branch above the window of their mother's room in the hospital while their mother and father converse happily below about their mother's forthcoming return home. Looking up, the mother tells their father that she "thought she saw Mei and Satsuki just now," to which the father responds, "That may be." He

Mei and Satsuki watch their parents in the hospital in
*My Neighbor Totoro,* Studio Ghibli, 1988.

points to an ear of corn that has mysteriously appeared on the windowsill with "For Mother" inscribed on it.

Miyazaki's decision to go for a magical resolution to real-life trauma underlines one of the film's key messages: that belief in the powers of nature and the imagination will give us the strength to go beyond ourselves and transcend the traumas of daily life. Satsuki's choice when she confronts what might be Mei's sandal and the real possibility of her death is not to turn to the villagers for comfort or help, nor toward prayer or religion. Instead, Miyazaki has her bypass a Shinto shrine to turn toward nature and the fantastic in the form of the long leafy tunnel leading to Totoro. Her journey down the tunnel can be seen as her decision to travel back into the faith and innocence of childhood and, equally important, to the world of the imagination. Her own creative reserves allow her to find her sister.

The villagers rallying together to search for the missing Mei has its own appeal and function. As Kaplan and Wang point out, "modernity . . . has shattered the . . . inherited ground of experience, and the intimate cultural networks of support and trust that humans hitherto relied on for a sense of security and meaningful life."[20] *Totoro* offers a possibility of the recovery of these "intimate cultural networks" through both fantasy and its vision of collective human decency.

The genre of the fantastic was long considered escapist at best, at worst irresponsible. In *Totoro*, however, the fantastic becomes not only a means of liberation and empowerment but also a form of utopian critique. In Miyazakiworld openness to and appreciation of Otherness can help us recover whatever has been forgotten or lost—the best parts of our culture and of ourselves. These parts may be hidden by shadows, but if we can only recover the right perspective, they become clearly visible, like acorns shining in the tall grass.

An urban legend that grew up around the movie in the early twenty-first century offered a darker interpretation of the film. Still disturbingly popular, it posits that *Totoro* contains a number of secret references to death, of the mother and Mei and even Satsuki. The legend, which transforms Totoro from a benign and helpful woodland spirit to a *shinigami,* literally a god of death, probably arose from a 2001 book on Miyazaki by the scholar and teacher Masashi Shimizu. Shimizu argues that the real inspiration for the movie was *Night Train to the Stars,* a classic fantasy by one of Miyazaki's favorite writers, Kenji Miyazawa. This haunting work follows two young boys, Giovanni and Campanella, on a surreal train journey across the galaxy, ending with the discovery that Campanella had drowned before the journey even began and that it was really his ghost who accompanied Giovanni on their journey.

In Shimizu's analysis, *Totoro* actually takes place in a world of death.[21]

The house itself, as Shimizu reminds us, is described as "haunted" by Nanny's grandson Kanta, and he suggests that Kanta's strong reaction to Satsuki is because "something alien had entered the countryside."[22]

Needless to say, as Shimizu acknowledges, there was immediate pushback to his theory, even among his own students. While generally seen as a preposterous bit of speculation, the idea of *Totoro* as a death-haunted saga grew popular enough in the early twenty-first century to generate websites and television "news" features on the premise that the movie had more to it than Studio Ghibli was willing to admit. "Evidence" was brought forth, such as the perception that the girls' shadows disappear toward the end of the movie and that the sandal found floating in the pond really did belong to Mei. Careful examination of the film, however, shows these "proofs" to be untrue, and the studio itself is on record as emphatically rejecting the theory.

Some suggested a historical base for the legend, a controversial murder case known as the Sayama incident. Occurring in the late 1950s in the area where the film is set and where Miyazaki lived, the case involved the murder of a sixteen-year-old girl. Its widespread notoriety arose from the fact that the accused was a member of the *burakumin,* an invisible underclass in Japan who are still discriminated against. It is certain that Miyazaki would have been aware of this case, both because of its geographical proximity and for its controversial nature, since many people remain convinced that the accused man was framed for the murder.[23]

If there is anything to be learned from these unhappy speculations, it is how the legend serves as a mirror for the changes in Japanese society in the decades since the film came out. At the time the film first appeared, Japan had reached its postwar economic peak. While mourning the loss of the agrarian past, the country still looked forward to a better future. In many ways the utopianism of *Totoro*—with its vision of a recovered idealized past and call for a new harmony between human and the nonhuman—piquantly emblemized this optimistic moment. After the film's release the postbubble recession deepened, however, and a darker mood took over Japan: an increasingly severe loss of faith in the possibility of national recovery, not only on an economic level but on a spiritual and emotional one as well. A world that can even imagine Totoro as a death god is a qualitatively different place from the heady Japan of the 1980s.

The legend is accurate in one respect, however: *My Neighbor Totoro* is indeed about death, or at least about mortality, an aspect of the world with which Miyazaki had been intimately familiar from early childhood on. The mother's potentially fatal illness overshadows the story and serves as the pivot for the final plot developments. When Satsuki finally admits that their mother might die, she not only terrifies her little sister but opens the floodgates to her own awareness of adult mortality, something that she had previously blocked by busily taking on the chores and persona of the "adult child." The realization that our parents can and eventually will die—indeed, that anything good can be taken from us—is both a terrible and a necessary one.

In the utopian world of Totoro, however, that realization is kept largely at arm's length, and filtered through fantasy. The sobering awareness that childhood, too, will ultimately end, and we will forget the radiant world of our youth is one that the movie elides on its surface but ultimately endorses. Time itself, relentless time, is the fearsome element in the movie, reminding us of the quotation from Hosoe that serves as this chapter's epigraph: "Utopia is a place where time stops."[24] *Totoro*'s final "magic," and the reason why its appeal is so profound and universal, is that it allows us to recover what we have forgotten and to luxuriate in innocence, beauty, and joy, if only for a few transitory moments.

# 8
# The Witch and the City

*Time, Space, and Gender in* Kiki's Delivery Service

A few years ago when I was teaching my seminar on Miyazaki, a student complained about the premise of *Kiki's Delivery Service* (Majo no takkyūbin, 1989), the director's next movie after *Totoro*. It wasn't "realistic," she said, that a young girl on her own should meet with such kindness from a bunch of strangers in a big city. Many of us disagreed, and I was the most vehement. Forty years before, I had gone to Tokyo by myself at the age of seventeen. I found work teaching English conversation and rented a six-mat room—about one hundred square feet—with its own private bath, a real luxury in those days. Above all, I found friends, a varied and wonderful group of people ranging from a Dutch bar hostess who became an older sister figure to a trio of Japanese English teachers who loved to drink beer and play Scrabble.

From my point of view, therefore, *Kiki* is a realistic movie, never mind the fact that it is about a young witch who flies on her broom and holds long conversations with her black cat, Jiji. Many young Japanese women also found it realistic, apparently. Working women in their twenties flocked to see the movie, along with children and their families. Together they helped to make *Kiki* Studio Ghibli's first major hit, further underlining independent young women and evocative visions of Europe as major tropes of Miyazaki-world.

*Kiki* almost didn't happen. When work began on the movie, both Miyazaki and the studio were in a tight place. Ghibli's first releases, *Laputa* and the double bill of *Grave of Fireflies* and *Totoro,* had taken in far less than *Nausicaä,* which had been produced by a different studio, Topcraft. Industry gossip suggested that Studio Ghibli, Miyazaki in particular, was incapable of producing a hit.

*Kiki*'s success turned the studio's fortunes around. Toshio Suzuki's connections and his efforts in producing and marketing Ghibli films were instrumental. Suzuki remembers the stress of making the movie, and a constant feeling of precariousness. He tried to arrange commercial tie-ins with Yamato Delivery Service (whose logo of a black cat carrying a kitten seemed perfect for a movie about a witch and her cat), but Suzuki found Yamato initially uncooperative. Asked why, Yamato's representative replied abruptly, "Miyazaki's pretty much washed up. . . . After all, since *Nausicaä* he's been steadily losing his audience."[1]

Although Yamato eventually did end up helping to sponsor the film, Suzuki remembers this discussion changing something inside him: "From that point on I started to work seriously at creating hits and began to pour all my energies into advertising." Miyazaki's own attitude toward this more clearly commercial shift was ambivalent. Suzuki recalls that the director opened a meeting with the Yamato representatives with the acerbic announcement, "The title may have 'Delivery Service' in it, but we have no plans to make this a movie to educate the employees of Yamato Delivery Service."[2]

*Kiki* is actually quite educational in its messages of independence and empowerment. At the same time its many appealing images create the magical panorama we now recognize as a Miyazakiworld trademark: sparkling natural scenery, elegant European architecture, and, of course, spectacular flying scenes, ranging from a girl on a broomstick riding with a flock of geese to a huge zeppelin trailing slowly across the sky. But the movie also has a brief episode never before seen in the director's work, a young girl on her way to the bathroom.

Kiki wakes up on her first morning in her new home, a little room above a bakery. She moves restlessly in bed, and finally gets up and heads out the door, still in her nightgown. From outside the bakery, we see Kiki trotting downstairs to a homely little shed with a heart carved on it: the bakery does not have indoor plumbing. We hear the sound of a toilet flushing, and Kiki peeps out the door to see the baker, a large, strapping man, limbering up for the new day. Kiki hastily shuts the door and opens it only after the baker has gone back inside. We see her scurrying up the steps back to her room, her cheeks flushed with embarrassment.

To be clear, there is nothing remotely salacious in this scene. Rather, as the critic Taiten Kawakami points out, the scene is a well-executed portrayal of a young girl's behavior in a new situation.[3] Miyazaki expresses the physical realities of living in someone else's house and overlays this with the kind of intimate psychological accuracy that would become an increasingly impressive element of his work.

But what makes the scene particularly memorable is that Kiki is not just any young girl. She is a witch in training, learning self-reliance by living for a year by herself in a strange new city, a traditional part of a witch's apprenticeship, according to the young adult novel by Eiko Kadono on which the movie is based. The movie follows Kadono's story in combining fantasy with a realistic and sympathetic portrayal of a young girl working through the typical traumas of adolescence while learning to survive on her own. The scene of Kiki shyly on her way to the bathroom reflects an unusual new reality for a Miyazaki film—an urban lifestyle in which virtual strangers come together in disparate modes and moments. This new reality was one increasingly shared by young people in 1980s Japan.

This mixture of detailed realism and fantasy elements gives *Kiki* its particular strength. Miyazaki had already made a name for himself by creating strong female characters in *Nausicaä, Laputa,* and the previous year's *Totoro,* but none has the intricate mixture of traits that makes Kiki such a believable character. We see her express a range of emotion—from the positive, such as childlike enthusiasm, simple joy, and sincere gratitude, to more complicated and often negative feelings: embarrassment and shyness, ano-

Lupin shows Clarisse the real treasure at the heart of Cagliostro Castle.
*The Castle of Cagliostro,* Toho Studio, 1979, see pages 55–56

Lupin and Jigen evade the count's minions.
*The Castle of Cagliostro,* Toho Studio, 1979, see pages 56–63

Nausicaä dances with Ohmu eyeshell deep in the Fukai.
*Nausicaä of the Valley of the Wind*, Topcraft Studio, 1984, see pages 73–80

Nausicaä is resurrected on a field of Ohmu feelers.

*Nausicaä of the Valley of the Wind*, Topcraft Studio, 1984, see page 84

Robot and wildlife

*Laputa: Castle in the Sky*, Studio Ghibli, 1986, see pages 95–96

The castle of Laputa takes leave into the open sky.
*Laputa: Castle in the Sky*, Studio Ghibli, 1986, see pages 97–100

Satsuki, Mei, and Totoro wait in the rain for a bus.
*My Neighbor Totoro,* Studio Ghibli, 1988, see pages 112–114

Totoro takes Satsuki, Mei, and the junior totoros on a flight above their rural community.
*My Neighbor Totoro,* Studio Ghibli, 1988, see page 115

Kiki flies over the beautiful town of Koriko.
*Kiki's Delivery Service,* Studio Ghibli, 1989, see pages 123–130

Marco's plane cannot join the others in the Valhalla in the sky.
*Porco Rosso,* Studio Ghibli, 1992, see pages 151–153

Princess Mononoke stands with her wolf mother, Moro.
*Princess Mononoke,* Studio Ghibli, 1997, see pages 183–184

The shishigami walks the mountains followed by kodama.

*Princess Mononoke*, Studio Ghibli, 1997, see pages 186–192

No Face, grown to giant size, rampages inside the bathhouse.

*Spirited Away*, Studio Ghibli, 2001, see pages 203–208

Chihiro and No Face on the train en route to Zeniba's house

*Spirited Away*, Studio Ghibli, 2001, see pages 208–210

Chihiro and No Face have a genteel tea party with Zeniba.

*Spirited Away*, Studio Ghibli, 2001, see page 210

Howl's castle appears over a mountain ridge.
*Howl's Moving Castle*, Studio Ghibli, 2004, see pages 218–220

Ponyo and Sosuke putter across a flooded world.
*Ponyo,* Studio Ghibli, 2008, see pages 238–240

The seascape that inspired *Ponyo*
Photo by Stephen Coit, see pages 229–230

Naoko tells Jiro to "live."
*The Wind Rises,* Studio Ghibli, 2013, see page 259

The forests of Yakushima Island: the green world that inspired *Princess Mononoke*

Photo by Stephen Coit, see page 189

mie and despair. Paradoxically, the young witch is one of Miyazaki's most human characters, and the movie itself one of the director's most heartfelt coming-of-age stories, a "small gem," as critic Shunsuke Sugita puts it.[4]

While Miyazaki has spoken repeatedly and at length about *Totoro*, *Nausicaä*, and *Laputa*, I find fewer comments on *Kiki*. Part of that may have been simple exhaustion: Miyazaki started work on *Kiki* the day after he finished *Totoro*. Furthermore, he stepped in after three other directors had already worked on the movie. It would not be the last time he took on the added responsibility of directing—a desire for aesthetic control and an almost masochistic perfectionism have been consistent key features in sustaining Miyazakiworld.

Miyazaki tied *Kiki* to a materialist and consumer culture for which he increasingly expressed contempt. The film came out during the last year of Japan's bubble period, and while Kiki's hard work, honor, and perseverance contrast with that era's culture of hedonism, Miyazaki includes skeptical glimpses of young people who appear to spend their lives partying.

Although Miyazaki had worked with Takahata on adapting children's classics and in *Cagliostro* had created his own version of the manga and anime *Lupin III*, *Kiki* was the first time he was solely responsible for making a film based on a novel. Moreover, the novel's author was alive. Miyazaki's departures from Kadono's novel inspired some heated discussions between author and filmmaker. Ultimately Miyazaki and Takahata brought in a female Ghibli staff member to persuade the reluctant author that film narrative needs its own kind of story.[5]

Overall, however, Miyazaki stays true to Kadono's basic blueprint—her use of a fantasy framework to create a believable female protagonist's rite-of-passage story. Kadono's novel takes elements from traditional Western folklore about witches, such as Kiki's black dress, broom, and black cat, and Miyazaki adheres to this vision while adding his own modern touches, particularly technological ones.

Although Japanese folklore abounds with powerful supernatural females, witches are not part of its traditions. By the late twentieth century, however, they had become a staple of Japanese manga and anime. In fact, while still at Tōei in the 1960s, Miyazaki had been involved in an early and extremely popular anime series called *Sally the Witch* (Mahōzukai Sari). Sally is now seen as the progenitrix of the many witches and "magical" girls who still populate anime and manga series.

Using folklore to tell a modern story can be challenging. But Kiki is far from being a conventional witch, and the movie is far from a conventional coming-of-age narrative. In her novel and in subsequent Kiki books, Kadono updates historical convention to create a witch who is not old, ugly, or exceptionally powerful, and places her in nontraditional situations. Her Kiki is a believable thirteen-year-old girl who happens to possess two supernatural powers, the ability to fly and the ability to talk to her cat. More intriguing than these rather clichéd powers is Kiki's willingness to leave her rural village and seek her fortune in a large city at a very young age, a quest more typical of a male protagonist. Kadono created an original modern fairy tale by updating the traditional trope of the witch and combining it with a more typically male story of development through adventure.

Quite atypically for a young Japanese woman of that period, Kadono had lived abroad for two years soon after graduation from college, in Brazil, and the experience of making her way in a foreign world probably helped inspire the books.

Further inpiration can be found in the political movements that roiled Japan from the 1960s on, particularly the women's liberation movement, which spread from the West late in the decade. It had led to significant changes in the way Japanese women saw themselves. By 1985, feminist stirrings had shaken up if not completely altered conventional assumptions about women's place in society.

By the 1980s women were more likely to go to college and work outside the home, at least for a while. Popular culture reflected this, as in the *shōjo manga* (girls' manga) that, from the 1970s, increasingly featured powerful and independent heroines. In a discussion of Kiki, Miyazaki related her story to the "young female staff members" at Ghibli, noting that "there is a similarity [in Kiki] with young women who come to big cities all alone, dreaming of making it as manga artists."[6] If anything, Miyazaki amplifies the novel's feminist aspects, bringing out some of the most groundbreaking elements more effectively than the book itself.

He does this in two significant ways. First is his highlighting of other female characters, in particular, the self-sufficient young artist Ursula, who becomes a role model for Kiki at a critical juncture in her life. Ursula has a far lower profile in the book; in fact, Kadono does not even give her a name. In many ways, Ursula is Kiki's older self, which the director underlines by having the same voice actress play both roles.

Another major difference is that Miyazaki darkens the tone of the novel by acknowledging the cost of independence and emphasizing the loneliness and self-questioning that accompany maturation.

Miyazaki's changes created a work that manages to be heartwarming yet provocative, even gently subversive. The movie offers subtle comments not only on the process of individual maturation but on some of the wider cultural issues sweeping Japan: the tensions between traditional and modern, and the clashing rhythms of traditional time and space coming up against the new chronotope of modernity. The critic Manabu Murase suggests that the work contains two or even three different forms of time: "witch's time," referring to the primordial traditions Kiki inherits from her mother; "society's time," reflected in the bustling urban world she settles in; and "forest time," the natural rhythms of the forest where Ursula dwells.[7] Miyazaki had touched on contrasting time periods in previous films, as in his vision of the ancient and protective camphor tree that Mei and Satsuki bow to in *Totoro*. In *Kiki*, he adds for the first time the dynamic dimension of urban time, something that is inferred only by its absence in *Totoro*.

All these tensions are embodied in Kiki's encounter with Koriko, the lovely city by the sea where she chooses to settle. Miyazaki's highlighting of the city is important for several reasons. Placing Kiki in a richly detailed urban and clearly capitalist environment amplifies the estranging aspects of this modern-day fairy tale, emphasizing the demarcation between "witch's time" and "society's time." Unlike traditional witches (including her own mother), Kiki draws her raison d'être (and financial well-being) not from handed-down tradition or organic inheritance but from the bustle of city life.

The city is also the traditional site of exploration and maturation for young male protagonists in the typical modern bildungsroman. Many modern Japanese classics are coming-of-age novels in which the protagonist leaves his country home to find fortune in the big city. The protagonists of such novels as Natsume Sōseki's *Sanshiro,* Kenzaburō Ōe's *A Personal Matter* (Kojinteki na taiken), and Haruki Murakami's *Norwegian Wood* (Noruwei no mori) find adventure, romance, and challenges in Tokyo. Kiki follows this pattern, growing in self-reliance as she moves through (and above) the noisy streets of Koriko in what might be called a magical and feminist bildungsroman.

Her story differs not only in its female protagonist and fantasy framework but in that the city where she settles is a fictional one, allowing Miyazaki to pick and choose elements from cities that had caught his fancy over time. In creating Koriko (the name appears only once, on the side of a bus), Miyazaki was inspired by some of his favorite European cities, especially the Swedish town of Visby, but including aspects of Stockholm and of Mediterranean cities. The artwork on Koriko was done by Hiroshi Ono, whose previous credits included work on the cyberpunk anime masterpiece *Akira.*

Not entirely unlike what he had created for Neo-Tokyo in *Akira,* Ono gives Koriko a similar if more homey energy, filling the screen with moving vehicles ranging from streetcars to perambulators. But he also offers lyrically beautiful set pieces, such as a classic European park with a gently splashing fountain, and a quiet city street lined with elegant residences through which a sudden summer gust scatters shining leaves. Far more than in the novel, the movie version of Koriko beckons us toward another version of Miyazakiworld's fantasy Europe, mixing fairy tale with an almost hyper-real urban energy.

Kiki's voyage away from home mimics Japanese society's increasingly outward orientation. The 1980s were characterized not only by economic materialism but by a wave of what politicians and the media termed *koku-saika,* or internationalization. Besides pursuing business ventures abroad, a significant number of Japanese were beginning to travel overseas for tourism. Young women used their salaries to enjoy a foreign adventure or two before marriage. *Kiki,* with its exquisitely imagined European setting and its adventurous young heroine, in many ways captures this glittering moment, and it is not surprising that the movie particularly appealed to young women in their twenties.

The movie's success was not predetermined, however. Suzuki orchestrated an extensive ad campaign, designing the posters and getting the movie mentioned on television. Miyazaki and Suzuki agonized over the movie poster, rejecting the initial simplistic tagline "An exciting story about a cute witch who flies through the sky" for something that would express the movie's adult complexities. They finally came up with "I was down for a while but now I'm feeling good," displayed over a picture of a glum-looking Kiki in the bakery. The catchphrase, combined with the use of a wistful theme song about a woman who leaves her husband, inevitably drew the attention of young female office workers, who would become a major part of Ghibli's audience.

But *Kiki*'s success is not simply a matter of presenting audiences with a version of an idealized Europe or an upbeat take on overcoming depression. Over the years, Kiki's story has become a touchstone for many young people, particularly but not exclusively girls, who see in her adventures a fantasy template for their own development.[8] While Koriko's architectural beauty beckons the romantic traveler, the heart of the film lies in the satisfying and diverse web of relationships, almost exclusively with women, that Kiki develops. As in *Totoro* and *Laputa,* Miyazaki creates an idealized community, but this time he places it in the city.

Time is another element that Kiki must contend with. Initially after arriving in Koriko, Kiki almost flies smack into the city's imposing clock tower. The clock tower is a reminder of "urban time," in contrast to the country rhythms that Kiki has grown up with. It also anticipates Kiki's frequent struggles not to be late for appointments as she begins to develop her delivery service.

Space, both aerial and urban, is also important. Miyazaki created many shots of Kiki flying over ocean, countryside, and city, suggesting Kiki's increasing sense of agency as she learns to master her broom both in the wildness of the sky and in the crowded jumble of Koriko. Kiki's journey may thus be seen as a movement away from tradition, in terms of "witch's time" and rural or natural space, into the urban space and time of modernity.

It is surely no accident that Kiki's story begins when she turns thirteen, an age when girls often begin menstruation. She is at a liminal period in her life, between childhood and maturity, a classic *shōjo*. Perhaps another reason for the movie's success is that while Kiki epitomizes the traditionally masculine traits of hard work and adventurousness, she retains the more feminine-coded traits of consumption and pleasure seeking. She worries about her clothes and wishes she could go to parties, but she combines these conventional shōjo concerns with an awareness of the value of money, and a commitment to self-reliance and independence in an urban technological world.

Our first glimpse of Kiki before she leaves home is bucolic and leisurely, far removed from the pressures of time or space. She lies in a green meadow, Jiji, her black cat, next to her, enjoying the late spring day as the wind whips around her. As in *Totoro* and *Nausicaä,* the wind plays a prominent role, acting as a catalyst for important events, but in this scene the wind is a supporting player, and the catalyst for action is technological: a transistor radio blaring out the weather report. Hearing a forecast for a beautiful night with a full moon, Kiki decides it is time to start her journey.

Technology remains a welcome guest on Kiki's voyage out; she takes the radio with her, strapped to her broomstick. The combination of broomstick and radio is symbolic in many ways. The radio is a gift from her father, and technology, as is typical in Miyazakiworld, tends to be associated with male characters, especially Kiki's aircraft-designing friend Tombo. The broomstick belongs to her mother. In the scene of her departure from home we see Kiki resisting her mother's gift of her old broom; she prefers the brand-new broom she herself has painstakingly crafted. Her mother holds sway, however. The implication is obvious—Kiki is still not fully independent of her mother at this point, although she thinks that she should be. She must use her mother's broom, a matrilineal legacy of literal support, as a basis for the next steps toward self-reliance.

Miyazaki later adds an intriguing scene in which Kiki explains to her new friend, the artist Ursula, that the ability to fly is in her "blood." In the English version of the movie, "blood" is translated as "spirit," but the rawness of the word "blood" (*chi*) in Japanese evokes the primordial essence of her power and her consanguineous connection with her mother. Miyazaki apparently pondered the question of Kiki's flying at great length, trying to decide between the broom as an autonomously flying object and having the power spring entirely from Kiki. In the original novel, it is Tombo whom Kiki tells that flying is in her blood. Tombo, who is fascinated by aviation and machinery, envies her ability to fly "naturally." By transferring the revelation to Ursula, who relates Kiki's flying power to her own ability to draw, Miyazaki emphasizes the importance of the organic in relation to art and talent, and also keeps these powers within a female context.

Kiki's radio stands in contrast to the broomstick's feminine principle. Strapped to her broomstick and blaring out music, news, and weather forecasts, the radio suggests a positive connection between technology and nature. Kiki's father's technological gift is also a supportive one, allowing Kiki to feel connected to the wider society that she will soon become a part of as she heads toward Koriko.

With one major exception (a forest in which Kiki has an adventure with birds and meets Ursula), nature largely takes second place in the film. The cacophony of urban life—cars, trucks, bicycles, and even the shouts of an overzealous policeman—immediately assails Kiki when she and her feline companion land in Koriko. In this new world, she must learn to live—socially, economically, romantically—assuming both the duties and the freedoms that maturity brings. To do this she becomes an entrepreneur, developing a business that mixes the prosaic and the magical. Her project is a delivery business; on her broomstick, she delivers objects ranging from pacifiers to heavy boxes, through windstorms and bad weather and through her own internal storms of self-doubt and depression.

Miyazaki's blending of the fairy tale with the everyday offers young audiences a glimpse of self-reliance that, while magic-based, stems from the fundamentally human qualities of perseverance, endurance, and a willingness to work hard. Kiki is fortunate in having many people around to help her. Whereas the original novel largely centered around the interesting or amusing objects Kiki had to deliver, Miyazaki's film concentrates more on her social encounters with the residents of Koriko. Most of the male characters she meets are disappointments. They range from bullying (the policeman who accosts her for flying), to bureaucratic (the hotel clerk who demands Kiki's identification), to simply immature (Tombo, Kiki's would-be boyfriend). In contrast, the female characters, with the exception of some "mean girls" who make fun of Kiki, are helpful and empathetic.

The prominence of the feminine is clear from the fortuitous beginning of Kiki's delivery service: after an exhausting first day in Koriko, she is standing disconsolate and lonely on a ledge above the town when a pregnant woman rushes by with a baby's pacifier in her hand. A baker's wife named Osono, she is trying to return the pacifier to a customer. Kiki volunteers to deliver it on her broomstick. Upon her return, the grateful Osono offers her and Jiji a place to stay above the bakery she owns with her husband.

Kiki's first entrepreneurial encounters are not only with women but with mothers, their babies either actual or incipient. The emphasis on women and babies supports the critic Tomohiko Murakami's comment that Kiki becomes increasingly part of a "network of women." To Murakami this "network" is not necessarily a positive phenomenon: "As a father watching this," he writes, "I couldn't help but feel brokenhearted and uneasy at the idea of having my daughter go far away."[9] From the point of view of the film's message, however, the variety and depth of this "network of women" provides a fresh perspective on the "hero's" journey, showing that women can serve as something beyond the clichéd "wise woman" role common to many such narratives.

Besides Osono, whose support for Kiki is constant and crucial, the female characters include a glamorous fashion designer who is Kiki's first customer, a grandmother referred to as Madam, and the elderly woman's housekeeper, Bertha, who encourage Kiki through their gratitude and enthusiasm for her. Miyazaki enlivens even these somewhat stereotypical characters with unique flourishes. The designer concerns herself mainly with work and family, while the kind grandmother is also stately and elegant. Bertha comes across as particularly idiosyncratic, exclaiming that she "loves adventures" and at one point sneaking off to see whether she can use Kiki's broom to fly.

Ursula is undoubtedly the most important of Kiki's female acquaintances. Their first encounter is a memorable one: Kiki and Jiji are flying over a forest to deliver a stuffed-cat toy, her fashion designer client's birthday gift to her nephew. A powerful gust of wind that Kiki had initially ignored takes Kiki's broom, causing the cage carrying the toy to drop deep into the dark forest. Trying to recover the toy, Kiki runs into a flock of angry crows that, Jiji explains, think she is about to steal their eggs. Kiki persuades Jiji to substitute for the toy. While the unhappy Jiji pretends to be a stuffed animal at the nephew's house, Kiki frantically searches for the real toy, conscious of the relentless pressure of time running out. She finds the stuffed cat in the window of a log cabin, a house owned by a young woman a few years older than Kiki, Ursula, who turns out to be a talented artist.

Kiki's attack by the angry crows and her obliviousness to the wind's force suggest her diminishing awareness of nature. In contrast, Ursula connects with both the natural, the forest around her, and the transcendent, in the form of her artistic creations. We first see her crouched casually on her rooftop, drawing the birds that had previously attacked Kiki, while Kiki, perched awkwardly on a ladder, ineffectually tries to get her attention. Ursula's ease with the crows contrasts with Kiki's fearful experience. The young artist treats them with respect and admiration, calling them "beautiful."

Ursula draws the crows in *Kiki's Delivery Service,* Studio Ghibli, 1989.

This comfortable interaction with the fierce-looking crows reflects Ursula's relaxed relationship with nature and her ease with the solitude and privacy necessary for artistic creativity.

In this regard, she resembles an important group of literary and artistic recluses in East Asian culture. Almost always male, they appear in paintings, essays, and poetry. In Japan the most famous of these recluses was the twelfth-century courtier Kamo no Chōmei, a poet, musician, and essayist who renounced the world at a relatively young age for the solitude of his "ten-foot-square hut." Miyazaki had long been an admirer of Chōmei's works, and seems to be creating a female version in the talented and self-sustaining Ursula. He is also clearly creating an older mentor figure for

Kiki, perhaps even an "alter ego," as Sugita suggests.[10] While Ursula lives in "forest" or "natural" time, she is portrayed as being at ease in the city, as when Miyazaki adds a scene of her visiting Kiki in Koriko.

Ursula's importance becomes even more obvious when Kiki loses her ability to fly, a crucial episode that does not occur in the book but serves as the emotional core of the movie. To Kiki the loss is the same as losing her identity. She cries out that she is "nothing" if she cannot fly.

The intensity of this scene has always made me wonder whether Miyazaki might be projecting onto his protagonist. By the time he began work on *Kiki,* he had been laboring essentially nonstop for two and a half decades. He was exhausted, irritable, and emotional. The industry gossip that *Kiki* would probably be his last film must have drained him psychologically as well. Shortly after finishing the film, he made a truly surprising request to Suzuki, asking him to "dissolve" Studio Ghibli. According to Suzuki, Miyazaki reasoned that there should be a three-film limit for any studio, arguing that "while making a movie there will be many clashes, and human relationships get difficult, so unless the studio resets itself, it can't go on being productive."[11]

Suzuki is too discreet to detail what "clashes" and "difficulties" Miyazaki is referring to, but this would be the first of several attempts by the director to walk away from the studio his energy and devotion had helped to create. At forty-eight, he would have felt more and more the responsibilities and pressures of helming an enterprise based on manufacturing hits to please an uncertain audience.

Fortunately, Suzuki came to the rescue in the rational manner of an elder brother. The two hammered out a vision of a "reset" Studio Ghibli with a new working environment. Its most important feature was offering full-time and permanent employment to its staff, almost unheard-of in a Japanese animation industry dominated by short-term contracts and freelancing.

It is Ursula who comes to Kiki's rescue. She does this not by helping her regain her ability, but by telling the distraught Kiki that she too has on occasion lost her ability to paint, essentially suffering from "artist's block."

When Kiki asks what she does in such circumstances, Ursula replies offhandedly that she "takes a nap" or "takes a walk." Ursula thus models a relaxed, nonpanicky mode of dealing with a genuinely traumatic situation.

Her laid-back advice does not lead immediately to Kiki's regaining her powers, but it is key to helping Kiki learn self-acceptance. Kiki's development is not simply psychological, however. Miyazaki also veers from the novel by introducing a strong economic dimension to the story. Whereas in the original work Kadono stresses that Kiki does *not* receive financial payment for her services, in the film the director lingers over scenes involving money; not only is Kiki paid for deliveries, but she discusses with Osono about how much to charge her bakery customers.

But the director also makes clear that Kiki's financial and psychological independence comes at a cost, the cost of the frivolous pleasures of adolescence. At the beginning of the movie Kiki tells Jiji that they must depart from home soon lest she get a "cool boyfriend" and get cold feet about leaving. Early on in Koriko, Kiki lingers in front of a shop window, coveting a pair of sparkling red shoes that she cannot possibly afford—perhaps a subliminal reference to Dorothy in *The Wizard of Oz,* another young girl who must find her way in the world without parental assistance. In several poignant later scenes, Kiki watches wistfully as young people her age enjoy the city's languid summer afternoons.

Miyazaki emphasizes the cost of Kiki's being an outsider. In one especially heartrending sequence, she has gone with Tombo to try out his new propeller-powered "flying" bicycle. The two barrel down a slope, zoom along the coastal road, and ultimately crash-land on a green lawn above the ocean. Relieved at being uninjured, Kiki breaks into cathartic laughter while Tombo asks whether she used her power of flight to contribute to their soft landing.

The director chooses that moment to bring in a discordant element, as a group of Tombo's pleasure-loving friends in a battered jalopy shout at him to join them on a tour of an enormous zeppelin that has been tethered farther down the beach. Tombo invites Kiki to join, and she stubbornly refuses. Standing alone, a dark shadow against the sea, she has heard one of the girls in the car say, "That's the delivery girl." Angrily telling Tombo that she needs to get back to work, Kiki trudges back uphill to the bakery.

It is no surprise that Kiki begins to lose her power to fly after this distressing end to her enjoyable time with Tombo. The other girl's defining Kiki by her job intensifies her sense of solitariness and vulnerability and reminds her keenly that, unlike these happy-go-lucky young people, she has to earn a living. Miyazaki emphasizes her solitude through her sudden loss of ability to talk with Jiji—again, a development that does not occur in the book. In a painfully self-aware moment, Kiki tells the indifferent Jiji that there must be something wrong with her. "I finally make friends and then I can't stand them," she laments, tossing in her bed.

Such complaints would hardly be out of place in a realistic young adult novel, where Kiki might simply reconcile herself to losing her powers and take her place in the world of ordinary people. In fact, Miyazaki joked that in a fictional sequel, Kiki would end up opening a bicycle delivery service.[12] Fortunately, he subverts such a trite conclusion by offering a boisterous finale, in which witchcraft and technology vie with each other to create a climactic rescue scene involving Koriko's clock tower, the zeppelin, a broom, and a young boy in distress.

The finale begins gently with Kiki's visit to Madam, her elegant elderly friend. While there Kiki sees a televised news report that strong winds have blown the zeppelin loose. It is impaled on the clock tower. Even worse, Tombo is hanging from it by the tethering rope. A distraught but determined Kiki borrows a broom from a street sweeper and once again tries to fly. She succeeds, although the clumsy broom bucks and sways beneath her. Eventually, she gains the altitude to fly close and zooms down to save Tombo as he loses hold of the rope, the crowd below erupting into a cheering frenzy.

Compared with the generally quiet tone of most of the movie, the turbulent ending stands out. Indeed, some Japanese critics lambasted the finale, calling it "gaudy" and "banal," dismissing the crowd scene and its action-movie theatrics.[13] In fact, however, the ending ties together a number of major themes in the movie while leaving room for further interesting developments. Miyazaki has subtly prepared this denouement, slipping in scenes of the zeppelin and references to it on the radio or in conversation. By ending the film with an all-out action scene framed by the townspeople, Miyazaki also allows us to see Kiki as a traditional hero, her rescue of Tombo helping her to incorporate into her new society. While the film's emotional climax probably comes when Kiki cries out that she is nothing without flying, the rousing finale once again brings together the natural and the supernatural, the human and the technological. It is Kiki and her belief in herself, signified by her renewed ability to fly, that allows her to take on both time and technology, symbolized by the clock tower and the zeppelin.

The movie makes harmony out of seemingly contradictory forces. In the scene of Kiki and Tombo racing down the beach road on his propeller bicycle, Miyazaki makes clear that technology and the supernatural can work together. Flying her broomstick above the lovely but thoroughly urban streets of Koriko, Kiki is an "intrusive anachronism," to use Michael Dylan Foster's felicitous phrase.[14] She is a jolt from the past traversing not only space but time as well. Miyazaki emphasizes the incongruity of her supernatural presence in Koriko by filling his frames with more conventional conveyances: trains, streetcars, cars, and the humble truck that picks up Ursula and Kiki as they hitchhike back to Ursula's forest home.

The climax of Kiki's witchcraft taking on both modern time and technology suggests an upbeat future in which tradition holds its own against modern encroachments. This is made even clearer in the mélange of ending scenes. The director shows us Kiki's happy incorporation into urban life, enjoying friendship with young people her age. At the same time she is seen flying her broomstick above Tombo on his propeller bicycle, a simple but effective representation of an accepting world that embraces both the technological and the magical.

Miyazaki ends the film with Kiki's parents reading a letter in which she writes of successfully settling into her new life. While they seem thrilled, the educator Sugita suggests that her parents might also experience a sense of mourning.[15] If *Totoro* is in some ways a movie about the fear of death, particularly a child's fear of the death of a parent, *Kiki* can be seen as relating to the fear of transition. On the one hand this fear is a form of mourning for the loss of childhood, from the point of view of a parent watching his or her child grow up, or perhaps a nostalgia for their own childhoods felt by young women office workers watching the movie. This complex undercurrent of adult nostalgia for the early stirrings of independence and sad awareness of what independence brings adds to the movie's emotional force. Intriguingly, while Kiki does recover her flying ability, she does not regain her ability to talk to Jiji. Flying above her new urban home, Kiki at the movie's end is stronger yet more limited than when she arrived, a bittersweet vision of what maturation can entail.

For the director, too, the future was rushing toward him. As Seiji Kano notes, "With *Kiki*, Ghibli entered its second stage ... offering an alternative to the previous common belief that only Hollywood movies could be hits and proving that Japanese movies could bring in audiences."[16] The next decade would bring Miyazaki's greatest directorial triumphs and see him stepping out, like Kiki, into an international arena.

# 9

# *Porco Rosso* Lands in Casablanca

A personal movie is a frightening thing!

——M I Y A Z A K I

Miyazaki's next film, *Porco Rosso* (Kurenai no buta), was released in 1992, three years after *Kiki* and light years from that movie's fantasy bildungs-roman scenario. The story of a former World War I airman who becomes a bounty hunter in the Adriatic, the movie contains clear fantasy elements but also deals with serious political, social, and moral issues. With *Porco* the director goes in a new direction, away from childhood or even adolescent fantasy to a world that, while still enchanted, also addresses war, history, and the complexities of adulthood, adding a new and more mature dimension to Miyazakiworld.

One scene in particular stands out: A beautiful woman stands singing a song in a nightclub. The words are in French and no subtitles are given, but the slow cadence and haunting melody suggest that it is a song about loss. As the woman sings, the camera travels outside to discover a lone seaplane traversing the sky through russet sunset clouds. While the plaintive song continues off screen, we see the little plane sliding into its berth outside the grand hotel that houses the club. We follow the pilot as he enters the bar. Standing alone at the top of the stairs, natty in his airman's suit and silk

Marco on the stairs at Gina's nightclub in *Porco Rosso,* Studio Ghibli, 1992

scarf, he looks down toward the woman as she sings in French, "But it is very short, the time of the cherries."

The scene would not be out of place in a classic black-and-white movie from the 1940s. But this movie is in color. Furthermore, it is animated. Finally, the natty airman is a pig, or rather, a man with the face of a pig.

In many ways, *Porco Rosso* is Miyazaki's fantasy redoing of the 1942 American film *Casablanca,* one of the most romantic and stirring movies ever made, cherished in Japan as well as in the West.[1] *Porco Rosso* resembles

*Casablanca* in its larger-than-life story, its connection with a war-torn Europe, and in the characterization of its star-crossed lovers, Marco and Gina, who are Miyazaki's equivalent of *Casablanca*'s central characters Rick and Ilsa. Like Rick, Marco, the protagonist of *Porco,* is a jaded man with a past, suggestively sexy in a well-fitting trench coat. Like Ilsa, Gina is a beautiful mystery woman with antifascist political connections, although in the case of Miyazaki's movie, it is Gina, not Rick, who runs a nightclub and, unlike in *Casablanca,* it is she who sings the film's signature song. A chanteuse, a political activist, and a hotelier, she is the next in Miyazaki's roster of impressively independent older women characters, and her hotel Adriatica, with its exotic setting and ragtag group of guests, would not be out of place in a Moroccan city. *Porco*'s politics—its underlying conflict, echoing *Casablanca,* between good and evil in the form of resistance and fascism—is unusually clear-cut for a Miyazaki film.

Perhaps *Porco*'s most interesting commonality with *Casablanca* is its highlighting of music to express the movie's theme. *Casablanca*'s bittersweet song "As Time Goes By" has an equivalent musical leitmotif in *Porco Rosso*'s "Les Temps des Cerises" (The time of the cherries). In the scene described above, Gina sings it in a moving moment at her nightclub, but we also hear it spilling softly from a radio in the movie's memorable opening scene. The film ends with another poignant lament over the final credits, this time a Japanese song invoking the days of student radicalism in 1960s Tokyo, "Once in a While Shall We Talk about the Old Times" (*Toki ni wa mukashi no hanashi o*).

Of course there are notable differences between the films. *Porco Rosso* is set in 1929, not 1941, and the European war that haunts it is World War I (although there are shadows of the coming war, as well). Rather than the Hollywood-ized North Africa of *Casablanca, Porco*'s setting is the lusciously realized Adriatic seacoast. Based loosely on the region around Dubrovnik in Yugoslavia, the setting is another addition to the roster of European settings that might be called Miyazaki's Euroworld, an important component of Miyazakiworld. Unlike Rick, Marco hides out in a deserted cove accessible only by seaplanes, rather than in a heavily patronized bar in a bustling city. Miyazaki also adds a second potential love interest for his male hero, the feisty young aircraft mechanic Fio: an appealing young girl he meets when he brings his airplane to Milan for repairs who has come to stay with her uncle in Milan, she is another in a long list of Miyazaki's shōjo heroines. And, while maintaining dark overtones, the movie is more lighthearted than *Casablanca,* a picaresque adventure with thrilling aerial sequences, slapstick combat, and a ridiculous, if rather appealing, villain in the form of Curtis, a boastful American airman. While the shadow of fascism hangs over both movies, *Porco*'s finale consists of a zany crowd scene, allowing viewers to walk out of the movie in a pleasantly nonpolitical haze.

*Porco Rosso* is also a highly personal film, perhaps the most personal in Miyazaki's oeuvre. The movie captures the director's disgust both with war and the military and with the constraints and disappointments of middle age. Its opening scene is a dreamy image of a man lazing under a parasol, a bottle of wine by his side, "Les Temps des Cerises" playing softly on a radio, while a bright red seaplane bobs gently on the azure sea in front of him. This scene is the ultimate escapist fantasy for overworked Japanese businessmen, who were the film's initial target audience, and also, in some ways, for Miyazaki himself.

As the camera travels across the prone figure lazing in the sun, it moves up to where his face should be but finds his countenance obscured by a film magazine. A phone beside him rings and he answers. It is a distress call for someone called Porco Rosso, whose help is needed against a gang of air pirates who have captured a group of schoolgirls. "That's going to cost you," the figure says, in a jaded tone of voice. As he puts the phone down we see that he has a pig's face.

One can imagine that many directors might want to create a post–World War I romance about a war-weary aviator and a beautiful chanteuse. Such a movie plays into our notions of a golden time that we are now locked away from, lost in the detritus of too many subsequent brutal wars and the more subtle brutalities of modernization. Few directors, however, would make that aviator a bounty hunter with a hideout in the Adriatic who entrusts a team of Milanese women, ranging from grandmothers to teenage girls, to rebuild his beloved plane. And no other director that I can imagine would make that aviator a pig in exile. Furthermore, this is not simply any porcine aviator but a former human flying ace who at one point tells an old comrade, "I'd rather be a pig than a fascist," suggesting that his exile is not only spatial but ideological. And finally, this is an antifascist pig who loves a woman whose signature song, "Les Temps des Cerise," comes out of the 1871 utopian socialist uprising that was known as the Paris Commune.

What would end up becoming one of the director's most personal movies was originally conceived as a short in-flight film for Japan Airlines business passengers—at the time mainly tired men whose brains, in Miyazaki's immortal words, had turned to tofu.[2] Stuck on a flight, they would want something light and entertaining as a means to escape the dreariness of business travel.

In fact, the director was himself looking for something light and entertaining. Miyazaki felt worn out, both physically and emotionally, from producing two major films, Takahata's *Only Yesterday* and his own *Kiki's Delivery Service*. The creative effort had exhausted him, and there were also practical questions to be addressed. He and Suzuki had been able to get much of the staff onto long-term employment contracts, something that he had long been concerned with, but now they had a growing company to feed.

Many of these employees were women, and it is not surprising that a scene of women working together in an aircraft factory would be one of *Porco Rosso*'s highlights. In real life among the practical issues confronting the director was the expansion of the women's bathroom. Miyazaki wanted to create a space for women featuring windows and light where they could take a break from the intense demands of making animation. Always planning for the future, Miyazaki was also thinking about making the studio more ecologically sound. Ultimately, he would add a grass roof to Ghibli's main building. Above all, the studio needed to continue creating hits to help maintain what would become a costly new environment.

But there seems to have been more than simple exhaustion behind Miyazaki's yearning for lightness. Although the previous two films were big hits, Miyazaki was ambivalent about them, in retrospect saying that they were "too close" to the bubble period and its culture of materialism and excess. The bubble period, with its "hysterical" emphasis on an "overflow of things" (as Miyazaki puts it), seems to have deeply shaken him.[3]

Miyazaki felt the need for what he called, using the English word, "rehab," apparently meaning a chance for relaxation and renewal. He also used another English word, "moratorium," to describe his initial plan for *Porco Rosso*. The word appeared frequently among Japanese intellectuals, signifying a kind of postponement of maturity, a way to linger in youthful irresponsibility. *Porco Rosso* would be Miyazaki's "moratorium" movie, offering something completely different from the coming-of-age issues tackled in *Only Yesterday* and *Kiki*.

Miyazaki's original plan with Japan Airlines called for a forty-minute in-flight entertainment based on the director's own lighthearted manga that he had collected in a rather random series entitled *Mōsō Nōtō* (Daydream Notes), all featuring good-natured pigs as heroes. According to Kano, these forays "offered [Miyazaki] a happy respite from the hard work of drawing the *Nausicaä* manga or doing film preparation, allowing him to immerse himself into a world of fantasy and wild notions."[4] Miyazaki and his producer Suzuki saw these madcap episodes as excellent material for a zany animated adventure.

It is likely that the original manga format and the initially short running time projected for the film combined to create refreshingly low expectations for a director and a studio that had been working at a feverish pace. Emancipation from the typical studio pressure seems to have allowed Miyazaki a flexible mental space to explore new and sometimes disturbing issues. As the movie went from forty-five to ninety minutes, with new characters and plot lines added, it evolved into something multilayered— simultaneously entertaining and diverting while also emotionally challenging. Jostling visions of nostalgia and escape versus engagement and commitment, the movie ends up being a profound and unexpected exploration of midlife crisis.

The project was initially conceived as a cheerful story about the adventures of a former Italian airman/pig who flies his wooden seaplane around the Adriatic as a bounty hunter and rescues people in distress. The plot gave Miyazaki the opportunity to indulge one of his great loves, drawing planes. He had drawn imaginative aerial machines in previous films such as *Nausicaä* and *Laputa,* but the ocean-based story of *Porco* featured not only vintage World War I aircraft but also the jaunty little seaplanes that the director believed represented a particularly golden era in aviation history. Entirely impractical, these aircraft seem to express an unfettered joy in flying for its own sake, and with their flat wings and jutting "feet," they strongly resemble dragonflies, a favorite symbol of ephemerality in Japanese culture. Miyazaki insisted on doing all the flight scenes himself and would capture that beauty and flexibility both in his designs of the planes and in the film's numerous aerial sequences.

Like its part-human, part-pig hero, the movie is a hybrid: an enthralling adventure that is also a unique commentary on political and moral commitment, middle age, masculinity, and desire. It is also in many ways the most naked expression of Miyazaki's own longing for a different life, a life of action, freedom, and intense moral significance, one that was far away from the constant work and pressures of the director's normal existence. Its gorgeous animation and fantastic plot can be seen as a kind of therapeutic processing of the traumas of middle age.

Both the personal and the political were at work here. Of the latter, what Miyazaki called a "body blow" (using the English term) hit him in 1992 when the former Eastern European–bloc nation of Yugoslavia began to fall apart.[5] Yugoslavia had been something of a poster child for seemingly enlightened and independent socialism during the Cold War, and its dissolution brought forth a tidal wave of violence, from widespread rape and massacre to ethnic cleansing.

Why would a Japanese film director half a world away react so strongly to conflicts in Eastern Europe? Why would any Japanese people care? It might first be noted that many Japanese citizens are far more tuned in to world events than Americans tend to be. Equally at play is that Miyazaki is an artist who loves Europe, has a solid grasp of its modern history, and deeply admires certain aspects of its way of life. That admiration for the European ideal made the downfall of Yugoslavia all the more bitter. The director had believed that such a bloodbath was no longer possible in an enlightened modern Europe. Indeed, to Miyazaki the conflict brought back echoes of the bloodshed of the First World War and even earlier.

Kano speculates that the song "Les Temps des Cerise," a litany of lament for the failed Paris Commune of 1871, became a proxy for expressing Miyazaki's own sense of loss and betrayal.[6] The fall of Yugoslavia was a body blow to Miyazaki's flickering optimism about the state of the world in general and the possibility of hope for the future. The director explained his feelings shortly after *Porco*'s release in a disarmingly candid discussion with the singer Tokiko Kato, who voices Gina in the movie. He emphasized that his generation of Japanese had grown up at a time where they believed in the possibility of a better world. Watching their country, battered and benumbed immediately after the war, grow into a site of new possibilities had inspired Japanese born in the 1940s. To many of that period a peaceful international world was a powerful and perhaps realizable ideal.

Even reading the discussion twenty-five years later, one feels the sense of puzzlement and sadness in Miyazaki's words: "We felt that the world was getting better, bit by bit. Our history was that things would get better. So when the Yugoslavian ethnic wars happened we were dumbfounded. What was going on? Were we just going backward? These last two years [since 1992] I've really been running around in a haze."[7]

In an interview a bit later Miyazaki is more direct and more personal, bringing up his deceased mother. He had been internally arguing with her all his life and here finally acknowledges her victory: "I used to fight constantly with my mother when I was an adolescent about whether people are stupid or not. My mother's cherished opinion was that people were hopeless. I always disagreed, but lately it's unconditional surrender!"[8]

Miyazaki had also been shaken by the first Gulf War, when the United States led an international coalition against Iraq in order to preserve Kuwait (and the oil interests of industrial states). It is surely no accident that the "villain" in *Porco Rosso* is Curtis, a bumptious young American who is equal parts arrogance and ignorance, although Miyazaki possibly tried to counterbalance that by making Fio, his secondary female character, a charming young girl recently returned from America.

Japan's involvement in the Gulf War, while hesitant and piecemeal, seemed to Miyazaki and many others on the left to be a betrayal of the country's pacifist constitution. The high-tech nature of the war and the fact that scenes of carnage were rarely shown in the media also greatly disturbed the director. In fact, he went so far as to state that, after *Kiki,* he had been planning a film about young love set in modern Tokyo but had abandoned that idea. As the critic Kōji Okuda puts it, "In a world of blood Miyazaki could not make a movie about youth."[9]

But one senses more than political disillusionment at work here. *Porco Rosso* is a radical departure from the director's previous films that had been Ghibli's bread and butter: *Kiki, Totoro,* and *Laputa* had all featured young heroes and delivered essentially upbeat endings. *Porco* takes us into a complicated world in which fascism is on the horizon and the future may be cloudy.

But why make the hero a middle-aged pig? Japanese critics also seemed bewildered. While the film's promotion campaign featured Marco in all his porcine glory with the catch phrase "This is what 'cool' is," the other aspects of its promotion, including a direct appeal to women who would "enjoy a bittersweet romance," muddied the waters. Can a pig be romantic?

Apparently yes, and more. Pigs have a complex and not necessarily benign reputation. This is true not only in the West but in Japan as well. In a provocative discussion, part interview and part interrogation, between the director and his most thoughtful interlocutor, the critic Yōichi Shibuya, the director is alternatively evasive and confessional.

When Shibuya prods the director with his own speculations about why Miyazaki has chosen a pig as his star, Miyazaki at first sounds slightly exasperated, insisting, "We just wanted to be funny." He mentions that the studio had offered the idea to Japan Airlines as a "joke. . . . We were sure they would turn us down."[10] Certainly the pigs in Miyazaki's original manga are quite humorous (and rather cute), and putting a pig in a cockpit makes for unforgettable animation.

When Shibuya presses further, however, the director brings up politics, pointing out that the name Porco Rosso (literally Red Pig), might suggest "Communist." Miyazaki then speaks of Yugoslavia, insisting, "I long ago swept away my belief in socialism," but then undercuts this assertion: "In making the film all this [disillusionment and regret] piled up and I had the feeling that 'I will be the last Red!' And [the vision] became that of a single pig flying alone."[11]

Shibuya relentlessly links Miyazaki's apparently political statement to the personal. He asks, "Isn't the idea of a single survivor turning into a pig after everyone else is dead—isn't that expressing a kind of self-punishment?"

To this leading question Miyazaki answers, "Well, yes. But it's not exactly because he is the only one left—the problem is that he is flying."[12]

It seems highly possible that the discussion is at least partly about what we now call survivor's guilt.[13] Miyazaki's family's refusal to help a neighbor with a child escape the flames of the Tokyo air raids remained a searing memory. A pig, after all, is often seen as a representation of greed and selfishness, as we see in Miyazaki's later film *Spirited Away*.

It is also possible that this "guilt" may connect to a broader sense of guilt on Miyazaki's part relating to his own family's relative affluence during the war and perhaps to Japanese war responsibility in general. This is borne out in his discussion with Tokiko Kato. Sharing Miyazaki's left-wing politics, the singer is married to the former head of the Zengakuren, a radical student organization that flourished during the 1960s.

For a public exchange the discussion is surprisingly intimate and probing, not only of the themes of the film but also of Miyazaki's inner psyche and political beliefs. Several times the director mentions feelings of guilt, then suddenly announces, "When it comes to guilt, it's a consistent theme inside me—my family in Japan, my household, and then Japan in the world, Japan in Asia."[14]

In a Japan that still has trouble engaging with its wartime past, this is a notable statement. But Miyazaki goes on to say something even more startling and revealing: "Getting to this age, I'm starting to dig up all kinds of memories from my childhood and my past. And after digging them up and arranging them, I come to see, 'Aah, this is what formed me.' And at the same time this guilt coils around my memories and if I lose that guilt then somehow I have the feeling that I'll lose the most important thing about myself. I even feel that the guilt is what really supports me."

To which Kato exclaims, "So that's the source of your energy!" Miyazaki says, "Embracing a divided self is how I must go on."[15]

When I read these words I felt I had finally understood one of *Porco Rosso*'s most crucial, eerie, and ethereally beautiful scenes, in which Marco reveals (more or less) what made him become a pig. The sequence is worth describing in some detail:

It is night. Marco is back at his coastal hideout, having barely escaped the fascist police in Milan, where he had gone to get his plane fixed at a small family factory. He has brought back Fio, the young niece of the factory owner and an excellent mechanic in her own right. To their mutual chagrin, however, Fio is not being appreciated for her engineering abilities. Instead, she has become the potential prize in an aerial competition between Marco and the annoying American pilot Curtis, who has fallen in love with her (having previously been rebuffed by Gina). Marco insists that he has no romantic designs on Fio himself but cannot bear that she become the bride of that "American asshole," as he charmingly describes Curtis.

Long after he should be asleep, Marco stays up getting his ammunition together for the upcoming dogfight that will constitute the film's climax. The waves lap on the shore while Fio pretends to doze. Gazing at the pig through sleepy eyes, she suddenly sees his human face—a handsome young man with a Roman nose and a silky mustache—but when she calls out to him and he turns, he is back to being a pig. Gathering her courage, she asks Marco, "How did you become a pig?" the question that everyone has wanted to ask since he returned from World War I.

His answer is vague. "Well, you know . . ."

But after a bit more conversation, including Fio's suggestion that perhaps a kiss from her would magically transform him back to human (Marco reacts with horror), he agrees to tell her a story. This story, magical and mysterious, is the closest thing to an explanation that Fio or the audience will ever receive.

In classic flashback fashion, the screen darkens and the music swells as Marco slowly draws on his cigarette and starts to speak. We see a group of planes scattered across an achingly blue sky. "It was the last summer of the war . . ." Marco begins.

He relates that he and his friend Berlini had just returned from Berlini's wedding to Gina, but with no time for a leave, they had been told to return to the sky (*tombogaeri:* literally, the way a dragonfly turns), where they quickly come under fire. Marco's description of the fight is harsh ("the bastards had blood in their eyes"), but the actual sequence is a lyrical one. To slow music we see the airplanes circling in and out around one another, as if in an air ballet, although the sound of their motors is consistent with Marco's description of them as buzzing "like flies."

"I was the only one left and thought it was all over," he says, then goes on to recollect that he suddenly found the plane flying itself inside a bright light, and describes a "strange cloud" across the sky. We see the cloud, like a vast vapor trail, etching across the heavens as Marco's plane comes to rest on the "cloud prairie" below. Marco's plane remains motionless, but around him other planes rise up toward the sky. Close by him he sees Berlini ascending steadily, and he shouts "Berlini! You made it through alright?" But Berlini doesn't answer, and his plane keeps ascending, even though Marco yells at him, "What about Gina?"

We see that the "strange cloud" above him is actually a vast silvery swarm of planes, all rising steadily and silently, accompanied by the quiet ringing tones of an ethereal chorus.

"When I recovered I was flying alone close to the sea," Marco continues.

Fio interjects "God was telling you, 'Not yet.'"

Marco laughs, "I thought he was telling me that I had to go on alone, forever."

Obviously sensing the despair behind Marco's laughter, Fio insists "No! You're a good person!"

Marco responds with a single bleak sentence, "The good guys are the ones who die."

Fio daringly kisses him on the cheek. He remains a pig and she dashes back into her sleeping bag.

The visuals in the flashback are striking, especially the immense silvery cloud of airplanes that seems to dwarf Marco but also to uplift his spirit, a vision of the sublime that, unusually for Miyazaki, has a clearly human component. The dead airmen from all different countries rising toward some kind of heavenly destiny—a kind of Valhalla, perhaps, as anime scholar Patrick Drazen suggests—evoke a vision that seems caught between dream and nightmare.[16] The scene touches on deep elements—death, guilt, even hope.

None of this is what one usually expects to see in an animated film. It seems like something we would find in a book. In fact, this episode is inspired by a short story by the English writer Roald Dahl. Children around the world love Dahl for his lush children's fantasies such as *Charlie and the Chocolate Factory,* but adult readers also appreciate his many short stories, works that can be cynical or tough-minded but often having a surprise ending. The latter is true of the story in question. "They Shall Not Grow Old" is narrated by a World War II airman whose fellow pilot, Fin, has a transcendent near-death experience while on patrol in the Middle East. Caught in a dogfight, Fin suddenly feels the embrace of a white light and sees a vast cloud of airplanes above him that his aircraft joins, becoming part of a silent aerial procession. However, when the pilot in front of him, whom he describes as a "lucky bastard," lands on a beautiful green field, his own plane refuses to follow. Fin returns to base and tries to explain his adventure to his colleagues, who are surprisingly accepting of his strange experience.

I finally read the story after seeing the movie many times and was impressed by how perfectly Miyazaki had realized Fin's narration. In fact, the saturated blues of sky and sea, the shimmering whiteness of the cloud, the silver planes rising like a flock of silent metal birds, and the eerie music create a picture of the sublime that reaches far beyond the airman's comparatively prosaic description. But there is another description in "They Shall Not Grow Old" that caught my eye. After hearing his comrade's story, the narrator says:

"There was a tension, a fine high-drawn tension in the room, because here for the first time was something which was neither bullets nor fire, nor the coughing of an engine nor burst tires nor blood in the cockpit."[17]

The "something" the narrator describes is the sense of Otherness, a tension that has crossed the boundary between dream and reality and settled itself in the aerodrome. A similar sense of Otherness permeates Marco's surreal flashback. But Miyazaki adds one more element of Otherness to Dahl's account: his image of hero as pig. As Tokiko Kato writes in an afterword to her discussion with Miyazaki, "I cannot help but think that Miyazaki is Porco."[18] Porco's idiosyncratic version of Dahl's story, which dives back and forth between the young and handsome Marco and the middle-aged pig that he has become, conveys the director's sense of his own "divided" identity.

It is hard not to imagine that this scene and the movie overall reflect Miyazaki's inner turmoil as a fifty-one-year-old man looking back at his life and forward to what will come. By using the magic of animation to make his other self a pig, Miyazaki pungently explores such issues as survivor's guilt, his disillusionment with ideology, the complexities of desire (embodied in Fio's kiss and Marco's reaction), and what we all face when, unlike the airmen of Dahl's title, we do indeed grow old. Marco, only a little younger than Miyazaki was at the time of the film's creation, is a flawed hero trying to come to terms with the loss of youth, the loss of idealistic dreams, and the pressures and disillusionments of middle age.

We never really do find out what transforms "Marco" into "Porco." We assume it is some kind of magical manifestation of survivor's guilt combined with Marco's contempt for a human race that can produce a fascist ideology and a war that sacrifices thousands of young men for nothing. But we are never told explicitly. In Dahl's story, Fin does eventually get his wish. A couple of weeks later, his engine on fire, Fin goes down, shouting exultantly, "I'm a lucky bastard. A lucky, lucky bastard."

Miyazaki does not give us this easy resolution, a solution that one might think would appeal to a Japanese man who had grown up hearing of the young kamikaze pilots who had sacrificed themselves in the last days of World War II. Instead, like so many of the director's characters, the hero must go on living. As Nausicaä says in the final line of the *Nausicaä* manga, "We must live." But the question remains: why live as a pig?

Shibuya seems to be probing for a possible relation between the pig and sexuality. In the interview he returns repeatedly to Miyazaki's choice of animal, suggesting at one point, "Having the protagonist be a middle-aged pig is surely a premise with some strongly private elements to it." When Miyazaki denies that that is the case, saying it was just a joke, Shibuya pushes back, saying, "Well, even if it is a joke, still, taking a subject like a middle-aged man as a protagonist, surely that comes down to a taboo."[19]

The "taboo" that Shibuya refers to is probably having a middle-aged man as the hero of an animated movie, but it is possible that he is referring to sexual implications as well. In East Asia the connection between pigs and lechery has a long history, dating at least to the medieval Chinese quest story *Journey to the West*, a classic work reimagined in anime as *Dragon Ball Z*. Of the four diverse main characters, the least appealing by far is Piggsy, a gluttonous, lecherous lump of a male who seems mainly to exist for comic relief. Miyazaki acknowledged the influence of Piggsy in creating *Porco,* but in his interview with Shibuya continues to insist on only the humorous aspect of making his hero a pig.

Certainly some of *Porco*'s imagery is suggestive.[20] The first year I taught my Miyazaki class I had a student who loved finding phallic imagery in Miyazaki's movies, from the clock towers in *Kiki* and *Cagliostro* to the many sharp-nosed planes that zoom through the director's works. It is hard to resist the idea that Marco's sleek shiny red plane is the embodiment of some powerful male fantasies.

The structure of Marco's Adriatic hideout is also suggestive. Entered by plane through a crevice in the mountains, its narrow passageway opens up to a welcoming vision of soft sand and gentle water. Miyazaki has long been fascinated by the notion of the "thatched hut" in the mountains outside the capital of Kyoto to which the medieval writer Kamo no Chōmei, disgusted with the chaos of the world, retreated. Marco's idyllic hideaway is clearly Miyazaki's vision of the "thatched hut," lovingly imagined by the director as a place of beauty and idleness but with worldly pleasures such as wine, cigarettes, and music. There is also, perhaps, the opportunity for other sensual joys as well, since at one point we see Marco en route to Milan and anticipating the "white sheets" and "beautiful women" he will find there. All this is underlined in the structure and constitution of the cove, which evokes a feeling of returning to the womb.

Although less overtly than the female-centered *Kiki,* the movie features a varied and appealing array of female characters. The beautiful and haunted Gina runs the Hotel Adriatica, a grand hotel straight out of Belle Époque Europe that is a welcoming home both to the coarse air pirates and to the dapper world-weary pig who fights them for bounty. Gina was not featured in the original manga, but with her introduction Miyazaki gives the movie a far more adult and melancholy tone. She has a story to fit her romantic demeanor—she is a three-time widow whose pilot husbands were all killed in action. Marco and Gina go back a long way, almost to childhood, and as the flashback episode makes clear, he had been her third husband's closest friend. It is obvious throughout the film that the two of them share a deep emotional bond and that, Gina, at least, would like to see the bond flower into romance.

Gina's foil is Fio. In contrast to Gina's wistful sophistication, Fio is enthusiastic, sprightly, and tough. It is she who confronts the air pirates when they try to invade Marco's seacoast hideaway, essentially taking over the masculine role for a few moments, although at the movie's climax she becomes briefly a damsel in distress, allowing Marco to fight for her virtue against the aggressive Curtis.

In *Porco Rosso*'s wish-fulfilling male fantasy, Fio and Gina occupy two ends of Miyazaki's dream continuum, the complicated, resourceful, and beautiful older woman and the cute, vivacious, and also resourceful young girl. Naturally, they both love Marco, and he responds to both of them. Gina's professional accomplishments and Fio's mechanical expertise make them more than simply idealized cardboard cutouts, however. One of the movie's most charming twists is that they become lifelong friends.

Miyazaki presents Fio's ability as a mechanic a little didactically when she must passionately defend herself against Marco's assertion that she cannot fix his plane because she is "too young" and "a girl." The scene does not occur in a vacuum, however. The director goes on to portray a positive association between women and technology in the striking sequence in which Marco brings his plane to the factory in Milan for repair.

This sequence envisions interwar Milan as a place of recession, where men are forced to leave home for work. Taking up the slack, at least in the case of the company that Marco depends on, are the female relatives of Piccolo, the feisty old factory owner. His niece Fio is the most important, but the movie also features amusing and memorable scenes of women of all ages working together to refurbish and rejuvenate Marco's shiny seaplane. These scenes are both a nod to Ghibli's many female workers and also a utopian vision of an industrial commune where women of all generations labor seamlessly together.

*Porco Rosso* thus highlights two forms of utopian vision, the communal, gender-transcending factory in Milan and the private joys of Marco's Adriatic hideaway. But the movie also dips into the past for a third vision of a utopian ideal, that of the Paris Commune. Although it lasted barely two months, the Commune embodied the budding leftist activism of 1870s Europe, offering stirring ideals of working-class rights, collective living, and feminist empowerment. In response the French government destroyed the

Commune in a bloody series of savage attacks, massacres of men, women, and children, and, at the end, mass executions.

The Japan of the 1960s in which Miyazaki had come to young manhood did not suffer such violence but did offer visions of an alternative and better society. These visions had sustained Miyazaki for many years. Now, as he looked at an ever more oppressive and ideologically bankrupt world, it is little wonder that "The Time of the Cherries" would come to haunt him. The song lyrics combine a nostalgia for a lost love with a sense of mourning for an idealistic revolution that collapsed almost before it began.

In *Porco Rosso* nostalgia and regret contend against a still flickering belief in the beauty and potential of the world, creating a bittersweet vision of middle-aged yearning. That this yearning may go unrealized only adds to the film's emotional complexity. If anything, its overall lightheartedness makes its darker passages more intriguing and meaningful. Miyazaki would never create anything quite like *Porco Rosso* again, but the film ushered in a decade of films and manga that put forth increasingly hard-hitting views of the human condition.

## 10

# From Messiah to Shaman

*The* Nausicaä *Manga Seeks Light in the Darkness*

I really wanted to punish humanity, but I realized that I was trying to play god and that didn't work.

— MIYAZAKI

The movie *Porco Rosso* introduced a more adult and in some ways darker aspect to Miyazakiworld. But the director's darkest and most expansive vision during this time was reserved for his manga, specifically his epic *Nausicaä of the Valley of the Wind,* which he finally completed in 1994. The movie version of *Nausicaä* had established Miyazaki and Studio Ghibli as household names in Japan by 1984. The film connected with audiences on issues of female empowerment and environmental catastrophe, both embodied in its smart and active heroine, whose compassion extends to insects, plants, and the Earth itself. The movie also has perhaps the most literally uplifting climax of any Miyazaki work, a vision out of Judeo-Christian mythology. Having sacrificed her life, Nausicaä is miraculously resurrected by the Ohmu, the giant insects that populate her postapocalyptic thirtieth-century world. Raised up on the tips of the Ohmu's gigantic golden antennae, she strides across the sky to the accompaniment of swelling symphonic music reminiscent of the end of the Hallelujah chorus.

This cathartic and redemptive scene could hardly contrast more with the final scenes of Miyazaki's graphic novel version of the film, the seven-volume *Nausicaä* manga. Begun in 1982, two years before the film was released, the manga ended not in the literal heights of the movie's climax but in an abyss, the crypt of Shuwa, to which Nausicaä has journeyed to seek enlightenment. The crypt, however, becomes a mass grave for much of the human race where the dead of ages past are brought back to life only to die again.

And who is it that brings about this genocidal moment? It is Nausicaä herself. In the manga's dozen years and thousand pages she has gone from a radiant messianic figure to what one character describes as a "chaos of destruction and mercy."[1] The movie ends with what some viewers criticized as an artificially redemptive message symbolized by its almost too perfect heroine. In contrast, the manga ends in dark ambiguity, still offering a flicker of hope for survival, but one dimmed by its suffering protagonist's decision to destroy much of the human race.

Nausicaä's agony exemplifies her creator's increasingly dark worldview as it evolved over the tumultuous years of 1982 to 1994. We have already seen hints of this in Miyazaki's *Porco Rosso*, which was released in 1992, but the *Nausicaä* manga goes deeper, offering an epic journey of despair mixed with fleeting moments of radiance. Working on it alone in his house at night after midnight, Miyazaki was able to retreat briefly from the pressures of studio responsibilities that had only increased with the success of a string of hit movies. While he has stated that the upbeat tone of the earlier films from that period (*Kiki, Laputa*) gave him the psychological support to wrestle with the dark issues of the manga, it is clear that during those twelve years he was developing a deepening pessimism regarding the future of the human race. While still profoundly passionate and engaged, the man who penned the manga's rueful last sentence, "We must live," was a considerably more somber individual than the ambitious young artist of a dozen years earlier.

The same is true of his manga alter ego, Nausicaä. While the movie's messiah figure offered the promise of redemption, the manga heroine is more of a shaman, a preternaturally gifted go-between among nature, the supernatural, and the human. The shaman, as Joan Halifax explains, is one who deals with both "terror" and the "light of day," a characterization suggesting the dark journeys a shaman must take while still holding on to a belief that light exists beneath and behind the shadows.[2]

It is no accident that the most beautiful line Miyazaki ever wrote is Nausicaä's declaration toward the end of the manga, "Life is the light that shines in the darkness." Light and dark play across the work in a way that goes beyond the movie's Judeo-Christian framework to encompass a far more East Asian and animistic worldview. Nausicaä's evolution toward shamanism reflects Miyazaki's own increasing turn toward East Asian traditions and culture. Her transition also reflects more personal aspects of the director's psyche, as Miyazaki strove to deal with the internal vicissitudes of aging and a painful awareness of the complexities of the world around him. The passion and rage that animate Nausicaä echoes her creator's increasingly angry frustration at a society seemingly bent on disaster.

As we saw in the previous chapter, world events during the manga's creation had conspired to dishearten the director. Global politics weighed deeply on Miyazaki and led to an ideological transformation in his thinking. A committed Marxist much of his adult life, he was shocked and disillusioned by the fall of the Soviet Union in 1991. The atrocities of the ensuing war in Yugoslavia were also deeply disturbing. Miyazaki lamented the lack of concerted efforts to confront the worldwide surge in environmental problems and the dangers of nuclear radiation. The Japanese economy was painfully deteriorating after the heady and arrogant 1980s, its seemingly endless recession and attendant emotional malaise still characterizing Japan today.

In the twelve years between beginning to write the manga at age forty-one and finishing it at fifty-three, Miyazaki entered middle age. "I discovered that I was understanding myself," he said, and "it was an entirely different self than the one at the beginning [of writing the manga]."[3]

We will probably never know exactly what Miyazaki was "understanding" about himself by the end of that period, although we can guess that part of those years was spent confronting the darker aspects of his own psyche. The manga's emphasis on sometimes problematic mother figures suggests the director's still painful experience of his mother's sickness in his childhood and her death a decade earlier. There are hints of a midlife crisis and escapism in the world-weary protagonist of *Porco Rosso*, but while Nausicaä, his other alter ego from this period, has moments of trying to escape the world, her angst is both more metaphysical and more visceral than that of *Porco Rosso*'s hero. Like her creator, she is beset on all sides by pressures, demands, and dependents, but in a world far more extreme than that of a movie studio in suburban Tokyo. Over the manga's thousand pages she must confront apocalyptic violence that is both within her own soul and in the savage world around her.

It is through Nausicaä's eyes that we see the main issues of the manga, and it is her moral and emotional growth that give the narrative the moral authority to comment profoundly on some of the most challenging problems that Miyazaki felt were confronting the world. While the manga is certainly an epic, it is also a deeply felt bildungsroman, a journey to maturity that belongs not only to the main character but to Miyazaki as well.

The solutions that Miyazaki proposes are subversive and extreme, even shocking from the Western anthropocentric point of view, implying a shift on Miyazaki's part toward a non-Western worldview. Nausicaä's journey contains a number of near-death experiences and revelations that suggest some of the agonies of self-doubt and change that the director was experiencing.

To understand Nausicaä's and ultimately Miyazaki's journey we need to plunge into the intense world of the manga. Although extremely popular, the *Nausicaä* manga is perhaps the most understudied work in Miyazaki's oeuvre. There are many reasons behind this lack of critical attention. Most obvious is the manga's epic structure, with its complicated plot, multiple scene shifts, and myriad characters. But its shifting emotional and moral landscape may also put off critics who enjoy seeing Miyazaki as a fundamentally positive and upbeat director. For audiences who loved the movie's inspirational heroine, the darker, indeed disturbing, Nausicaä of the manga may have been simply too challenging a figure.

That said, the work is generally considered a masterpiece, offering a haunting look at a postapocalyptic future and a radical vision of humanity's place in the cosmos. Some of this quality may be found in the film, most notably when a blind seer who is present at Nausicaä's miraculous resurrection lauds the powers of "compassion and mercy." She is admiring not the powers of humanity, however, but rather those of the insect Ohmu, hinting at a fundamental shift away from anthropocentrism. The overall ideological structure of the film remains human-centered, however, with its main struggles between the empires of the imperialist Torumekia and the industrial Pejite. Furthermore, the movie's final cathartic scenes suggest a pastoral kingdom on Earth guided by humanity.

In contrast, while the manga retains and actually expands these human empires to include the priest nation of the Doroks, it also brings in other contesting powers, including more mysterious human collectivities. These range from the spiritual "forest people" and degraded "worm handlers," to monks and priests, and, at the end, the voices of the dead from a millennium before, who engage Nausicaä in a final debate. But the manga version also amplifies the role of nonhuman species. These include a particularly virulent form of "miasma," sentient toxic spores that become bioweapons in the hands of the warring humans and develop into an enormous mutating mold with incredible life force that engulfs entire populations.

Of humanesque figures the crypt of Shuwa—an organic entity complete with human flesh—is one of the most distinctive. But perhaps the most emotionally affecting is the God Warrior, a gigantic artificial being awakened by the Doroks and originally created as a weapon more than a thousand years earlier. While in the film the God Warriors were simply humanoid weapons, in the manga they become a single being that evolves into a sentient and tragic creature, imprinting onto Nausicaä as its "mother" and exercising along with her a form of ultimate power at the manga's end. In this evolution of Miyazakiworld, technology has not only power but sentience.

The most significant completely nonhuman creatures, the giant Ohmu, play a far larger and more responsible role in the manga than in the film. With their immense size, impervious carapaces, and myriad feelers, they intimidate and terrify most humans, who would destroy them if they could. In the manga Miyazaki develops the Ohmu, who are linked in a kind of hive mind, into a clear alternative to humanity, a life force that creates and heals rather than wreaking chaos in its every action. In the manga's final, climactic scene Nausicaä names the Ohmu as representing the moral force left in the world.

The manga's action thus flows in two different but often interlocking currents, that of the Torumekian and Dorok empires, struggling over the scarce resources and land that their depredations have left them, and the world of the nonhuman sentient organisms. It is this world of myriad contesting forces that Nausicaä must navigate. Philip Brophy's assessment of the movie, that "*Nausicaä* is a military epic that subverts the narrative binary of warring sides and their principles and in its place offers them a far greater force for them to combat—the very Earth which they contest and attempt to possess," is even more accurate concerning the manga.[4]

Ultimately the manga asks a two-part question, one that would increasingly be asked in later versions of Miyazakiworld: what does it mean to be human, and what role does humanity have to play in a larger interspecies world? *Nausicaä* radically deconstructs the notion of what it is to be human while refusing to acknowledge the Judeo-Christian vision of humanity as the sole source of moral and environmental stewardship. While the work encompasses significant Christian references, it also has Buddhist, Taoist, and animistic touchpoints, subverting the conventional view of humans' relationship with nature in fascinating and significant ways.

*Nausicaä* is filled with distinct and memorable characters: the brooding Torumekian commander Princess Kushana, who, with her toughness and steely ambition, is Nausicaä's obvious foil; Teto, the wild fox squirrel whom Nausicaä tames and whose love and loyalty at one point rescue her from death; the shadowy Dorok priest-king Miralupa, whose evil actions were initially inspired by beneficent motives uncomfortably close to Nausicaä's own.

But it is Nausicaä who weaves the narrative's threads together and provides it with its provocative moral center. Far from the movie's optimistic young girl, she grows increasingly pessimistic and finally apocalyptic. By making Nausicaä a shamanic figure, Miyazaki changes the dynamics between human and nature, rendering the natural environment not only a stronger but a more multidimensional force. Unlike a messiah, the shaman is in and of the world, as much an agent of the wind and the water as a representative of humanity.

As Halifax writes, "In many societies the shaman is the focus of basic human values that define relationships between human beings, the culture's relationship to the cosmos and the society's relationship to the environment."[5] Nausicaä certainly encompasses these aspects, although at times she seems dangerously close to giving up on "human values" to enter into an individual pact with the cosmos. At other times she still bears traces of the messianic role from the film, inspiring others as a moral leader, and rescuing them from physical danger and suffering.

She is the go-between who mediates among every single faction in the narrative, using her formidable arsenal of skills. These range from the practical—wind riding and military abilities—to the spiritual, her ability to psychically commune with nonhuman creatures and her empathy and compassion, which inspire humans to love and follow her. Like a messiah figure, Nausicaä in the manga still carries the weight of the world on her shoulders. But unlike a messiah, she cannot or perhaps will not lead her people out of exile to some promised land or heavenly place. The shaman knows that there may be no other home than the place around us and that we must contend with the natural world to find our proper identity therein.

In Nausicaä's case we see this struggle for identity and, not coincidentally, the beginnings of her disaffection from humanity early on. In a flashback (also seen in the movie) a very young Nausicaä attempts to protect a small Ohmu larva. In this episode we see Nausicaä as a vulnerable little girl attempting to conceal the baby insect under her robe. Instead, the little

Ohmu wanders out obliviously and is captured by adults, including Nausicaä's mother and father.

The brief dialogue is both heartbreaking and revelatory:

**NAUSICAÄ'S FATHER:** So, you've been possessed by an insect. Hand it over, Nausicaä.
**NAUSICAÄ:** But it's not doing anything wrong!
**FATHER:** Insects and people can't live in the same world—you know that.
(Many adult hands reach down and take the baby away.)
**NAUSICAÄ:** Don't kill it! Please don't kill it![6]

But of course that is precisely what the adults intend to do.

This short interlude contains many important clues to Nausicaä's shamanic destiny. Most obvious is the fact that Nausicaä is seen by her father as being "possessed" by insects. To him this is the worst fate possible, since he sees no connection between the world of insects and that of humans. But Nausicaä has the opposite reaction. She wants to commune with the Ohmu because even as a child she senses that they have powers and qualities that make them at least equal to humanity.

The scene with the Ohmu larva has other implications. As Masahiro Koyama points out, the baby Ohmu, crawling out between Nausicaä's legs, seems to be enacting a kind of birth scene.[7] Incidentally, this is the only birth that Nausicaä will ever deliver. She will remain unmarried and childless all her life. This does not mean that she is not a maternal figure. In fact, she is the most powerful of the many maternal figures in Miyazaki's work. Throughout her journey she will "mother" a variety of nonhuman creatures, from the little Ohmu to the giant God Warrior, whom she comes to call "child."

Nausicaä begins her journey of discovery in her basement laboratory beneath her father's castle. Not surprisingly, given her inclination toward nature, the laboratory is overflowing with plant life rather than steely with technological instruments. But Nausicaä's investigations are for the purpose not of controlling the natural world but rather of understanding it. It is by breeding these plants that she believes she has discovered one of the secrets of the Fukai, the "sea" of decay that is actually a forest. Her revelation concerns the plants of the Fukai, conventionally believed to be poisonous since they emit toxic spores. Nausicaä discovers, however, that it is the Earth's deep pollution caused by the Ceramic wars of a thousand years before that distorts the plants and makes their emissions toxic. When she gives them clean water in her laboratory, the plants thrive and bloom harmoniously and safely.

Nausicaä's hypothesis is reaffirmed when she and Asbel, a Pejitean prince and warrior, crash-land in the Fukai and are rescued by the Ohmu. The Ohmu then leave her and Asbel, and the humans sink farther beneath the forest to discover at its heart a crystalline world of peace and purity, where they are able to breathe unpolluted air and walk freely. Nausicaä discovers that the Fukai "takes into its body the pollution left in the soil by the old civilizations" and "turns it into harmless crystal." More shocking, she realizes that "the forest no longer needs us" and becomes aware that "we humans are the real pollution."[8] This revelation will begin to lead her beyond her childhood sense of the Ohmu as beings equal to humans down a darker path where she must puzzle over the status of humanity in an interspecies world where the Ohmu increasingly seem superior.

The episode at the heart of the Fukai can also be seen as the first of a number of near-death experiences that Nausicaä must undergo, each one leading to a revelation. Another is the episode in which Nausicaä rescues an Ohmu infant from torture by enemy humans. In the movie version this leads to the clearly messianic scene of Nausicaä sacrificing her life for the Ohmu baby and being resurrected by the compassionate Ohmu collectivity, giving the film its upbeat closure. The film concludes with Nausicaä staying in her beloved valley and guiding her people into a promising future.

In the manga Nausicaä is only severely wounded in this episode. As in the movie, the Ohmu heal her wounds, and she walks through a field of golden feelers and is identified with a prophesied figure from an ancient tapestry. There is no hint of a Christlike death and resurrection. Rather, the emphasis is on the healing power of the Ohmu; although Nausicaä returns briefly to the Valley of the Wind, this is no utopian homecoming but rather a quick stop on the way to war. Leaving the beautiful valley, perhaps forever, Nausicaä turns toward seemingly endless violence and death.

Much of the rest of the seven volumes is occupied with battles, both aerial and terrestrial, and Nausicaä encounters scenes of sickening chaos and bloodshed, including an entire village dead from miasma. "Death, nothing but death wherever I go," she muses.[9]

Yet Nausicaä continues her journey, unwillingly engaging in a bloody and damaging battle with the Dorok empire, part of her reluctant agreement with the Torumekian Princess Kushana. While the battle is one of the more thrilling set pieces of the manga, revealing Nausicaä's military prowess, her real work is of a quieter kind that suggests both a messianic and a shamanistic side. For a brief time she finds a strange refuge, a temple where priests of the now forbidden religion of the ancient Doroks still survive in nearly mummified state. A picture of a winged creature in blue at the temple suggests to the priests that Nausicaä may be the winged messenger announcing an apocalypse. They tell her, "Destruction is inevitable. . . . All suffering is but a trial for the rebirth of the world."[10]

While Nausicaä is with the priests a terrifying miasma has begun to spread, engulfing planes, fields, cities, and armies and ushering in the final apocalyptic wave of insect attacks called the Daikaisho. The Dorok peasants believe that the Daikaisho will bring about a cleansing of the world, and they, like the mummified priests, take Nausicaä for a heavenly messenger. Nausicaä uses their belief in her, plus her telepathic powers, to rescue some of the Doroks, but all around them swarm chaos and violence. Children's bodies are left in ovens, and corpses litter the roadsides.

Even in these bloodiest of volumes, however, the action slows at times for Nausicaä to continue putting the pieces of the ecological puzzle together. She realizes that the miasma's mold spores are angry about their short life, overwhelmed by the hatred that they feel around them, desperate for food, and searching for one another. It is this search that brings the mold together into a gigantic wave of death. As Nausicaä says, "I've never encountered so wretched a creature. Any form of life knows joy and satisfaction . . . but they know only hatred and fear."[11] Even at this catastrophic moment, Nausicaä insists on seeing the mold as simply another life form rather than as an antagonistic force.

Exhausted, she falls asleep and confronts a giant skeletal creature that she calls Nothingness (*kyomu*, which can also mean "emptiness"). The Nothingness returns later and seems to represent Nausicaä's own inner darkness and the temptations of nihilism. The scenes with the Nothingness have a more psychoanalytic than mystical flavor, suggesting Miyazaki's own struggle with despair. Returned to the real world, she realizes that, in attacking, the Ohmu are deliberately sacrificing themselves to the miasma. They eat the mold, then use their bodies to form seedbeds from which a new forest will grow, one that will ultimately clean the Earth. To Nausicaä, the insects "were trying to eat up the mold's suffering."[12]

Her final and most significant near-death experience occurs as the apocalyptic Daikaisho rumbles around her. Taunted by the Nothingness, which points out that she herself has killed and calls her "a bloody woman of a cursed people," Nausicaä decides to die along with the Ohmu. Determining to become "part of the forest," she allows the Ohmu to swallow her.[13]

This is an almost textbook example of the shaman's "stepping over the threshold." Nausicaä does not die, but her mind goes into an altered state of consciousness and her body is discovered by her former companions. With them are a group of outsiders known as the Forest People, who live deep in the Fukai, in harmony with the forest, subsisting on insect eggs. The unconscious Nausicaä is given a place of honor by Selm, the young man who heads the Forest People, who declares, "Nausicaä is the Forest in human form. She stands at the center of both worlds."[14]

While her companions watch over her, hoping for her reawakening, Nausicaä slips first into memories and then into another world. She goes back to her failed attempt to protect the Ohmu larva when she was a child; then she is visited by the shadow spirit of Miralupa, the evil Dorok emperor who, although dead, remains in the world to search for her. In her dream state Nausicaä acknowledges the darkness in herself as well, and she, Selm, and the emperor journey together through a forest. Beyond the forest they see a pastoral landscape that has sprung up after a thousand years of purification. Nausicaä longs to stay there but cannot, acknowledging that humans "would eat up this newly born, fragile land and do the same thing over again." Leaving this oasis, she says, "If we can only survive and grow a little smarter . . . then we can come and join you here."[15]

As Andrew Osmond points out, this episode would make for an obvious and upbeat finale in a conventional science fiction narrative.[16] By crossing the threshold into near death, Nausicaä has discovered the "truth": that the Fukai is, albeit slowly, cleansing the world of human pollution and that perhaps humans may someday live in a "pure green land" again. The reader would be left cautiously hopeful.

In fact, however, the manga continues for one more volume toward a final, infinitely more disturbing vision of the fate of humanity. Reawakening to life, Nausicaä refuses Selm's invitation to stay with him and the Forest People. Telling him that she loves "the people of this world too much," she goes back to face the endgame being played out by the remnants of the Torumekian and Dorok empires. But the last volume of the manga is less about apocalyptic battles and more about temptation and power.

Nausicaä's final journey is toward the crypt of Shuwa, where a revelation concerning humanity's role on Earth awaits her. Along the way she encounters an Edenic garden and mushroom clouds, then meets two awesomely destructive forces that take on humanoid form. The first of these is the God Warrior, the humanoid weapon created in the last moments of the old Earth before the Seven Days of Fire. Brought back to life by the Doroks, the God Warrior "imprints" on Nausicaä, whom it calls Mama. Nausicaä decides to use the gargantuan creature to fly to Shuwa, but on their flight they pick up two Torumekian princes, the brothers of Nausicaä's erstwhile comrade in arms Princess Kushana. Their flight leads to one of the most important revelations of the manga.

Stopping to bury Teto, who was killed by Ohma's radiation, Nausicaä and the princes discover an Edenic place of healing known as the Garden. There she is fed, bathed, clothed, and left in a serene state of joy. Reminiscent of preindustrial Europe, the Garden contains fruit, flowers, libraries, and even a music room where all the great treasures of humankind have been stored. In a truly delightful scene that offers brief relief from the manga's earlier miseries, the two pudgy princes find themselves playing piano duets in a large sun-filled room full of books and "all the music mankind has produced."[17] Refreshed and tranquil, Nausicaä forgets her past and seems ready to succumb to an invitation from the Master of the Garden to stay there permanently. A beautiful and immortal being, the Master occasionally resembles Nausicaä's dead mother.

There is a catch, of course. Nausicaä begins to realize that she is betraying her responsibilities. The Master, however, refuses to let her go. Nausicaä becomes aware that the Garden is actually a storehouse for the crypt of Shuwa and that "the image of her mother was a trap, [her] own desires the lure," but she also reveals that she had never been certain as to whether her mother had really loved her.[18] The Master continues to remonstrate with her, pointing out that others had come to the Garden and left it to save the world but only ended up in disillusion and despair. Still Nausicaä struggles, and with the help of Selm eventually breaks out of the trap of this pseudo-Eden.

However, the real revelation is not about the Garden but about the world outside the Garden. In her discussion with the Master and with Selm, Nausicaä discovers that she had been mistaken in believing that the Ohmu and the Fukai were naturally purifying the world. To her horror she learns that the entire ecosystem of her world was engineered by the last humans during the final apocalyptic moments a millennium earlier. Not only did these humans remake the ecosystem, creating the Fukai to gradually get rid of the contaminants caused by industrial civilization, but they also remade human beings themselves so that they could live in the world. Even more disturbing is the fact that the current humans, the residents of Nausicaä's world, will not be able to live in the new purified world that the ecosystem is building toward.

Armed with this revelation, Nausicaä and the God Warrior journey to the crypt of Shuwa, where Nausicaaä confronts one last form of distorted life, the living walls of flesh that form the crypt. On these walls, at the pace of one line every summer and winter solstice, appear technological instructions for the scholars who guard or, more accurately, nurture the crypt. In a narrative that has so far progressed through images and conversation, Nausicaä and the reader are suddenly confronted with a literal writing on the wall. These instructions will ultimately add up to a blueprint for creating the new human race that will live in the purified world. In order to persuade her to cooperate in this utopian plan, the Master of the crypt takes human form and engages in a last debate.

But Nausicaä rejects this deus ex machina. In the manga's final confrontation, she argues with the Master of the crypt over the future of the human race, using the Master's own images of purity and light to envision a world in which impurity and darkness must also have a place. While the Master insists that "Life is light," she counters with the memorable sentence "No! Life is the light that shines in the darkness," adding, "All things are born from darkness and all things return to darkness."[19]

The Master attempts to convince her that the crypt safeguards humanity, in the form of the engineered eggs that the last humans before the apocalypse had deposited there, waiting for the world to be reborn in purified form. If Nausicaä destroys the crypt, he argues, she will essentially have destroyed humanity, since her people will not be able to live in the new dawn but will only spit up blood and die.

In words that sound even more chillingly accurate now than in 1994, the Master of the crypt describes the world before the invention of the Fukai —"poisoned air, punishing sunlight, parched earth, new illnesses coming into being every day. Death was everywhere." He explains, "We decided to entrust everything to the future."[20]

Nausicaä acknowledges at least part of this argument, saying, "I have no doubt that you were created out of idealism and a sense of purpose in an age of despair." But she castigates the relentless pursuit of purity, asking,

"Why didn't those men and women realize that both purity and corruption are the very stuff of life?" When the Master reminds her that her own form of humanity will not be able to live beyond "that morning" of the new world, she asserts, "That is for the planet to decide." The Master exclaims, "That is nihilism! Nothingess!" But she invokes a nonhuman example, countering that "the sympathy and love of the Ohmu were born from the depth of the nothingness."[21] For Nausicaä it is the nonhuman world that sets the moral tone, and the real nihilists are the people who built the crypt to create a future artificial race that would have no genuine connection to the planet.

She tells the resurrected dead that they are nothing but shadows that keep her fellow humans alive only so that they may serve the plan of the crypt. "We can know the beauty and cruelty of the world without the help of a giant tomb and its servants," she insists, adding, "Our god inhabits even a single leaf and the smallest insects."[22]

With that final remark she summons the God Warrior, who has already been busy around Shuwa creating catastrophic explosions that take the form of mushroom clouds. She tells him, "Send your light to this place." But the God Warrior's light is lethal. We see its fatal radiance explode the crypt, which begins to die. It is the crypt rather than Nausicaä and her fellow humans that emits blood, crying out that its eggs are dying. With a groan of agony the crypt disintegrates. Debilitated by this final expenditure of energy, the God Warrior dies, asking its "mother," Nausicaä, whether it had become a "good person." Nausicaä replies, "You are my son, and I am very proud of you."[23]

Leaving the God Warrior in the remains of the crypt, Nausicaä escapes to reunite with her fellow humans, who have huddled together outside. Departing from a conventional utopian science fiction ending, Miyazaki has these few remnants of humanity facing not a new purified morning but rather their old "twilight world." Nausicaä's last words are, "Let us depart. No matter how difficult it is . . . we must live."[24] The manga ends with a brief coda telling us that Nausicaä remained in the Dorok lands but that, according to one legend, she returned to the Valley of the Wind, and according to another, she did, after all, rejoin the Forest People.

This shattering conclusion has provoked a good deal of debate. The manga "captures readers' hearts, shakes their souls and changes their lives," writes Kaoru Nagayama, summing it up as "an awe-inspiring work of great depth." Masahiro Koyama describes it as a "turning point" and discusses its "dark power." Yoko Goi refers to it as a "work of purifying darkness." More troubled is Shunsuke Sugita, who insists that by "summoning Ohma to destroy the unborn eggs, [Nausicaä] has committed genocide." As Kano sums it up, *Nausicaä* "is a fantasy masterpiece, a severe work that [embodies] Miyazaki's suffering and philosophical vicissitudes over the decade from the 1980s to 1990s."[25]

The *Nausicaä* manga may also have been a way for Miyazaki to process some of his own psychological issues from childhood. As Sugita suggests, the repeated scenes of rescuing babies (both Ohmu and human) recall the traumatic incident that occurred in Miyazaki's childhood when his family was unable to provide a ride for neighbors attempting to escape the American air raids. Nausicaä's continual risking her life to save others can be seen as a kind of working through of guilt and even a form of expiation.

But Miyazaki's decision to allow his heroine to destroy myriad unborn children suggests even deeper inner conflicts, a combination of guilt over the past and despair about the future, or at least a future of Westernized technology.

To understand this, we must return to his decision to have his heroine shift from messiah to shaman mode. This is seen most saliently in her "threshold experience," when in despair she tries to join the Ohmu and gives herself up to death. Instead, she comes back to life to live in the world again, not as a messianic leader or savior but as someone who loves all things on the Earth. As Eriko Ogihara-Schuck states, "The two religious traditions [Christian and East Asian] are conflated in the anime but in the manga they oppose each other with animism triumphing at the end."[26]

Christianity or something very close to it is represented by both the Dorok peasants and another group, the despised Wormhandlers, who, respectively, view Nausicaä as an "apostle" or as a deity herself. Nausicaä is not above using her "apostle" status to lead the Doroks to safety, but she takes pains to show the Wormhandlers that she is not a god, having them touch her face to experience her fleshly humanity. But her continuous insistence on loving and privileging all life, as summed up in her final speech to the Master of the crypt, underlines her profound connection with nature. Nausicaä's final judgment, in destroying the unborn eggs, is not so much against humanity but for a larger vision of the Earth: humanity may or may not survive, but it will in any case live or die by natural means rather than through artificial technological engineering.

Nausicaä's choice is both away from the West and away from what Lamarre calls the "technological condition" that traps humanity in an ever-increasing race to exploit and destroy the planet. This notion is supported by her sojourn in the Edenic Garden that was also the storehouse for the great artifacts of Western civilization. In an interview with Yōichi Shibuya, Miyazaki acknowledges that this episode was a turning point in the narrative. As he says, "I hadn't planned on the Garden, but then, in order to have the Garden appear, I had to extend the manga." To which Shibuya responds, "Well, so the Garden happened naturally? I thought for sure that it represented the temptation of European ideas in a general way." Although Miyazaki does not specifically agree with this statement, nor does he disagree with the interviewer's assertion that the manga had "boiled down into a really East Asian worldview."[27]

This "East Asian worldview" consists most clearly of an animistic vision in which all species intermingle and no one type is superior to any other. This animistic approach further underlines the different strategies toward technology. If the Earth does not exist to be subjugated, then technology should work with nature rather than against it. The Forest People represent a clear rejection of all technology, but Miyazaki's vision is far from simplistically draconian in this regard. In both manga and film he offers the image of the windmill that functions as the technological underpinning of Nausicaä's pastoral Valley of the Wind. Not only does the windmill work with the wind to create energy that supports a bucolic and harmonious society, but in an animistic world, it can also be seen as working with the god (or gods) of the wind who are occasionally invoked throughout the narrative. Nausicaä's wind glider is another example of a technological instrument that takes advantage of natural forces without putting stress on them.

Finally, East Asian philosophy is based not on the Judeo-Christian dichotomies of good versus evil but rather on the admission that light and dark interact within all of us. This vision is shown most saliently in Nausicaä's insistence on rescuing one of the few objectively evil characters in the narrative—the recently dead priest-king Miralupa—admitting that she too has darkness in her heart. Miyazakiworld is striking for how few conventional evil villains can be found in it. Even Miralupa, who has caused great suffering, is allowed a glimpse of the Earth's beauty.

Nausicaä's decision to leave the utopian but artificially maintained world of the Garden may be seen as a rejection of the fundamental ideals of Western culture, and her refusal to be a messiah may be considered a turning away from simplistic idealism that, as Miyazaki saw in Eastern Europe, can ironically lead to more destruction and despair. But the final message of the manga is surely one that is particularly Miyazaki's own: "We must live." Simple as that message is, it is also immensely powerful. It appears implicitly in his earlier works and explicitly in his next movie, *Princess Mononoke,* whose catchphrase was "Ikiro!" (Live), and in his most recent film, *The Wind Rises,* whose protagonist quotes Valéry: "Le vent se lève! . . . il faut tenter de vivre!" (The wind rises. We must try to live).

By denying life to the technologically created artificial eggs of the "new morning," Nausicaä issues a challenge to the "twilight world," which is the only one we have. As she says, "We are birds who, though we may spit up blood, will go on flying beyond that morning, on and on. To live is to change . . . the Ohmu, the mold, the grasses and trees, we human beings . . . we will go on changing . . ."[28]

In her final holistic vision Nausicaä rejects the artificialities of eternal unchanging life to plunge deep into a world where light and darkness, death and life, blood and purity intermingle. Whether humanity can remain in that world is, she suggests, up to us.

# 11

# The Faces of Others

*Boundary Crossing in* Princess Mononoke

How do you live with a true heart when everything around
you is collapsing?

—— M I Y A Z A K I

I brought a friend with me the first time I saw *Princess Mononoke* in an American movie theater. He had no experience with Miyazaki or with Japanese culture or animation, but he was intrigued to see what promised to be a grand adventure story, especially one that was appearing in the United States under the auspices of the Disney Corporation. In the middle of watching the movie, however, he started nudging me. "Who's the good guy?" he hissed irritably. "I can't tell which is the good guy and which is the bad guy!" "That's the whole point!" I whispered back.[1]

*Princess Mononoke* inaugurated a new chapter in Miyazakiworld. Ambitious and angry, it expressed the director's increasingly complex worldview, putting on film the tight intermixture of frustration, brutality, animistic spirituality, and cautious hope that he had honed in the *Nausicaä* manga. The film offered a mythic scope, unprecedented depictions of violence and environmental collapse, and a powerful vision of the sublime, all within the director's first ever attempt at a *jidaigeki,* or historical film. It also moved farther away from the family fare that had made him a treasured household name in Japan.

In the complicated universe of *Princess Mononoke* there was no longer room for villains such as *Conan*'s power-hungry Repka, the greedy Count of *Cagliostro,* or the evil Muska of *Laputa.* Miyazaki instead gave his audiences the ambitious but generous Lady Eboshi and the enigmatic monk Jiko-bō, who insists that we live in a cursed world. It is not only Jiko-bō who thinks this, apparently. In the darkest moments of his tale of humans battling the "wild gods" of the natural world in fourteenth-century Japan, Miyazaki seems to be saying that all the dwellers of this realm, human and nonhuman, were equally cursed. *Princess Mononoke* raised questions Miyazaki had implicitly asked in the *Nausicaä* manga: Given what humanity has done to the planet, do we have a right to keep on waging war against the nonhuman Other? Is there any way that human and nonhuman can coexist?[2]

These questions struck a deep chord in Japanese audiences, and the movie opened a new chapter in Miyazaki's influence on Japanese society. *Princess Mononoke* became not simply a hit but a cultural phenomenon. The Japanese media celebrated the more than two thousand eager fans who lined up for the movie's first screening in Tokyo, then vociferously commemorated the moment when the film surpassed the country's previous highest earning movie, Steven Spielberg's *E.T.* Magazine articles and even special issues on the film flooded Japan, tackling everything from the movie's reworking of traditional history and its varied and impressive group of voice actors to its innovative animation techniques, including Studio Ghibli's first use of computers and digital painting.[3]

Miyazaki was interviewed on subjects ranging from environmental degradation to his judgment as to whether children should see such a violent movie (on which he reversed himself, initially saying that they should not see it and then insisting that they would make the "best" audience). His fame among anime fans had been building for many years, and *Kiki*'s success opened up a still wider audience, but it is with *Princess Mononoke* that Miyazaki became a celebrity of sorts. This does not mean that he built a flashy house and started dating supermodels. He remained in the unpretentious Tokyo suburb of Tokorozawa, and continued to welcome friends and staff members to the rustic cabin his father-in-law had built in the mountains of Nagano prefecture. In an interview after *Princess Mononoke*'s release, he spoke longingly of a desire "just to go away and live in a cabin in the mountains."[4]

This desire for retreat was understandable. As numerous articles and a six-hour documentary on the making of the film make clear, *Princess Mononoke* was the most stress-inducing film the director had created. Notably longer and far more expensive than any previous Ghibli film, the work required almost superhuman efforts on the part of Miyazaki and his increasingly weary staff. Given Miyazaki's obsessive attention to detail, the film's epic scope, historical setting, and wide cast of characters made the preparation period alone intensely time-consuming, to say nothing of the time that the actual production took. Exhausted by the experience, some of the veterans who had worked on *Princess Mononoke* left the company when the film was finished to be replaced by new animators.

Toshio Suzuki, who produced *Princess Mononoke,* recalls a moment when Miyazaki finally "exploded" after being asked to do too many things in too short a time. The director was "correcting the storyboards, checking the originals, aligning the music to the story, and presiding over the 'after recordings'"—vocals added after the initial animation is complete. He was also giving interviews on television and to newspapers and magazines, all while being involved with the marketing and with introducing the film to audiences as it was rolled out over Japan. As Suzuki puts it, Miyazaki had "given his body and soul" to the movie and was beyond exhaustion. Suzuki remembers being with the director the night before the movie's premier in the provincial city of Kochi. Miyazaki lay in bed and with a felt pen drew a sketch of his own face. Handing the paper to Suzuki, he said curtly, "Here, you put this on and go out and pretend to be me at the movie tomorrow."[5] *Princess Mononoke*'s aftermath would mark the beginning of the director's retreat from extensive public relations responsibilities.

The all-out marketing campaign that surrounded the movie marked a first: the studio marketed it as a Ghibli rather than a Miyazaki film. This change was more than symbolic, attesting to the ascendance of Suzuki as Ghibli's main producer in the widening realm of Miyazakiworld. Involved with Miyazaki and Takahata since his days as an editor at *Animage,* he was widely credited with successfully marketing *Kiki.* But *Princess Mononoke*'s record-breaking box-office performance was deemed Suzuki's most spectacular success to date, launching him firmly into a highly visible position in the animation industry. Viewed as the pragmatist who enables Miyazaki to express his idealistic vision, Suzuki became an increasingly dominant force at Ghibli.[6] Indeed, the documentary on the making of *Princess Mononoke* sometimes appears to be allotting almost as much face time to the producer as to the man who actually directed the film.

New faces were also coming in from overseas. In 1997 Ghibli's parent company Tokuma Shoten announced a deal with the Walt Disney Corporation to distribute its products worldwide. Suzuki had arranged the agreement, and it was a huge achievement for him and for Ghibli. The deal expanded Ghibli's influence globally in one stroke and achieved an enormous public relations coup at home. More than a thousand reporters attended the press conference announcing the deal and presided over by Yasuyoshi Tokuma, the head of Tokuma Publishing, while two representatives from Disney chimed in by satellite. As Suzuki disarmingly explained, "The announcement that [*Princess Mononoke*] would be opening across America was important only in that it helped us capture market share at home."[7]

In fact, *Princess Mononoke,* despite an elegant English-language script written by the fantasy writer Neil Gaiman and an impressive roster of American and English voice actors, did not perform particularly well in the United States. While the prominent film critic Janet Maslin of the *New York Times* praised the film's "exotically beautiful action" and Miyazaki's construction of "an elaborate moral universe," she also felt compelled to mention its occasionally "knotty" plot and sometimes "gruesome" imagery. A Japanese journalist wondered later, "How could [Americans who were] used to stories about good versus evil, full of musical numbers and comical sidekicks, and always with a happy ending, be expected to appreciate the appeal of Studio Ghibli's offerings?"[8]

Miyazaki's feelings about the new arrangement with Disney are cloudy. Beyond a rather vague speech at the press conference, I can find no public pronouncement by him on the subject. Over the years neither he nor Suzuki had had much good to say about Disney, so it seems likely that the arrangement was a purely practical one for the benefit of both parties.[9] But Miyazaki and Suzuki could at least be satisfied that they had broken new ground for quality Japanese animation. Furthermore, the Oscar later awarded to Miyazaki's 2001 film *Spirited Away* would show that American audiences could indeed appreciate something beyond "happily ever after."

Although groundbreaking in many ways, *Princess Mononoke* did not come out of nowhere. By the early 1990s Miyazaki had completed his first adult-oriented feature film, *Porco Rosso,* and was finally finishing the *Nausicaä* manga. Always searching for new inspirations, he became intrigued by the idea of doing something with the *Hōjōki,* a classic work from the thirteenth century. A brief, beautifully written reflection on the world and the transience of life, the *Hōjōki* is still part of the curriculum in most Japanese schools.

The *Hōjōki* is not an obvious candidate for a movie, animated or otherwise. Written by Miyazaki's much-admired author Kamo no Chōmei, a former courtier who had grown disillusioned by the ways of the world and become a Buddhist monk, the work appeared in 1223, at a time when military takeovers, famine, pestilence, and natural disasters such as earthquakes and floods rocked the capital and claimed thousands of lives. The *Hōjōki* chronicles these disasters from a safe distance, through the viewpoint of a thoughtful, poetic man who saw in the apocalyptic events around him a reason for retreat and reflection.

Miyazaki's interest in the *Hōjōki* was stimulated by a book called *Hōjōkiden,* by a favorite novelist, Yoshie Hotta. But beyond such influences Miyazaki's own frame of mind played a part in sending the director's art in grimmer directions than the largely upbeat family-oriented works of the

1970s and 1980s. As evidenced by both *Porco Rosso* and *Nausicaä,* he had grown increasingly disillusioned with authoritarian ideologies, and his growing anxieties about the vulnerability of the natural environment were reflected in *Nausicaä*'s apocalyptic themes.

Miyazaki admired the great live-action film director Akira Kurosawa, whose *jidaigeki*—period films featuring samurai—had hugely influenced postwar Japanese cinema. But Miyazaki wanted to do much more than create a piece of historical entertainment. Building on Hotta's view of *Hōjōki* as a critique of the militarism and false ideologies of Kamo no Chōmei's period, he hoped to create a work that would comment on Japan's emptiness and confusion in the postbubble era. A country that had worshiped materialism and success seemed now to be floundering in a spiritual vacuum, reflected in the increasing use among contemporary Japanese of the word *kyomu:* emptiness.

Two major incidents in 1995 had traumatized Japan. The first was the Kobe earthquake in February, which killed between four thousand and six thousand people and was the worst earthquake to hit the country since the Great Kantō earthquake of 1923. For a modern industrialized nation the scale of destruction was truly shocking. It seemed as if nature itself was seeking vengeance on human civilization. The earthquake was followed a month later by the Aum Shinrikyo incident, when members of an apocalyptic religious cult released sarin gas in a busy station in the Tokyo subway system, killing twelve people and injuring thousands more. These two terrifying episodes underlined the increasing sense of vulnerability felt by the Japanese, on both a psychological and an environmental level.

As a dweller in perilous times, Kamo no Chōmei would have been all too familiar with experiences like the horror of the Kobe earthquake and with the apocalyptic despair that inspired the Aum Shinrikyo incident. While Miyazaki ultimately abandoned the idea of filming the *Hōjōki,* he continued to consider a medieval period piece treating natural and technological catastrophe and the question of how to live in a complicated and terrible world. Unlike Chōmei or Kurosawa, Miyazaki wanted to give equal agency to human, natural, and supernatural forces.

Considered by many to be Miyazaki's most important work, *Princess Mononoke* expands on some of the themes developed in the *Nausicaä* manga.[10] Environmental catastrophe, the role of technology and warfare, and human interactions with nonhuman species are now cast, however, in fourteenth-century Japan, the so-called Muromachi period. While the film's title (literally "the possessed princess") refers to San, a young woman raised by wolves, Miyazaki felt that the real hero of the film was Ashitaka, a young prince of the peaceful Emishi clan in far northern Japan. Ashitaka sets the narrative in motion by going on a quest of healing and discovery. He has been cursed by a *tatarigami,* a demon boar god, Nago, who, sent into a maddened state by an iron musket ball that had lodged in his body, attacks him. The wounded Ashitaka must leave his village and go to western Japan to find the source of the iron ball.

Ashitaka's curse is embodied by a tattoolike mark covering his right arm that may end up destroying him. To Miyazaki, Ashitaka's curse exemplifies such contemporary ills as the scourge of ectopic dermatitis that had affected many Japanese children. It also marks Ashitaka as an outcast and connects him with others of Miyazaki's male characters, such as Marco or Howl, who also bear curses.[11] Less world-weary than Marco and less filled with rage than Howl, Ashitaka endeavors to see the world "with eyes unclouded," an entreaty he has learned from the wise woman of the Emishi.

Ashitaka's quest will take him to two unforgettable and antithetical places, an enchanted forest ruled by a divine entity known as the *shishigami*, and Tatara, a community of ironworkers, physical and social outcasts led by Eboshi, an aggressive woman who wishes to destroy the forest. Although loath to do so, Ashitaka will ultimately be forced to participate in an all-out war between the two sides.

Ashitaka's gentleness, perseverance, and tolerance suggest an idealized version of the romantic young Miyazaki, the adolescent who long before fell in love with the beautiful and pure heroine of *Panda and the White Serpent*. In fact, Miyazaki's original title for the movie had been *The Tale of Ashitaka* (Ashitaka no sekki), but he had been persuaded to change it by

Suzuki, who preemptively issued a press release calling the film *Princess Mononoke*.[12] On his journey west Ashitaka encounters San, a fierce young girl raised by wolves, who initially wants to kill him, seeing only a member of the despised human race, from which she is exiled. Just as she is about to put a knife to his throat, however, Ashitaka stops San by telling her that she is beautiful. With this one remark Ashitaka establishes a connection with her.

San seems to be an embodiment of Miyazaki's anger with what he increasingly perceived as a stupid and chaotic world. In his drawings the director shows her as a terrifying force of nature. The audience first sees her as she stands with her wolf mother, Moro, her mouth rimmed with blood. Later on, wearing a fearsome red mask, she attacks the human settlement of Tatara, which threatens the wolves' forest. Neither fully human nor fully animal, San is alone.

Miyazaki counterbalances San's rather one-note rage with one of his most complex and fascinating characters, Lady Eboshi, the leader of the Tatara ironworkers community, who is building an arsenal of rifles for use against the forest. She hopes to kill the shishigami, the god of the forest, and deliver its head to the Japanese emperor.

As previously mentioned, when I first met Miyazaki, he told me that Eboshi was his favorite character in the movie. Though that surprised me, over the years I came to realize that Eboshi is a remarkable portrait of leadership—a character tough, smart, and driven, but also capable of startling generosity and, ultimately, of compromise. That Eboshi is female is important as well. As I have written elsewhere, Miyazaki's ability to defamiliarize long-held conventions is one of his most striking talents.[13] He subverts many Japanese traditions in *Princess Mononoke*—the sacredness of the emperor, the nobility of the samurai—but his most impressive piece of subversion is his incorporation of so many dominant female characters. It not only refreshes the traditional *jidaigeki* format but it also stimulates the audience to see the world from a different angle. As a female, Lady Eboshi forces the audience members to reconsider their notion of the conventional villain role.

It is likely that Miyazaki saw part of himself in Eboshi. She is, after all, the head of a community who is forced to make tough decisions and still not lose her humanity, a complex dynamic that Miyazaki faced every day at Studio Ghibli. He demonstrates these complications most strikingly in his portrayal of Eboshi's workforce, which consists mainly of former prostitutes and sufferers of Hansen's disease, leprosy. Miyazaki had long been interested in medieval ironworkers, who often formed outcast communities in wild mountains and forests. His decision to make them female, however, contravenes the historical view of women as polluting forces who might contaminate ironworkers' work sites. Even more radical was his notion of having Eboshi employ lepers to make rifles, the weapons that she plans to use against the forest gods. The combination of Eboshi's compassion in employing the lepers with the fearsome nature of the work she has them do strikingly illustrates the kind of moral compromises that being a leader, or simply being human, can force upon us.

Miyazaki deliberately created characters outside of the traditional *jidaigeki* to show a more diverse and rich version of Japanese history. But perhaps his most interesting inclusion was the sufferers from Hansen's disease. According to Kano, he was inspired to do this by his visit to the Tama Zenshōen, a leprosy sanatorium near his house. Though leprosy is only mildly contagious, the Japanese government in the 1990s still considered it a "fearsome disease" and imposed a strict isolation on sufferers. Miyazaki spoke of his shock when interacting with the inhabitants of the sanatorium, who somehow carried on with their lives in a robust and positive ways. Afterward he noted in wonderment, "In the middle of no matter what kind of misery there is joy and laughter. In human life which tends toward ambiguity I have never seen a place which shows this with such clarity."[14]

I find these sentences to be some of Miyazaki's most affecting ever, resonating more deeply than his diatribes against the stupidity and carelessness of humans. That the director could still, at a time of social troubles and inner stress, at some level believe in humanity suggests the idealism that still burned inside him. But Miyazaki does not take his idealism to unrealistic extremes. As he said in a later interview, "The inhabitants of Tatara are not all good people; there are stupid elements and crazy elements, because that's what people are."[15]

*Princess Mononoke* is more than social or political commentary, however. It is clearly Miyazaki's attempt to offer a new approach both to Japanese history and to human interaction with the environment. Using the magic of animation, Miyazaki creates a vividly realized world in which a wide range of human and nonhuman characters cross conventional boundary lines of physicality, gender, species, and the natural and supernatural. Ultimately the movie offers a vision of life as a densely interwoven design, rather than a simple allegory of dichotomized opposites.

Historians traditionally view the Muromachi period as a time when Zen aesthetics developed, giving rise to the classic Japanese garden. In *Princess Mononoke,* however, nature in the Muromachi period comes across in a completely different form—still largely beautiful, but wild, dangerous, remote, and thoroughly nonhuman. It also has agency, at times spiritual and transcendent and at other times violent and terrifying. One of the film's great achievements is that it gives voices and faces not only to marginalized humanity but also to nature itself.

Miyazaki needed to go beyond realism to do this, and *Princess Mononoke* can be seen as a historical epic that is also a richly realized fantasy. Miyazaki's partner, Takahata, took the film to task as a well-done fantasy that "differed from reality and [was] dangerously liable to give the audiences misconceived impressions of history."[16] On the contrary, Miyazaki's intertwining of the fantastic and the historical gives the film its particular impact, suggesting a more thought-provoking human/nature dynamic than would have been possible in a more realistic work.

The director treats both humans and nature evenhandedly in the movie. The film is not simply an environmentalist paean that blames humanity and suggests that a return to nature is a simple and easy solution. Instead, the movie presents a radical vision of hybridity and interdependence between natural, supernatural, and human that only the animated medium with its transformative possibilities could express. In the long run, this vision calls into question not only humans' right to dominate nature but queries what place humanity can and should have in a challenging and unstable world.

At its most fundamental level the movie asks: Can we live ethically in a cursed world? And if so, how? *Princess Mononoke* offers two related possible solutions. The first is simply to "Live!" (*Ikiro!*), the catchphrase emblazoned on the movie posters and uttered by Ashitaka to the desperate San as she struggles to deal with her fear and resentment of humanity. In context it tells us we cannot give up, no matter what, a message that Miyazaki felt imperative in the emotionally apathetic landscape of 1990s Japan. The second is "to see with eyes unclouded"—a challenge, as the movie presents both bloodthirsty beast attacks and relentless human industrialization and asks us to observe all sides with clarity and objectivity.

That an animated rather than a live-action film should ask such deep and provocative questions may seem surprising. Yet animation is a particularly appropriate medium for dealing with these difficult questions. Themes of metamorphosis, hybridity, and boundary crossing, which force us to consider our place in the world and in relation to others, have long been staples of animation and its favorite genres of science fiction and fantasy. As environmental scholar Ursula Heise points out, the animated medium is particularly adept at "open[ing] up a world being worked on by nonhuman agents in ways that resonate with environmentalist thought—all the more so if they are not simply presented as humans in another guise but inhabit modes of thought and being all their own."[17]

It is this notion of sentient nonhuman entities "inhabit[ing] modes of thought and being all their own" that *Princess Mononoke* explores with urgency and animates with vivacity. The movie envisions a world on the brink of crisis, making an awkward transition from a nature-based conception of life toward one dependent on technology symbolized by the ironworkers. In this transitional world the wild gods of the forest are being threatened with extinction. But these gods are not "humans in another guise." The film's sophisticated animation allows for a distinctive variety of nonhuman faces,

The shishigami in *Princess Mononoke,* Studio Ghibli, 1997

from the appealing and expressive visage of Yakkul, Ashitaka's red elk steed, to the simplified, masklike countenances of the little tree spirits known as *kodama.*

In the movie's most provocative touch, Miyazaki offers the gentle otherworldly countenance of the shishigami. Monstrous, awe-inspiring, and fundamentally Other, the shishigami is a creation that pushes the film well past the clichés of the many admirable but obvious artworks on environmental issues that tend to simplify nature as noble/vulnerable or cuddly/vulnerable. In this film not only can we envision the Other in ways never before presented, but the Other looks back at us. From the impishly smiling visages of the kodama to the fearsome hatred emanating from a wounded boar's eyes, *Princess Mononoke* offers a panoply of gazes from the Other.

Rendering the shishigami in all its simultaneous beauty and grotesqueness, Miyazaki takes the film squarely in an ethical direction that goes beyond the truism of humans' dominating nature. In this regard, the film contrasts with Disney films in which even enthusiasts acknowledge a "cute-ification" of nature occurs. In his analysis of *Bambi,* for example, Disney scholar David Whitley acknowledges the movie's sentimentalizing of nature, noting that "the choreographed interactions between animal 'friends' of different species, the wide-eyed enhancement of facial features designed to appeal to human ideals of attractiveness and the elimination of natural predators to create a world of idyllic innocence all combine to create a sentimental viewpoint that is difficult to reconcile with full respect for the integrity and otherness of the natural world."[18]

*Princess Mononoke* depicts engagement with the natural world on a level that manages to avoid much of the typical anthropomorphizing tendencies of conventional nature representations. Through the brilliance of its animation, the movie offers what the French philosopher Emmanuel Levinas calls the "strangeness of the Other," although it goes beyond Levinas's concern with the human to suggest a whole new category of Otherness. The film's revelation of this "strangeness" wakes the human audience to its proximity to, and intimacy and interdependence with, the natural world. To see how Miyazaki accomplishes this, let us turn to the film's narrative, beginning with its famous opening sequence of the maddened boar god Nago in *tatarigami* (demon god) form attacking Ashitaka.

The sequence starts with an ethereal image of vast mountaintops wreathed in mist. We glimpse a grassy spot suddenly covered in what looks like steaming brown leeches. In fact, these leechlike forms, which are erupting from the boar, express the natural, supernatural, and technological—they symbolize the boar's supernatural transformation into a tatarigami. But the transformation is forced by technology—the iron ball that has lodged in the Nago's flesh and is destroying it. Thus the boar/tatarigami is a hybrid, a supernatural beast with a trace of human technology embedded within.

By taking on the boar's curse, Ashitaka becomes a hybrid himself. As with the boar, the curse represented by the scar threatens to destroy him. Before doing so, however, it will give him superhuman strength, energy, and proficiency in warfare. At the same time this superhuman power is inspired by the hatred and anger welling up inside him, just as was the case with Nago. In Nago's agonized last moments he addresses the "disgusting humans," telling them that they will soon suffer his anger and agony as well. From the movie's opening, therefore, we see human society not simply confronting the natural/supernatural world but interwoven within it, part of a complex totality wherein the nonhuman speaks directly to us and penetrates our emotional and physical identity.

Ashitaka and his Emishi tribe are mediators between nature and humanity, a peaceful people whose actions stand in stark contrast with the warring communities of the Yamato (Japanese) nation. Ashitaka is not allowed to continue this peaceful and tolerant lifestyle, however. Cutting off his topknot and setting out on Yakkul, his red elk steed, he himself now becomes an Other, in exile from his land and people and crosses into the lush green forest of the shishigami, the powerful nature spirit whom Ashitaka has learned about from the enigmatic monk Jiko-bō. These early forest scenes take the audience into the spiritual heart of the movie, depicting an enchanted place where humans, beasts, and supernatural creatures cross boundaries of perception and belonging. Based on Miyazaki's travels to the extraordinary World Heritage site of Yakushima, where two thousand–year–old cedars still grow, the forest of the shishigami is a place of deep clear pools, glittering butterflies, and gigantic old trees of an intense emerald hue.

In the forest Ashitaka has three major encounters with the natural/supernatural, ranging from the forbidding to the playful and finally to the numinous. In the first, stumbling across two injured men who had been abandoned by Lady Eboshi, he suddenly becomes aware of a presence across the river from them. Peeking through the branches of a fallen tree he sees three enormous silver wolves and a young human girl wearing a wolf pelt with a red mask slung over her back. The girl, of course, is San, the "princess mononoke" of the movie's title. "Mononoke" literally refers to spirit possession, but in this case suggests both San's otherness and separation from humanity and her corresponding closeness to the family of wolf gods, who, we discover, have adopted her as one of their own.

Ashitaka's second encounter with the supernatural, more playful and lighthearted, is with the *kodama* nature spirits. When one of the injured men whom Ashitaka is helping screams in horror at a kodama gaily perched on Yakkul's saddle, Ashitaka simply remarks, "So they have kodama here too." Ashitaka's relaxed acceptance of the creatures strongly hints that he is familiar with them from his homeland in the north.

Ashitaka's last encounter with the supernatural Other is the most overtly spiritual. He penetrates ever more deeply into the forest, despite the pleas of one of the injured men, who warns that "this is the entrance to the spirit world." Ashitaka's eyes are drawn across a mossy forest glade and then upward to a golden radiance emanating from a copse across the water. Outlined against the light come several small deer, and then a larger, many antlered deerlike form appears, the shishigami in daylight incarnation. As the ethereal animal turns toward him, Ashitaka experiences intense pain in his scarred arm, which he plunges into the water for relief as the deer spirit silently departs.

Elsewhere Ashitaka's pain had telegraphed hatred and rage, but in this quieter scene it symbolizes the shared pain between the species. The agony that Ashitaka experiences is a reminder of the dying boar god and may also anticipate the later death agonies of the shishigami itself.

Ashitaka's next discovery is the giant iron manufacturing foundry of Tatara, a dark fortresslike place whose products and processes have laid waste to the region around it, creating a sterile land of dead trees and bare rock. In Tatara Ashitaka again walks the challenging and dangerous line of mediator between a variety of Others, though this time they are human.

In this regard, perhaps his most surprising encounter is with Tatara's leader Lady Eboshi when she leads him through her secret garden to the place where her muskets are manufactured. There he finds the group of bandaged lepers who eagerly produce sturdy rifles on Lady Eboshi's orders. Again hatred and anger enflame Ashitaka, and his arm takes on a life of its own, seemingly about to attack Eboshi for inciting this willful and savage destructiveness. Before he can act, however, a different kind of Other, the most extensively bandaged and apparently blind leper, stops him by showing the arguing duo his bandaged arm encasing "rotting flesh." "Life is suffering," he tells them. "It is hard. The world is cursed." He then adds, "But still, you find reasons to go on living."

Coming at a crucial moment in the movie, the leper's pronouncement is significant for several reasons. While his initial words echo those of Jiko-bō concerning a world of suffering, his final statement affirms one of the movie's basic themes—"Live!"—at the same time acknowledging how difficult living can be. The leper's presence also underlines both the separateness of being in the world and the inherent links among all living entities. Faceless and swathed head to toe in bandages, he seems initially to represent almost a different kind of life form from Eboshi and Ashitaka, but all three of them belong, each in his or her own way, to a community of outcasts who still believe in living against all odds.

Another kind of boundary crossing Otherness is played out in the subsequent scene, when San attacks Tatara, intent on murdering Eboshi. Ultimately, San fails in her mission to murder Eboshi and severely wounds Ashitaka instead.

It is just after this point in the movie that San begins to show glimmers of humanity, perhaps recognizing in Ashitaka a fellow outcast. Rather than kill him, San transports Ashitaka back to the heart of the forest and leaves the young man on a small island with only Yakkul to guard him. This action leads to one of the most sustained scenes of numinous beauty that Miyazaki has ever created.

The camera slowly moves upward from Ashitaka's prone figure on the island, through the lush green trees of the forest ending finally with a vision of towering mountains. The scene cuts to a group of kodama, growing steadily numerous as they gather on the mountaintops, seemingly waiting for something to occur. The full moon appears and through it, in a gorgeous feat of animation, we see the *daidarabochi*—the night version of the shishigami—slowly manifest itself. Gigantic, unearthly, and yet with a vaguely humanoid body and an even more vaguely human face, the daidarabochi strides slowly forward. The camera cuts to the kodama, who react to the god's coming by rotating their heads 180 degrees with an eerie rattling sound. We next see the god in profile, now looking more beastlike, with stripes on its sides and many antlers down its back, as it seems to dive down toward the forest lake below.

In a surprising transition, however, we suddenly see bearlike shapes crouching in the forest. These are hunters, led by Jiko-bō, hoping to catch a glimpse of the god in its nightwalker form. While Jiko-bō is fascinated, the hunters quake in fear, telling the monk that looking at the daidarabochi will render them blind. Jiko-bō reminds them that they have an official order from the emperor. Along with the kodama, the hunting band watches as the god dives toward the lake where Ashitaka lies.

This manifestation of the nightwalker/daidarabochi above the mountains is the visual and spiritual high point of the movie, verging on the textbook definition of the sublime as something terrifying, beautiful, and awe-inspiring. This sense is reinforced by the reaction shots of the kodama— not only do their rotating heads and strange rattling noises add to the otherworldliness of the scene, but the tight circle between the two forms of nonhuman entities—the giant ectoplasmic shishigami and the tiny almost doll-like kodama—reinforces the sense that the viewer is being allowed to see something utterly strange, a sacred moment that has nothing to do with humanity. Miyazaki supports this sense of taboo by having the hunters close their eyes in fear of seeing something forbidden. The feeling of the sublime is carried even further when, as the shishigami falls toward the forest, a strong wind blows and the kodama smile and wave their arms as the trees flutter in an intense wind, like whitecaps on a tremendous green wave. Nowhere in the rest of Miyazaki's oeuvre is there such a vision of otherworldly joy.

One more supernatural vision occurs in this episode. After the shishigami dives toward the forest, it takes on its daytime deerlike form. This time, however, the god approaches Ashitaka closely. As if in a trance, Ashitaka sees the face of the shishigami, a surprisingly human countenance, albeit with unblinking red eyes—the face of the Other, or perhaps the face of Nature itself.

After these sublime and slow moments in the forest *Princess Mono-*

*noke* returns to its previous action-packed style. The second half of the film consists largely of warfare on an epic scale worthy of Kurosawa: samurai, peasants, scenes of terrible bloodshed and body counts (unthinkable in previous Miyazaki movies), swords, arrows, spears, and guns and hopeless, death-defying final charges.

While Eboshi and her community fight savagely and suffer terrible losses, perhaps the most emotionally fraught battle is the last stand of the boars, led by their blind and tottering chief, Okkotonushi. Renouncing her humanity, San takes her stand alongside Okkotonushi.

In Okkotonushi's devouring anger and crazed willingness to sacrifice his fellow boars on a useless mission, he is reminiscent not simply of a wild beast but of the worst elements of humanity, an object lesson in the stupidity and futility of war. Okkotonushi behaves ever more recklessly, slowly becoming a tatarigami like Nago before him. In a final moment of boundary crossing, Okkotonushi's snakelike tentacles engulf San, threatening to transform her into a tatarigami as well. At the last moment, Ashitaka, with the help of the shishigami, is able to find her in the wilderness of tentacles and rescue her.

The nearby Eboshi takes advantage of the shishigami's presence to shoot at it and finally succeeds in severing its head. In the film's last apocalyptic minutes, the god transforms once again. Growing to enormous size, the headless body spews toxic slime all over the countryside, turning the green landscape into a wasteland. In the final moments before the land becomes totally waste, Ashitaka persuades San to stand united with him and return the shishigami's head, insisting that this must be done by "human hands." Although its head is restored, the giant god totters and falls onto Tatara, breaking apart Eboshi's community in a cataclysmic storm of destruction. In its dying agonies the shishigami covers the sky and turns it into darkness. This is in direct contrast to the apocalyptic end of *Nausicaä;* there a new hope for the future was heralded by the gentle blue of the sky above the Valley of the Wind.

Miyazaki does not end with a vision of catastrophe, however. Although the film leaves open the question of whether the shishigami will ever return, it does offer the audience hope of a restored green land. This land is a gentler, more pastoral place than the wild and towering forests. The new landscape resembles modern Japan far more closely, implying that wild nature has been finally tamed.

Or has it? Our final glimpse of San is as she says goodbye to Ashitaka, telling him that, though she loves him, she cannot forgive humanity and will return to the forest. The ultimate fate of Ashitaka and San as a couple remains ambiguous. Is San an embittered person returning, like Kamo no Chōmei, to a reclusive existence in the forest, far from the noise, filth, and misery of the world?

If Ashitaka is a mediator between worlds, San expresses both or even several worlds—beast, god, and human, a fitting emblem of the inclusiveness of Miyazakiworld. The poster for the movie shows her standing with her wolf family looking out with hostility at the human world. Her face is marked with blood and tattoos, but underneath we still perceive a vulnerable human girl. While San never rises to the rarefied moral heights of Nausicaä, her face, with its tattoos and its occasional mask, parallels the human/inhuman countenance of the shishigami, asking us to measure our own accountability as we stand face to face with the Other.

The film's final two shots are even more ambiguous, or perhaps ironic. We see a single kodama, and we are left uncertain whether this is the last kodama in the forest or the beginning of the forest's spiritual revitalization. We then see a quick shot of the formidable monk Jiko-bō throwing up his hands and saying, "I give up. I give up. You can't win against fools."

The despairing Jiko-bō may well be another, more cynical version of Miyazaki himself. The director's final quartet of movies, however, suggests that *Princess Mononoke* was at least partly a means for the director to work through a sense of cursedness and provide more optimistic visions. As the Hansen's disease sufferer in Tatara puts it, "But still, you find reasons to go on living."

# 12

# The Intimate Apocalypse of *Spirited Away*

I didn't want to destroy the bathhouse.

—— M I Y A Z A K I

Over the years my students have asked me what my favorite Miyazaki film is. To some extent, my answer depends on the time of day, how I'm feeling, maybe what I've read in the news that morning. But there is no question that the Miyazaki work that consistently captivates me is his 2001 Academy Award–winning film *Spirited Away* (Sen to Chihiro no Kamikakushi). In its depth, compassion, and dreamlike strangeness it epitomizes the most intriguing and distinctive elements of Miyazakiworld.

Appearing five years after the blockbuster epic *Princess Mononoke*, *Spirited Away* was very different from the previous film in scope and tone. Miyazaki had actually quit Ghibli on January 14, 1998, but less than a week later the director Yoshifumi Kondo died, and Miyazaki stepped back in. The forty-six-year-old Kondo had been Miyazaki's "heir apparent," a new-generation director who would lead the studio into the twenty-first century. *Spirited Away* was thus born out of some turmoil in the studio, which the movie's sometimes chaotic structure seems to reflect. But to my mind its intensity, opulent imagery, and sheer originality make it among the greatest, if not the greatest, of Miyazaki's films.

Like *Princess Mononoke*, *Spirited Away* also became a megahit in Japan and won a much wider audience overseas than had the previous film. The film impresses its audience in many ways. A coming-of-age story about a young girl, Chihiro, who must rescue her parents from a magical spell, the movie is a brilliant blend of fantasy and psychological realism. The fantasy is supported by Miyazaki's most flamboyant animation, a swirling riot of reds and blues, sometimes dazzlingly illuminated, at other times tinged by twilight hues. The animation gives life to the film's extraordinary locale, a magical village dominated by a towering red bathhouse. The bathhouse exists to nurture "tired gods" who are in need of purification, relaxation, and good food and are themselves as bizarre and memorable as the bathhouse they seek solace in.

The bathhouse is also suggestive of Ghibli itself. Within are harried male and female workers (in the film's vision they are frog men and slug women), and an even more overworked junior staff—the "soot sprites" of *Totoro* returning in a memorable and comic fashion. The soot sprites chatter, quarrel, and shirk work in a remarkably human way.

The management is even more distinctive. The head of the bathhouse is Yubaba, a powerful witch who can be as cantankerous and exacting with her staff as she is oily to customers. Yubaba occupies richly decorated rooms on the highest floor of the bathhouse and flies out at night on mysterious errands. Her enigmatic henchman is the handsome young boy Haku, who we eventually discover is a river spirit who came to learn magic from Yubaba and ended up being trapped by her. Finally, at the very bottom of the bathhouse lurks Kamaji, the many-armed boiler man, without whom the entire business would come to a halt.

Miyazaki has humorously suggested that Yubaba is actually Suzuki, whose work forces (or allows) him to leave the studio on interesting errands; later he acknowledged that Yubaba may actually be a hybrid of the two of them.[1] Yubaba also has an alter ego, her kindly twin sister Zeniba, who lives alone in an enchanting fairy-tale cottage, where she serves tea and cakes far from the hustle and bustle of the bathhouse. Given Miyazaki's tendency to explode and then apologize, it is quite possible that Yubaba and Zeniba manifest the two sides of his personality. Furthermore, Zeniba's fairy-tale-style thatched cottage may represent Miyazaki's yearnings for the "thatched hut" of the medieval hermit Kamo no Chōmei, combined with his youthful longing for Europe.

Miyazaki's admirer and follower the director Hideaki Anno, however, offers still another possibility. He suggests that it is Kamaji, the boiler man, who serves as Miyazaki's rueful fantasy of himself.[2] Without Kamaji's constant labor (aided by the soot sprites), the bathhouse would collapse. Furthermore, it is Kamaji who introduces the young human girl Chihiro, the movie's heroine, into the bathhouse and starts her on her adventures.

Kamaji or not, Miyazaki needed every ounce of energy and assistance he could find in the making of *Spirited Away*. Drawing on his own psyche, he created a work that is beautiful, moving, and spectacularly imaginative—and also outrageous, grotesque, and disturbing. Some of the disturbing elements are intentional—a means for Miyazaki to critique contemporary society using unforgettable imagery—but others seem to have emerged almost unconsciously. As he said to one interviewer, "When working on [*Spirited Away*] I frankly felt like I was lifting the lid on areas of my brain that I wasn't supposed to expose."[3] More generally he acknowledges, "When I'm creating a work I get the feeling that the general direction is always deep in my subconscious, in a place that I can't be fully aware of."[4] *Spirited Away*'s second half, with its Rabelaisian rampages followed by a quietly eerie train journey, evokes a nightmarish/dreamlike intensity unlike anything in Miyazaki's previous work.

Notwithstanding, the movie's frame narrative is both realistic and contemporary. In the course of its huge marketing campaign, the movie acquired the tagline "On the other side of the tunnel there was a mysterious and wonderful [*fushigi*] village." The phrase suggests the film's overall structure: a young girl named Chihiro and her parents, while moving to a new home, go through a tunnel and emerge into a fantastic realm. Within this fantasy realm Chihiro endures many trials and setbacks but works her way toward triumph and returns through the tunnel to the real world.

The term *fushigi* has connotations of the weird or strange (in the popular Japanese translation of *Alice's Adventures in Wonderland*, "Wonderland" is translated as the "fushigi country"), and the movie clearly separates its world into two spheres, the realm of fantasy and the space of reality. On one side of the tunnel is the drab reality of moving and starting at a new school. On the "other side" is a domain where anything can happen—and does. But the tunnel motif also suggests that these realms are connected, in ways that are mysterious and wonderful, just as our subconscious domain of feelings, memories, dreams, and nightmares connects to our waking life.

Like many dream (and nightmare) worlds, the bathhouse is full of monsters and spirits, unexpected friendships and shocking reversals, terrifying and amazing events. It is subversive yet seductive, transgressive and transformative. A "stink spirit," suspiciously resembling a slithering pile of excrement, forces its way into a bath and metamorphoses into an aged and very clean river god. Another spirit, fittingly known as No Face, transforms from a wispy blank-faced ghost into a colossus that devours the bathhouse inhabitants, only to vomit them up shortly afterward.

Perhaps most shocking of all is the transformation of Chihiro's parents, an out-of-the-blue event that starts the narrative moving. Soon after emerging from the tunnel, the three enter a mysterious restaurant. No one is there to serve them, so the parents start helping themselves to food and end up in an orgy of gorging. As anyone who has ever read a fairy tale knows, eating food in magical places without permission is sure to bring bad luck. Having gone exploring rather than join her greedy parents, Chihiro returns to find them transformed into two enormous pigs. Lurching off their stools, they fall comatose at her terrified feet. Later on she will discover her metamorphosed parents imprisoned in a sty, apparently slated to be turned into dinner for the bathhouse denizens.

The parents' transformation is genuinely terrifying and is meant to be so. I have mentioned previously the many "intimate apocalypses" that occur in Miyazaki's work, usually involving children dealing with an intimate and potentially traumatic loss.[5] These range from the mother's hospitalization

Chihiro's parents are transformed into pigs in *Spirited Away*, Studio Ghibli, 2001.

in *Totoro* to Kiki's separation from her parents in *Kiki's Delivery Service*. Chihiro's "apocalypse" is by far the most dramatic. She is separated from her parents not just physically but psychologically, in the most traumatic way possible. While we all may at moments consider our parents inhuman, Chihiro's parents have literally become beasts. It is left up to Chihiro to save them, by seeking employment at the bathhouse, the very place that cast the magic spell on them. Quaking and shaking, Chihiro enters the bathhouse to confront situations that at times will alienate and isolate her but that will ultimately transform her into a stronger and more mature individual.

Miyazaki wanted to send a message in *Spirited Away*. By the time he finished the film the director was sixty years old, old enough to understand the complexities of modern life but still vigorous enough to be angry and disappointed. The movie shares *Princess Mononoke*'s multilayered world that does not divide simplistically between good and evil, and retains its angry subtext. This time, however, Miyazaki leaves the distant world of the past to direct his anger at contemporary Japan.

By 2001, when the film opened, the country was mired in a culture of materialism that seemed an effort to allay a debilitating sense of spiritual emptiness through incessant consumption. While Miyazaki had once criticized American culture as one of excess, now excess was all around him. Even more disturbing, the Japanese landscape, both rural and urban, which was already under threat when *Totoro* came out, now seemed to be on life support. The government, in an attempt to jump-start the nation's long economic decline, had for decades promoted huge construction projects around the country. The flood of concrete destroyed forests, poured over beaches and mountains, and dammed up virtually every waterway that still flowed freely. Fast-food outlets and vending machines invaded the highways, and convenience stores took over city streets.

In Miyazaki's eyes the distortions of money and industry darkened not only the external landscape of Japan but the interior spiritual landscape of its citizens. Never one to mince words, the director had become increasingly impassioned in his denunciations of the modern world. "The whole world seemed covered in concrete," he declared.[6] His film images had even more potency. It is no accident that two of the most memorable characters in *Spirited Away* are river spirits, one shackled by pollution, the other by urban construction.

Miyazaki directed much of his message at parents, or more specifically the generation of Japanese in their thirties and forties whom he saw as gluttonous, consumption-mad, and uncaring. In *Spirited Away* he shows Chihiro's father driving a flashy new Audi and boasting of his cash and credit cards as he obliviously gobbles vast quantities of food at the mysterious restaurant. Miyazaki also marks Chihiro's mother as passive and cold, calmly following her husband while reprimanding Chihiro for "clinging" to her.

But the director also wanted to send a message to Chihiro's generation, or more specifically to the ten-year-old daughter of a colleague. With characteristic forcefulness, in a discussion of the film Miyazaki referred to this girl and her friends as "dullards."[7] Their pursuits increasingly alarmed him. The director had long bemoaned the fact that so few children played outside any more. He suggested that they should stop watching Ghibli videos on television and go outside to experience the real world for a change. Overall, Miyazki hated the waves of apathy and indifference emanating from the young "dullards" around him. It is not surprising that the path to redemption taken by *Spirited Away*'s ten-year-old heroine leads through hard physical labor, self-discipline, acceptance of and kindness to others, and a willingness to take on challenges.

To create the bathhouse world in which Chihiro labors, Miyazaki reworked elements of old Japan and the new affluent Japan. He drew inspiration both from traditional bathhouses scattered across Japan and from a modern, flamboyant wedding palace in Tokyo, the Meguro Gajoen: multistoried with vast high-ceilinged rooms, enormous elegant elevators, and gorgeously appointed restrooms, the Gajoen is a contemporary dream world.

He based the "wonderful and strange" village encircling his bathhouse on an open-air architectural museum of prewar buildings in the Tokyo suburbs near Ghibli that the director loved to visit. As the scholar Shiro Yoshioka points out, in *Spirited Away* Miyazaki "infused" the past with his personal memories, creating a sense of "collective identity."[8] As with *Totoro,* he seduced viewers with emotionally resonant images of a lost Japan combined with contemporary references. The bathhouse symbolizes centuries-old traditions of cleanliness and purification now used to revitalize the exhausted gods, who no longer seem welcome in the contemporary world.

As a film director and a master animator, Miyazaki had the tools to do something more practical and exciting than simply berate the younger generation with angry words. Almost miraculously, he constructed a "message" movie that was neither bullying nor boring. *Spirited Away* uses adventure, magic, and a touch of romance to invite the viewer into a topsy-turvy world

Gajoen, the modern wedding palace that inspired *Spirited Away*'s bathhouse

Photo by Stephen Coit

The Edo-Tokyo museum that inspired *Spirited Away*'s village. Photo by Stephen Coit

that critiques our own but leaves open the possibility of transcending the darkness it sometimes evokes.

This is accomplished partly through the beauty of Miyazaki's animation, including some startling metamorphoses, but also through the audience's identification with the movie's wide-ranging group of strange yet often appealing characters. In addition to the bathhouse workers and management are the varied spirits who visit, most notably, the black-robed creature No Face. No Face plays a dominant role in the film's second half, his protean weirdness suggesting not simply fantasy monstrosity but also the alienation Miyazaki saw everywhere among young Japanese. More universally sympathetic is Chihiro, who evolves from "dullard" to competent young heroine. Miyazaki described her as an "utterly ordinary young girl," and at the movie's beginning her whiny ways and bratty behavior contrast significantly with even his most realistic heroines from earlier movies, such as Kiki or Satsuki.[9] In the complex world of twenty-first-century Japan, such an "ordinary" character who still manages to triumph against the odds might have seemed particularly appealing.

Even by Miyazaki's somewhat elastic standards, *Spirited Away* was an unconventional piece of filmmaking, producing blood, sweat, and tears at Studio Ghibli. Miyazaki describes his staff as "crumbling" (*boroboro*) by the time work on the movie finally ended.[10] *Princess Mononoke* had exhausted the veteran staff to the point where some had left the studio, replaced by enthusiastic but inexperienced newcomers. As a result, the filmmaking moved so slowly that for the first time the studio had to outsource to non-Japanese contractors. The director Hideaki Anno, in discussing the film, spoke approvingly of its "Asian" look, especially its flamboyant colors and architecture. In truth, the movie is a visual hodgepodge that includes Western, Asian, and traditional Japanese elements.[11] Its final third is partly an homage to one of Japan's best-loved fantasy stories.

The movie somehow weaves all these factors together to create a seamless filmic experience. But it almost didn't. Midway through the movie, members of the senior Ghibli staff realized that they could not possibly finish it according to plan. As Miyazaki became ever more mired in exploring details ranging from Yubaba's backstory to the economic structures supporting the bathhouse, the film grew more complicated, unwieldy, and long.

As Miyazaki tells it: "On a nonwork day I happened to come to the studio and found that the producer [Suzuki] was wandering around, and I also noticed the screen director suddenly appear, and then the art director. So the four of us got together and, using a blackboard, I explained to them how the story was going to develop. And I realized as I was explaining it to them that we were in deep trouble—if we went on like this we would never be able to finish the story." Not wanting to extend the filmmaking for another year, the group realized that they needed to "throw out the entire framework." What next? "We suddenly changed the story or rather we narrowed it down. . . . There was that strange figure, No Face, that stood on the bridge and we decided to bring him into the story more. And very hastily in two or three days the whole project was rethought and only after that we finally began to see how it could come together."[12]

What had been a fairly conventional fantasy adventure now became something very different. Miyazaki's original proposal had Chihiro making an alliance with Haku, Yubaba's henchman, and the two overthrowing Yubaba. At another point he considered having No Face grow to giant size and destroy the bathhouse.

Neither scenario occurred. Although Chihiro and Haku do develop a positive, even potentially romantic relationship, and No Face at one point does grow to an alarming size, the film's focus remains strongly on Chihiro's moral and emotional evolution in relationship to the evolving monstrous personality of No Face. The film's real excitement lies in Chihiro's growing maturity confronting No Face's increasingly bizarre actions rather than in an obvious and violent climax.

The new direction required some major additions and changes. Miyazaki had already constructed scenes of Chihiro's gaining admission to the bathhouse's labor force and had worked out a memorable episode of her scrubbing down the stink spirit to reveal his true identity as a river god soiled by pollution. But now, he added an eerie scene midway through the movie in which Chihiro glimpses No Face standing lonely outside in the rain and invites him in. From this point on Chihiro's relationship with No Face plays a dominant role in the film.

Chihiro's admittance of No Face creates havoc. The creature first tries to buy her love with gold pieces and magical services and, when thwarted, begins to terrorize the bathhouse. Sometimes he bribes the bathhouse workers with gold so that they dance attendance on him, plying him with boatloads of delicious-looking food; at other times he simply stuffs the workers themselves down his gigantic sharp-toothed mouth in a cannibalistic feeding frenzy. It is finally up to Chihiro to contain him. She does so by offering him part of a magic dumpling that she had hoped to feed her parents, thereby breaking their spell. Her offering is effective, but not until the bathhouse has becomes a spectacle of appetite grown to truly grotesque proportions as No Face rampages. Ultimately he begins vomiting out the bath attendants, along with copious amounts of what looks to be bile or black blood.

Miyazaki does not allow the chaos to continue to all-out destruction, but No Face's appetites threaten the stability of the bathhouse. In response, Chihiro rejects excess appetite; she becomes a small, sturdy beacon of self-control in a world of extravagance. Food—its absence or presence—becomes the force that shapes the two of them. Neither outright denial nor feverish consumption, Miyazaki suggests, can really support a satisfying life.

Food has played a role, usually a positive one, in every Miyazaki film. But in *Spirited Away* nourishment comes across in a variety of intricate and seemingly antithetical ways, as the early scene of Chihiro's parent's transformation augurs. Sometimes food appears as bitter medicine, sometimes as comfort cuisine. There is a lovely scene, for example, when Haku offers rice balls to a miserable Chihiro, telling her that he has "put a spell on them." The real spell is the nurturing, homey quality of the rice balls themselves, a signifier of traditional Japanese culture.

At other times the movie pathologizes food. With Chihiro's parents and with No Face, food is dangerous and addictive. At still other times it performs an openly transgressive role linked to vomitus (No Face) and excrement (the stink spirit). Ultimately, however, food not only serves as commentary on the excesses of contemporary society but provides a path to a more meaningful existence.

At the beginning the film depicts Chihiro as a literal manifestation of anorexia, pointedly rejecting the food her parents are gorging on.[13] After they turn into pigs, she finds that her own body is beginning to disappear: "I'm see-through!" she wails. It is at this point she encounters Haku, who forces her to eat a magic berry that will restore her corporeality. Even here, however, we see her trying to reject the berry, screwing up her face in horror. In these early stages, Miyazaki defines Chihiro by abnegation, as if the only way to deal with the world is to reject it. For a director so concerned with children, the vision of a vanishing child is a serious one indeed.

Chihiro in this early scene is disgusted by and alienated from a world over which she has no control. Cultural critic Susan Bordo has linked anorexia to "our modern fear of loss of control over our future," pointing out that the body is "perhaps one of the few areas of control we have left in the twentieth century."[14] Chihiro's rejection of food begins as a rejection of parental authority and ends up, when she tries to reject the food that Haku gives her, as an attempted denial of the frightening outside world.

No Face is Chihiro's opposite. The creature goes from a virtually bodiless spectral presence to a gigantic monster of consumption, characterized by his enormous gaping mouth. Even more disturbing, he then becomes an emblem of bulimia, vomiting what he has ingested. The scenes of No Face's rampage are as disgusting as they are unforgettable, far more extreme than anything Miyazaki had previously created. Viewers can appreciate them simply for their sheer outrageousness or as intriguing social criticism.

While anorexia is about a desperate search for control, bulimia is about excess and self-punishment for excess. Both are linked to the very real ills of contemporary society. Bordo connects bulimia to consumer capitalism, suggesting that it is a characteristic of "modern personality construction."[15] But No Face can also be viewed in specifically Japanese terms. Another tagline emblazoned on one of the posters for *Spirited Away* was a rather surprising one: "There is a bit of No Face in all of us."

In three decades as an animator, Miyazaki had created an exceptional pantheon of supernatural characters, from the Rock Man of *Horus: Prince of the Sun* to the ectoplasmic shishigami who rules the forest in *Princess Mononoke*, but No Face is perhaps both the simplest and most complicated of Miyazaki's inventions. His archetypal black garb and white masklike face make him an easy target for projection of our own fears and desires.

Initially, No Face seems shy and lonely, a sad ghost unable to speak except for plaintive-sounding grunts. Once inside the dream world of the bath-house and its extravagant sensual pleasures, he becomes a demonic force of greed, his gigantic gaping mouth emblemizing an unquenchable desire. On his own, No Face can find no middle course that would allow him to inter-act with the other bathhouse denizens in a wholesome or fulfilling way. His frenzied actions suggest anger but conceal more complicated inner conflicts.

It bears repeating that No Face sprang almost spontaneously from a part of Miyazaki's brain that had gone into overdrive as time ticked down on the movie's production process. In relation to the vomiting scene, the direc-tor specifically speaks of the "need to spit everything out."[16] An emanation from the dark side of the unconscious, this raging id of aggression and other antisocial behaviors apparently struck a chord among viewers. Especially in Japan, a nation that still places an enormous priority on conformity, disci-pline, and self-control, No Face's antisocial actions seem strangely liberating.

These antisocial elements may include sexuality. Miyazaki has men-tioned that Suzuki describes No Face as a "stalker."[17] At one moment No Face cries out longingly for "Sen" (Chihiro), but it is clear that he wants to control her and hoard her love. Bathhouses in Japan have also served as places of prostitution, and the fact that No Face offers Chihiro money in exchange for her love is suggestive.

But sexual services can serve as metaphors for many other things, and it is clear that the void that animates No Face is more than carnal. In his emptiness and despair, and with his desires that can never be satisfied, he becomes a symbol for the most alienating aspects of modern life. Miyazaki's solution to this behavior, embodied in *Spirited Away*'s final twenty minutes, is as original and imaginative as the rest of the film. We have seen that he had considered having No Face grow ever more enormous to the point where he would become a shishigami-type monster, destroying the bathhouse in a frenzy of cathartic destruction. Instead, Miyazaki offers something very dif-ferent, a train ride into yet another fantasy world, this time one of tranquility and simplicity.

Realizing that No Face is "only bad in the bathhouse," Chihiro resigns herself to bringing the creature along on a personal quest, riding on a magical train above a glittering sea, and then taking a short walk to the cottage owned by Zeniba, Yubaba's more kindly but still powerful twin sister. The ostensible purpose of the journey is to return a magical seal stolen by Haku in his role as Yubaba's henchman. Haku himself has metamorphosed into dragon form and lies at the point of death, despite Chihiro's giving him the last of the magic dumpling that she had been saving for her parents.

It is Chihiro's love for Haku that makes her willing to seek out Zeniba, hoping that the return of the seal will save him. Accompanying Chihiro and No Face are two other bathhouse refugees, a bird now turned into a buzzing insect and Yubaba's own baby boy, Bo, a bratty, querulous child whom Zeniba has transformed into a surprisingly cute mouse.

Other directorial hands might have made this journey into a rollicking quest, with Chihiro as an adventurous heroine accompanied by her oddly assorted trio of friends, concluding, perhaps, with a final confrontation with Zeniba reminiscent of *The Wizard of Oz*. Miyazaki does something radically different. Again digging into his subconscious, he creates a vision that is not quite escapist, not quite sublime, but suggestive of a therapeutic progression into the depths of the soul.

The train ride itself is like a dream within a dream. Besides Chihiro and her friends, the only other passengers are shadows. Shadows also appear at the few stops the train makes—we see a silhouette of a man in a hat and a little girl in an old-fashioned dress. The distinctions drawn between the train and the brilliantly colored, populous world of the bathhouse could not be more obvious. This is a ride away from stress, pressure, noise, and complexity.

Miyazaki was intensely proud of this sequence. In a long interview about *Spirited Away* with the critic Yōichi Shibuya he returns frequently to his decision to create the train ride. It was immensely important to him, and he had planned it for a long time, telling his increasingly worried staff, "Eventually, she's going to catch the train." He calls it the "climax" of the movie, saying, "All the chasing around, it was leading up to this."[18]

Why did Miyazaki place such importance on this quiet climax? Revealingly, he says, "I didn't want to destroy the bathhouse. I was worried about how tough it would be on the poor sad gods who went to the bathhouse."[19] After the stresses of *Princess Mononoke* the director seemed to be ready for something calmer, both in his life and in his art.

Chihiro's decision to take the train indicates her final step toward independence. Miyazaki explains, "I wanted to write a story where the girl catches the train with her own will in a world that she experiences for the first time. We know that she is very afraid and unsure of what to do."[20]

The haunting quality of the train journey might suggest that it is a metaphor for death. Although this interpretation could have a source as early as Freud's *The Interpretation of Dreams,* there is also a more local inspiration, for the journey was partly an homage to the director's favorite Japanese fantasy writer, Kenji Miyazawa. Writing in the early twentieth century, Miyazawa had created an array of extraordinary fantasies, most famous the novella *Night on the Galactic Railroad* (Ginga Tetsudō no yoru, 1934). *Night on the Galactic Railroad* features two young boys taking a train to the stars. One of them, we discover at the end of the story, is dead, having drowned in a pond during a festival.

Miyazaki acknowledges the novella's influence on *Spirited Away,* but he does not discuss its implications of death, probably because his own version of the railroad trip is so clearly a journey into life. After Chihiro and her friends leave the train, they find another world of serenity and coziness inside Zeniba's rustic thatched cottage. There she feeds the travelers tea and cakes, offering an alternative culinary path of moderation in contrast to No Face's bulimic outbursts in the bathhouse or Chihiro's panicked abnegation at the beginning of the film. If Yubaba is the "bad" or at least strict mother of the bathhouse, Zeniba is the mother who comforts and cares.[21] She even offers No Face a place to live, promising to give him fulfilling work.

This vision of moderation and a healthy, wholesome lifestyle undoubtedly appealed to Miyazaki. Over the previous decade the director had begun to envision a separate studio for senior Ghibli staff members—himself included, of course. In his idealized vision, the senior staff members would give wise advice (tea and cakes perhaps?), while the new young talent produced another generation of films.

Appealing though the vision was, it was never quite realized. In this regard it is interesting that Miyazaki couldn't bring himself to "destroy the bathhouse" and that at the film's end he sends the newly independent and empowered Chihiro back to it one last time. Once there, however, she sees her former place of employment and her fellow workers in a new light, kissing Yubaba on the cheek and waving merrily at her former colleagues.

Most important, she realizes that her parents are not the pigs that Yubaba shows to her. Chihiro's enlightened vision can be read as a child's maturation into understanding that her parents are not, in fact, beasts, Miyazaki's ultimate message to the ten-year-old girls whom he wanted to reach through the film. But it is also possible, as Shibuya rather boldly suggests, that Chihiro's new vision implies a new Miyazaki, with a "different worldview" that incorporates and accepts friends and foe.[22] Miyazaki would go on to both strengthen and test that new worldview in his next film, *Howl's Moving Castle,* another work that revolves around journeys, both inner and outer.

# 13
# The Castle, the Curse, and the Collectivity
## Howl's Moving Castle

Old age hath yet his honor and his toil.

—ALFRED, LORD TENNYSON

*Spirited Away*'s climax, according to Miyazaki, was the magical train ride that took Chihiro and her friends away from the hectic pace of the bathhouse to a space of peace and nurturing comfort. As its title suggests, his next feature film, *Howl's Moving Castle,* also emphasizes activity, but this time of a more random and more extreme nature. *Howl* features an imaginatively rendered castle that is large and imposing but also ramshackle, higgledy-piggledy and in danger of breaking apart. If *Spirited Away*'s bathhouse hierarchy was one vision of Studio Ghibli, it seems likely that the precariously moving castle of *Howl* is another vision of the studio. Howl's castle dominates the movie, and first its dissolution against a fiery background of a world at war, then its ultimate rebuilding into a site of support and security suggest both Miyazaki's despair at present-day circumstances and his utopian hopes for a better future.

Miyazaki had just begun work on *Howl's Moving Castle* when *Spirited Away* received the Academy Award for best animated film in 2003. The Academy had established the award the previous year, when it had gone to *Shrek.*

For a Japanese movie to win an Oscar in competition with American films (including, this time, two from Disney) was an unprecedented honor. The media in Japan went wild.

Miyazaki, however, did not go to Los Angeles to accept the Oscar. He had experienced the Hollywood scene, thanks to the enthusiastic ministrations of John Lasseter, the brilliant head of Pixar Animation Studio. It was Lasseter whom Suzuki had approached to help with the marketing of *Spirited Away*, a task that the studio head performed admirably. He persuaded Disney to get behind the movie and also helped in the all-important casting of English-language voice actors for the film's many distinctive characters. Lasseter had hosted Suzuki and Miyazaki, proudly giving the director a ride on an antique plane and plying him with fancy meals and a visit to his California vineyard.[1]

It was not satiety with Hollywood that caused Miyazaki's nonappearance at what would have been for most people a major celebratory moment. The director would later explain his disgust at the American-led invasion of Iraq as the prime motivator: "I felt an intense rage. For that reason I hesitated to accept the Academy Award.... The war in Iraq had a great influence on me."[2]

Miyazaki's fury over the Iraq invasion was strong enough to make him add a war theme to *Howl*, but he may have been angry for other reasons as well. In an interview following *Howl*'s completion, Suzuki mentions that Miyazaki had become furious on hearing rumors that *Spirited Away*'s success had been due solely to its all-out marketing campaign (led, of course, by Suzuki). The producer describes a tense confrontation between the director and Ghibli staffers in which Miyazaki asked, "Which do you think? Was *Spirited Away* a hit because of the quality of the story or the quality of the marketing?" When one lone staffer insisted on the importance of the marketing campaign, Miyazaki lost his temper. "In that case, Mr. Suzuki," he said, "there will be no marketing for *Howl's Moving Castle*."[3]

Given how much effort the studio and its parent company Tokuma had put into marketing previous Ghibli films, this was a stunning announcement. The marketing campaign for *Howl* indeed proved low-profile, Miyazaki notably absent from it. But the strong reaction he displayed at the staff meeting (Suzuki describes the director as being "traumatized") underlined a complex set of dissatisfactions.[4]

As was the case with *Kiki,* Miyazaki stepped in only after a great deal of preliminary work had been done on the film. A fan of the book *Howl* is based on, he traveled to the United Kingdom to meet with its author Diana Wynne Jones, who remembers a "wonderful conversation" while the two consumed a huge cake. The studio, however, had initially slated the movie to be directed by someone outside Ghibli, the talented young director Mamoru Hosoda. A team had gone on location to Great Britain, and work was well under way when most of the team was let go and Miyazaki stepped in as director. The reasons were vague; the Ghibli historian Seiji Kano speaks of some kind of "trouble," using the English word.[5]

While staff changes had happened before, the amount of chopping and changing at such a late date points to stresses at the studio. In some ways this might seem counterintuitive. By 2003 Miyazaki and his fellow senior Ghibli associates had established a thriving company. Located in a spacious modern building in a quiet suburb outside of Tokyo that was still directly accessible to downtown, the studio stood next door to Miyazaki's own dedicated workplace, a charming European-looking atelier with high ceilings and a circular staircase.

What the director had envisioned as early as *Kiki's Delivery Service* had largely been achieved. The company's one hundred–plus workers had unusual job security in the uncertain animation business. The studio had even added a nursery for the children of the staff. Over the previous decade, under Miyazaki's direction and with the design help of his son Goro, Ghibli had also established the Ghibli Museum nearby, an enchanting place that manages to be simultaneously low-key and enthralling, so much so that there are monthlong waits to buy tickets. Structured on the principle of art being created out of "an accumulation of things of the past," the collection parallels the "accumulated" quality of the castle's architecture in *Howl* and the multiple inspirations for *Spirited Away.*[6]

Ghibli's most impressive achievement was its decade long string of hits, not only films by Miyazaki but such works as Takahata's *Pom Poko* (Heisei tanuki gassen pompoko, 1994) and the subtle romance *Whisper of the Heart* (Mimi o sumaseba, 1995), directed by the deceased Yoshifumi Kondo. Box-office records secured Ghibli's economic foundations, and the *Spirited Away* Oscar had made Miyazaki even more of a celebrity than had *Princess Mononoke.*

Increasingly unwilling to appear in public and, in the few interviews he gave, pessimistic to the edge of nihilism, Miyazaki kept his distance. Undoubtedly the studio's success led to further feelings of pressure. Although he often talked about retiring and of the need for raising a new generation of directors, his taking over the helm of *Howl,* combined with Hosoda's subsequent departure to establish his own studio, hinted at internal conflicts. Whereas Hosoda had spoken of creating a movie that would be "fun," Miyazaki expressed his wish to make a "melodrama set among the fires of war."[7]

The final product, despite its relative lack of advertising, was another blockbuster hit in Japan; with an international première at the Venice Film Festival, *Howl* would go on to become Miyazaki's highest-grossing film overseas. Admittedly, some critics in Japan and elsewhere had issues with its quality, finding it hard to understand. More recently Shunsuke Sugita has called the movie a "failure."[8] To these critics, Miyazaki's single-minded portrait of melodrama combined with war was a rough-edged work, difficult to comprehend, tied awkwardly together, and with a forced and artificial happy ending.

On the whole, I tend to agree with Seiji Kano's positive assessment of *Howl* as a work more poetic than narrative, stringing together a tapestry of images to create a multifaceted whole.[9] Overall it remains an idiosyncratic and appealing creation—ambitious and angry, while offering indelible visions of solace, beauty, and love.

One of its most poignant scenes is a brief flashback to when the film's wizard protagonist, Howl, captured a shooting star. Miyazaki had been haunted by such a vision from his college days, and he has said that one of the reasons he became an animator was to create just this scene. In many ways the movie itself can be likened to a shooting star, sometimes dark and dense, at other times sending off radiant sparks, reaffirming Nausicaä's dictum that "Life is the light that shines in the darkness."

The movie combines scenes of battle and destruction with episodes of romance and tenderness between its unlikely protagonists, a narcissistic young wizard and a young girl, Sophie, who has been changed into an aged crone by a witch's curse, a potentially dark premise. Through Sophie *Howl* deals unflinchingly with the pains of old age, an issue of huge concern in Japan, where the rapid aging of its population is viewed with alarm. At the same time the movie uses fantasy to process fears of aging and death in an ultimately optimistic fashion. While it acknowledges the darkness of human nature, the movie's upbeat ending offers a collectivity that is diverse, loving, and supportive. The movie is a kind of valentine to the director's older colleagues, especially his many older female staff members, demonstrating that old age can be liberating rather than diminishing.

The first in Miyazaki's final trio of films, *Howl* encapsulates many elements of what we might call "late Miyazakiworld." It shares with the subsequent *Ponyo* and *The Wind Rises* a youthful energy that belies its creator's age, showing his still vital desire to shock audiences out of complacency. In all three films Miyazaki actively confronts a twenty-first-century world in which tradition, history, and even magic seem to be fading fast. While *Spirited Away* also critiqued contemporary life, the final three films can be seen as even more activist. Rather than simply indictments, they are conscious and sometimes angry forms of resistance confronting a universe that appears to have become increasingly fragmented, anomic, and indifferent.

Howl's castle can be seen as its own form of resistance to a sterile materialistic world. In this regard Miyazaki is probably building on Diana Wynne Jones's conception of the castle as a liberating and magical entity, but the director uses the original novel more as a base upon which to put his own idiosyncratic scaffolding.

He does keep the novel's basic story line: After Sophie is transformed by the Witch of the Waste into a ninety-year-old woman, she leaves her town and wanders out into the wasteland, where she finds shelter in a mysterious castle that moves from place to place on what appear to be chicken legs. Sophie discovers that the castle is owned by the notorious wizard Howl, who turns out to be a narcissistic young man prone to breaking hearts and "slithering out" of any difficult situation. She also discovers that Howl has made a secret pact with a fire demon, Calcifer, to whom he has given control of his heart in exchange for magical powers. Sophie manages to get Howl to take her on as castle housekeeper, and the relationship between the two of them, initially cantankerous, gradually evolves into something sweeter. Sophie's crotchety love ultimately rescues Howl from his egoism and cowardice, and the story ends with Sophie returning (more or less) to young womanhood and the two of them marrying.

A good deal of critical attention focused on the significant differences between the book and the movie. Jones's novel was inspired by the *Ballad of Tamlin,* a song from British folklore concerning a young girl who rescues her lover from the clutches of the fairy queen who has him under a spell. The novel plays with the classic rules of the fairy-tale genre to create a fantasy romance that comments on the nature of fairy tales and the paradoxes of fate.

Miyazaki kept the magic spell and love story motif but added war as a central theme in the movie. While Jones's novel contains a brief mention of a war that the cowardly and frivolous Howl is trying to "slither out of," war becomes the framework against which the movie's action takes place. Miyazaki grafts onto the book a vivid depiction of brutal and unnecessary combat in which magicians turn into winged weapons of destruction, cities burst into flames, and the castle of the novel's title falls catastrophically apart. Howl, initially passive and vain, becomes a fierce and angry resister to the war.

Miyazaki also creates a charming visual tapestry for the movie, centering on traditional half-timbered European-style towns (a trip to Alsace provided inspiration). While Miyazaki incorporates gloomy images of industrialization, such as the smoke-belching trains that rumble by the hat shop where Sophie works, he balances these with light-filled gardens and sumptuous natural vistas. In one characteristically distinctive scene he offers an image of a shimmering lake amid alpine mountains. Beside it Sophie and two companions, Howl's acolyte Markl and a magically transformed scarecrow, hang up laundry in a sequence that mixes fantasy with domesticity.

The castle in Jones's book had magical properties, not only in its ability to move but in its many doors that opened on to different parts of the world. Miyazaki retains these powers but makes the castle even more formidable, creating a contradictory space that is both organic and mechanical, one that evokes the past, permanency, and tradition while at the same time suggesting speed, change, and fragmentation.

Long fascinated by castles, Miyazaki makes Howl's castle virtually a "star" in its own right, a visual tour de force encapsulating many properties that castles have shown throughout history. A place of power but also a site of intimacy and security, it evolves from being a source of both supernatural and military force into a refuge for a hodgepodge of creatures, a site for lovers' quarrels and trials, and also a repository for Howl's heart, literally encased at the center of the castle. Unlike the edifice in Miyazaki's earlier *Castle of Cagliostro,* the castle imprisons (while apparently empowering) not a beautiful young woman but rather the wizard Howl. In a reverse of traditional fairy-tale motifs, it is he who must be rescued, and not by a young girl, but by an old woman.

Howl's castle takes center stage from the film's opening image, a gigantic lumbering *thing* emerging through the mists on the horizon to swelling music. The opening shots concentrate totally on the castle's exterior. Miyazaki grants us glimpses through rolling clouds of a rugged metallic façade studded with towers, drainpipes, eyelike formations, and even a large tongue protruding from the object's front. Another shot shows us the castle's bony legs and feet, proceeding, almost prancing, across a steep ridge.

The Japanese critic Mari Kotani sees the castle as a "symbol of postmodernism," describing it as a "distorted collection of junk, resembling a monster assembled out of scrap iron but, despite that, still looking like a gigantic living creature." To my mind, this jumbled aspect is not simply aesthetic but also spiritual, suggesting what Carl Cassegard, in discussing contemporary Japanese society, describes as the "fragmented consciousness" of the modern condition.[10]

In a thought-provoking essay on the movie, Dominick Chen describes the castle as a dynamic "autopoetic system," a living thing continually regenerating itself based on Howl's and the fire demon Calcifer's "emotional feedback." Chen sees the castle's many portals as a metaphor for the internet, with Howl as a "lone hacker" who "uses his magic techniques (technology), builds a network, collects data and tries to change the world through his own talents."[11] Whether we see Howl as a bona fide hacker, his ability to go freely between worlds marks the castle's openness (and vulnerability) to the outside environment.

Howl's castle, in its crazy-quilt construction, ability to zip across space, and openness to its surroundings, suggests the complex and unstable conditions that characterize the contemporary world. At the same time it can also trace its history back over a long line of Miyazaki's castles. These go beyond the obvious castles such as the ones in *Cagliostro* or *Laputa*. The fortress of Tatara in *Princess Mononoke* and the towering bathhouse in *Spirited Away*, both ruled by female leaders, are castlelike structures. The castle in *Howl* initially seems to go against this paradigm of feminine control, since it is explicitly referred to as "Howl's Moving Castle," and the wizard is not only its owner but also apparently its creator. In fact, the situation is more complicated. Howl operates his castle through his contract with the fire demon Calcifer, voiced by a male actor. Thus control of the castle, while masculine, is inherently fragmented from its inception.

Then Sophie appears, adding a feminine note. Although she has forced her way into the castle out of cold and desperation, once inside she imposes her own element of control, by cooking and cleaning. While Sophie's position as housekeeper suggests a more conventional role for her than many of Miyazaki's other heroines, Kotani points out that Sophie's cleaning of the castle is really the cleaning up of Howl's personality, a daunting task.[12] In her nurturing zeal, Sophie becomes another in Miyazaki's pantheon of rescuing mother figures, going back at least as far as Nausicaä.

Far from being beautiful or even imposing, the castle when Sophie discovers it is essentially a den of a vain and superficial adolescent boy. Filthy, cobwebbed, and uncomfortable, the castle has one interior luxury, Howl's bathroom, but even that is so covered with oozing unguents that Sophie has to avert her eyes when she first cleans it. Her determined tackling of the castle's filth and untidiness not only harks back to Chihiro's valiant efforts to clean up the pollution in the bathhouse in *Spirited Away* but also suggests a means of working through the trauma of her curse of old age by summoning up reserves of perseverance and energy.

The power of curses and spells is another major theme in *Howl's Moving Castle,* and it links the movie with other important works in Miyazaki-world. Curses have far-ranging connotations—relating to issues of magic, ritual, fate, and identity. Although magic plays an important and positive role in *Laputa* and *Kiki,* curses and spells are virtually absent in Miyazaki's earlier works. It is perhaps no accident that they begin to surge into view as Miyazaki reached middle age, appearing first in Marco, the protagonist of 1992's *Porco Rosso.*

Curses and spells in Miyazaki's fantasies frequently have devastating effects, such as the dying boar's curse that exiles Ashitaka from his tribe and threatens his ultimate death in *Princess Mononoke,* or Yubaba's spell on Haku that deprives him of his memory in *Spirited Away.* Even when they are not always totally effective, such as in *Ponyo,* when Ponyo's father attempts to return her to fish form, they are examples of attempts at power and control. Overall, the proliferation of curses and spells in Miyazaki's later work adds a darker undercurrent to his films, evoking a world that seems increasingly arbitrary, ungovernable, and mysterious.

Curses abound in *Howl* and include the curse of old age inflicted on Sophie by the Witch of the Waste. Rather than causing Sophie to despair, however, this forced metamorphosis spurs her into action, as she quickly finds employment in Howl's castle. In a conventional fantasy one might expect the rest of the story to revolve around Sophie's attempts to dispel her curse, but Sophie's spell seems to work itself out rather painlessly, through her diligent cleaning and her increasing fondness for and nurturing of Howl. Her growing strength and maturity and her love for Howl bring her to an increasingly active position in the castle. By the movie's end, while Howl is learning to protect her, she becomes determined to protect not only him but the other inhabitants in the castle, who by this time include Calcifer, Howl's young disciple Markl, a transformed and reformed Witch of the Waste, and the wheezy old dog Heen.

Indeed, Sophie's curse, even with all the attendant aches and pains that her transformed ninety-year-old body accumulates, can be seen as a form of liberation. She gains confidence in the castle. Whereas the eighteen-year-old, physically fit Sophie would have been too shy to ask for lodging, the ninety-year-old Sophie's physical decrepitude compels her to force her way inside. Although initially she is a supplicant, asking Calcifer to allow her to stay, Sophie soon becomes a formidable presence, developing a new identity through work, a characteristic shared with Miyazaki's younger heroines such as Kiki or Chihiro.

Sophie's transformation into an elderly woman also aids in her developing relationship with Howl, because she cannot use flirtatiousness or sexuality, which the shy eighteen-year-old Sophie would have been loath to do in any case. She must rely on her intelligence and wit and her shared concern with Howl for the welfare of the castle and its denizens.

Kotani makes the radical suggestion that Sophie's real curse was a more insidious and earlier one—to be a young girl.[13] It is, after all, young girls who are constrained by society and expected to behave in certain ways, such as being charming or flirtatious. When we first encounter Sophie, she seems to be rejecting that role, even insisting on wearing a dowdy hat, in marked contrast to the gorgeous headwear available in her shop. But it is her metamorphosis into old age that allows her to reject the constraints of young femininity most definitively.

Although Miyazaki has consistently shown young girls breaking this

Sophie snores while Calcifer looks on in *Howl's Moving Castle,* Studio Ghibli, 2004.

constrained paradigm in terms of both action and attitude, his previous shōjo characters were feminine and cute. In contrast, the elderly Sophie, with her protruding nose, wrinkled visage, and sagging, stumpy body is decidedly not cute in the conventional meaning of the term. The director even includes a scene of her snoring by the fireside, an inconceivable image for any of his other young heroines. Even at the film's end she retains the traits of self-reliance, compassion, and forthrightness that her metamorphosis had nurtured, symbolized by her retention of silver hair while the rest of her body regains its youth.

If Sophie's aging is not "really" a curse, then is there a genuine curse in the movie? Actually, there are many, including the traditional types of spells that hold Calcifer imprisoned in the castle's hearth or transform a prince into a scarecrow. But from the point of view of contemporary society, a more meaningful, albeit a more amorphous, form of curse is the constrained condition that shackles the young wizard Howl. Following the original novel, Miyazaki initially presents Howl as a selfish and conceited breaker of hearts, who apparently uses his magic simply for his own egocentric purposes. Ultimately we understand, as in the book, that Howl is shackled by his contract with the fire demon Calcifer, who possesses his heart. While perhaps not a curse in the technical sense, this spell dictates his inability to develop into a compassionate adult; his heart/soul remains that of a callow adolescent.

But Miyazaki adds another kind of constraint for Howl, one that could properly be called a spiritual form of curse. This is Howl's growing indignation and horror at the war that is widening around him and the other denizens of the castle. Howl's fury at the war ultimately turns him into a terrifying beast of prey, a transformation that almost becomes permanent.

The film version of *Howl* goes beyond Jones's idiosyncratic magical romance to offer a vision of a world in which armaments are turning the environment into a "sea of fire" that threatens to engulf not only Sophie and Howl but the other innocent civilians who inhabit the towns around them. Howl's relationship with Sophie spurs the development of his own moral consciousness, and he becomes unable to tolerate the war or the actions of his fellow magicians who lend their powers to warmongers. As he says to Sophie at a climactic point of the narrative, "I've finally found something I wanted to protect. And that is you."

Howl's justifiable rage at the indiscriminate brutality around him is not necessarily a negative condition. Initially his metamorphosis into a winged creature fighting the other magicians suggests new depths of passion and righteousness in his soul. But his continued transformation begins to threaten his human identity. Calcifer warns Howl that he may ultimately not be able to turn back into a human being.

As Howl makes nightly sorties against the enemy, he grows closer and closer to becoming what he despises, a mindless weapon of war. In this re-

Sophie confronts a transformed Howl in *Howl's Moving Castle,* Studio Ghibli, 2004.

gard, he resembles San in *Princess Mononoke*. While San, unlike Ashitaka, is not under an explicit curse, fate itself has cursed her to be an outcast from humanity by reason of her parents' abandoning her to wolves when she was still a baby. Like San, Howl echoes Kamo no Chōmei, who attempted to turn his back on the twelfth century's brutality. Howl even has a secret house and garden where, like Chōmei, he finds respite from the disappointing world outside. But San and Howl differ from the medieval monk in their ultimate willingness to take up arms to preserve the good that still exists around them.

In his depiction of Howl as a fighter and in his magnification of the war, Miyazaki differs strikingly from the original book, though it must be acknowledged that the war is presented in a curiously offhand manner. In contrast to its charmingly detailed domestic scenes of hanging laundry or cooking breakfast, the movie gets rid of the bloody reality of war and instead offers a distanced perspective. While the director includes his trademark original flying machines, this time with memorably animalistic or even insectlike qualities, these machines are noticeable for their lack of any human presence. This is also true of the victims. Miyazaki presents numerous aerial depictions of bombings, showing a night sky full of flames and houses on fire. The images suggest the firebombings of Tokyo that he witnessed as a child and also the bombing of Kobe depicted in his partner Takahata's celebrated film *Grave of Fireflies*. Unlike in *Grave*, however, the camera never turns earthward. We are not privy to the life and death struggles of bombed victims and can only presume that they occur.

The most personal aspect of the war therefore becomes Howl's blistering anger embodied in his risky metamorphosis into a nonhuman creature. His nonhuman aspect is ironic—it is clear that he is the only participant in the combat who actually cares about humanity, a compassion expressed in his lamentation to Calcifer, that the other warring magicians "have forgotten how to cry."

Howl's warlike transformation is an attempt not only to protect Sophie but to protect the other members of his pseudo-family, which has expanded to include, rather surprisingly, the Witch of the Waste. The witch, who had been a formidable and glamorous presence when she first appeared and put the curse on Sophie, has now been reduced by another female magician, the king's adviser Madame Suliman, to a pathetic old lady who conspicuously resembles a layer cake that has been left out in the rain. It transpires that the witch, like Howl, had entered into a contract with a fire demon that kept her artificially young and beautiful. Miyazaki's retransformation of her (again, not in the original) not only is supremely visually entertaining but also implicitly contrasts Sophie's intelligence and wholesome nature with the witch's obsessive and ultimately futile quest for artificial youth and beauty.

Howl's passion to protect his territory and community underlines an evolving masculinity that seems both traditional and subversive. Andrew Osmond compares Howl to Marco, the hero of *Porco Rosso,* suggesting that each movie "become[s a] reflection on the limits of masculinity, portrayed as both nobly idealist and incorrigibly childish, except when redeemed by love."[14] But, unlike Marco, Howl does not end up hiding outside his lover's garden, performing drive-by aerial stunts. In fact, he creates a garden for Sophie, reconstitutes the castle as a house, and transforms himself permanently (we assume) back into a human being.

As previously noted, many critics dismiss *Howl*'s explicitly "happy ending," regarding it as artificial and sentimental. Critics point out that there is no real explanation for the war's end beyond the king's adviser Madame Suliman's declaring, "Let's put an end to this silly war." In fact, at the time of the movie's release, the *Asahi Shimbun* newspaper published an article detailing "Three Riddles" of *Howl:* How does Sophie's curse get removed? Why was the castle reconstructed? And how did the war get settled?[15]

The director does not provide clear answers to any of these questions, leaving some viewers dissatisfied with the film's lack of resolution. What Miyazaki does offer at the movie's end is a vision of resistance to the anomie of modern society, in the form of the "family" that Sophie and Howl create around them. This new family incorporates the very old (the Witch of the Waste), the very young (Howl's boy apprentice Markl), and even a pet, the old dog Heen, not to mention a magical creature, Calcifer, returning to the family because he misses its other members.

While family issues are important and contentious around the world, it is reasonable to suggest that Japanese society has particular difficulties in this regard. As Sugita points out, the Japanese family underwent major shifts in the last two decades of the twentieth century.[16] While the divorce rate in Japan remained far lower than that of other industrialized countries, relations between the generations grew increasingly negative, leading to such phenomena as the *hikkikomori,* young people (usually but not always male) who stayed at home with their parents but refused to interact with them or with the outside world. During this period youth violence also rose, and the media detailed truly shocking stories of bullying and abuse by young people whose families apparently had no idea of or concern about what they were doing.

It is this state of toxicity within the family that the director is clearly attempting to combat in *Howl*. While Howl is hardly a textbook hikkiko-mori, his narcissism, lack of responsibility, and isolation at the beginning of the film suggest a socially unevolved young man. The other characters also initially seem to have little interest in family relationships, though Sophie rather perfunctorily visits her sister Lettie at the beginning of the film.

Miyazaki emphasizes the power of family ties with a scene inserted late in the film in which Howl's young apprentice Markl asks Sophie whether they are a "family." Her reply is strongly affirmative, and we see Markl clutching tightly to her skirts in a gesture that suggests both desperation and relief. Sophie's taking in of the now virtually senile Witch of the Waste is also an element added by the director. Her kindness to her former enemy not only emphasizes Sophie's developing maturity and compassion but suggests a model of acceptance and love toward infirm and elderly people. Whether Sophie is actually capable of magic herself (and there are hints in both movie and book that she is), her ability to see the best in people, from Howl to Calcifer to the witch, suggests a form of special talent.

At the movie's end Sophie and the witch unwittingly destroy the castle. In Sophie's case she does this in order to protect Howl, fearing that the castle will lead his enemies to him. The witch's part in the destruction is more selfish; she wants Howl's heart and, in taking it, extinguishes Calcifer's power to defend the castle. Paradoxically, however, this final encounter between castle and curse becomes a form of liberation. Whereas Miyazaki had not allowed the destruction of the bathhouse in *Spirited Away*, perhaps fearing that it would comment implicitly on the state of Studio Ghibli, in *Howl* he permits destruction in order to create a newer, better form of community. As Chen suggests, "the destruction of the castle is a manifestation of [Howl]'s personal transition, his liberation from being closed off."[17] No longer an isolated adolescent hiding behind the protective shield of magical spells, Howl now faces the world, but this time with his new family to support him.

The movie's final image is of the castle, again magically transformed. This time, however, it is a welcoming abode, a green, floating manor house. As with the castle in *Laputa*, it can fly, but unlike *Laputa*'s castle, it supports a family rather than a theoretical utopian ideal—and it still keeps its ties to the Earth.

# 14
# Rich and Strange

*The Apocalypse of the Innocents in* Ponyo

Full fathom five thy father lies; . . .
Nothing of him that doth fade
But doth suffer a sea-change
Into something rich and strange

——SHAKESPEARE, *The Tempest*

I want to see the sea rise over Tokyo . . .

——MIYAZAKI

In April 2013 I stood with my husband on a hill above the harbor of Tomo-noura, the picturesque fishing village in western Japan that inspired the location of *Ponyo,* Miyazaki's second-to-last movie. Miyazaki spent a month in a small villa above the village and harbor in 2005, reenergizing from his work on *Howl's Moving Castle.* Refusing even to take a cell phone, the director spent much of his time listening to classical music and reading the works of Natsume Sōseki. Sōseki's favorite painting, John Everett Millais's portrayal of the drowned Ophelia in London's Tate Gallery, would serve as inspiration for a memorable scene in the watery world of *Ponyo.*[1]

Since *Ponyo*'s release Tomonoura had become something of a tourist destination, although it remains remarkably unspoiled. In our case it was the middle stop on what I called our "Miyazakiworld Tour," which had also included a visit to the ancient Dōgo Onsen (hot springs) in Matsuyama, said to have served as a model for the bathhouse in *Spirited Away,* and would end with a trek to the transcendently beautiful island of Yakushima, whose deep forests and crystalline pools appear in animated form in *Princess Mononoke.*

Tomonoura Harbor was also beautiful. Like Dōgo Onsen, the place had been inhabited for centuries, but as with Yakushima, it was nature that had created the exquisite circular harbor, with its placid ocean waves. The day we were there was a classic Japanese spring day—bright and calm with a soft breeze—and the little town and seascape a perfect illustration of what the Japanese call *satoumi* (literally "village plus sea"), the liminal area where the sea laps up against the human community. Yet standing there looking over the harbor, I found myself immersed in a question: "How on earth did Miyazaki go from this beautiful tranquil vision to the stormy apocalypse of *Ponyo?*"

In a way the question is inane. As I have attempted to show, Miyazakiworld is protean, untrammeled, and extraordinary. If the director wishes to gaze at a calm harbor and imagine gigantic fishlike waves, a falling moon, and a "graveyard of ships" (all of which appear in *Ponyo*), this is a testament to his greatest strength—the ability to develop anything in his head into full-blown fantasy.

Apocalyptic imagery has invaded Miyazakiworld from as early as *Future Boy Conan.* Yet the catastrophic events in *Ponyo* are perhaps the most distinctive and memorable in all of Miyazaki's oeuvre, a working through of trauma on a level that is both profound and expansive. The volatile narrative suggests an artist liberated from conventional narrative constraints and opening himself up to extremes. *Howl*'s central themes of family (or pseudo-family) and love become more intense and exaggerated—a passionate "romance" between two five-year-olds and a "family" of hundreds of fish, whose mother is a sea goddess and whose once-human father is a sea magician. Thematic and visual elements are extreme as well, suggesting a world in which things are literally falling apart.

Amid all the chaos and uncanny beauty various versions of Miyazaki appear. Most obvious is the magician Fujimoto, an angry exile whose desire to see humanity destroyed echoes many of the director's more nihilistic pronouncements. But there is also a representation of a youthful Miyazaki, the "good kid" who took care of his ailing mother, in the film's young male protagonist, Sōsuke, who caresses his mother's brow while she lies in bed, disconsolate at her husband's absence from dinner. In her aggressive enthusiasm and constant movement, even the movie's protagonist, the eponymous Ponyo, evokes the young animator of the 1960s whom colleagues described as "running like the wind."

In *Ponyo* Miyazaki seems to be working through his life and times in a white-hot fever, a passion and intensity reminiscent of what critics such as Edward Said have called "late style," a term describing works of an artist's final creative years. As Linda and Michael Hutcheon explain, the term can be an ambiguous, even contradictory one, embracing both "the extremes of rage/pessimism/despair" and "serenity/contemplation/resignation."[2]

*Ponyo* encompasses both aspects. *Ponyo*'s gorgeous hand-drawn animation suggests a serene return to a childhood world, but the movie's apocalyptic themes express a deep and abiding rage against what humanity has done to the Earth. As with Shakespeare's *The Tempest,* another "late" work, the movie takes us through stormy waters but ends with an expression of tranquil acceptance in its final moments, as love, forgiveness, and redemption are celebrated at its climax. Unlike in previous Miyazaki movies, the cataclysmic events depicted in *Ponyo* are not due (at least not directly) to war or technology but, again not unlike *The Tempest,* are the result of magic and passion. Its apocalypse is caused by a child, a little girl who is half-fish, half-human and who meddles with her magician-father's attempts to punish a world he views as corrupt and despoiled. No blame is attached to her, and even her father is offered redemption at the end.

The catastrophe is seen almost entirely through children's eyes—as an amalgam of wonder, terror, sadness, and joy. *Ponyo* is an extreme version of the most common narrative paradigm in Miyazakiworld—the "world-ending" event, in this case a gigantic tsunami—and shows children successfully working through it by means of a combination of perseverance, cour-age, and curiosity.

This vision of trauma and recovery turned out to be eerily prescient. Two years after *Ponyo*'s release, a powerful earthquake and ensuing tsu-nami struck Fukushima in northeast Japan, killing more than fifteen thou-sand people and displacing hundreds of thousands more. Even worse, the cataclysm caused a meltdown at a regional nuclear power plant, leading to lingering radiation that is still being cleaned up today. Traumatizing Japan and shocking the world, the triple disaster was to Miyazaki a "warning," an ominous suggestion of more disasters to come.[3] The movie is also a warn-ing. Even though it ends on a cathartic note with the "balance of nature" restored, much of the film shows us an out-of-joint world in which nature and even time itself become twisted and disrupted. Miyazaki takes us into some truly disturbing waters.

*Ponyo*'s narrative is fairly simple—an archetypal romance in which a boy and a girl meet, endure complications, and go on to live happily ever after. Miyazaki then introduces a number of elements and themes not usu-ally seen in a movie explicitly marketed for young children, including not only a child's-eye view of apocalypse but visions of aging, intimations of death and a world beyond death, a call to arms on the environment, and, finally, an implicit call for a utopia of tolerance, love, and acceptance.

Along the way Miyazaki produces an indelible picture of the sea in all its power and mystery that stacks up with his other great natural and unnatural landscape "characters"—the forest of the shishigami in *Princess Mononoke*, the insect-haunted Fukai (sea of corruption) in *Nausicaä,* and the dreamy European city of *Kiki's Delivery Service*. In *Ponyo* the sea frames the lives of the various characters and drives their fates as well. While the ro-mance between the two children is the catalyst for the tale, it is the charac-ters' interactions with the sea (and often their interaction with boats) that propel the narrative forward.

In an interview around that time with Yōichi Shibuya, visions of "run-ning aground" and "sinking" seemed to be filling Miyazaki's head as he contemplated his age, his responsibility toward Studio Ghibli, and his desire to retire, to just "go away somewhere." The studio had been doing well, with *Howl* a major hit, but expenses were mounting. As always, the director felt that new blood was needed, but he seemed unsure who might succeed him. The industry itself was changing, relying increasingly on computers, and the audience was changing as well. Beginning to question whether he or the studio could continue making movies popular enough to keep the Ghibli ship on course, Miyazaki spoke of powerful "waves" in the animation industry and likened himself and Suzuki to captains of a ship, describing himself and his producer as "the two men on the bridge."[4]

It is perhaps not coincidental that the first character who appears in the movie, Ponyo's magician father, Fujimoto, is shown standing on what looks like the bridge of a sunken tower deep underneath the water. Fujimoto is signaling passing fish, although whether for help or companionship is never made clear. Haggard and rather dandified, with long red hair and striped trousers, Fujmoto claims that he "used to be human." Now, however, he abominates humanity and is working to transform the world back into the Devonian period, the so-called Age of Fish, when vast seas covered the Earth. Fujimoto's loathing of humanity stems from his disgust at what humans have done to the world, illustrated early in the movie by a scene of a trawler dragging a load of human trash through the ocean shallows.

The critic Shunsuke Sugita describes Fujimoto as trying to foment an "ecological revolution," seeing him as a figure who will stop at nothing to purify a corrupted world.[5] Fujimoto's scorn and anger suggest the darker side of Miyazaki's temperament, while his formidable magical talents evoke the power of animation and of the animator.

While Fujimoto is a human who attempts to become a creature of the sea, his favorite daughter, Ponyo, is a fish whom he vainly attempts to prevent becoming a human. Like Fujimoto, Ponyo has supernatural powers, but hers are even more impressive and ultimately more damaging, not because she is evil but because she loves too much. Her determined and reckless love for the human boy Sōsuke will almost destroy the world.

The third character we meet after Fujimoto and Ponyo, Sōsuke is named after the protagonist of *The Gate,* a novel by Sōseki. *Ponyo*'s Sōsuke, however, has little in common with the novel's gloomy, prematurely middle-aged protagonist beyond the fact that both characters are associated with cliffs. Mature, thoughtful, and compassionate, the five-year-old Sōsuke is one of Miyazaki's most appealing characters.

Sōsuke lives with his mother, Lisa, and his ship-captain father, Kōichi, on a cliff above the sea. His comfort with the sea clearly started at an early age. He loves to play with his toy boat on his own in the ocean waters. It is in the sea beneath the cliff that Sōsuke finds Ponyo. Still in fish form but with a human face, she has escaped Fujimoto but is now trapped in a glass jar, from which Sōsuke sets her free. Enchanted by his new friend, Sōsuke decides to introduce Ponyo to a trio of old women who spend their days at the retirement home next to his preschool. The old ladies know Sōsuke well because Lisa works at the home. Two are pleased to meet Sōsuke's "goldfish" but Toki, the third elderly woman, is terrified by Ponyo. She is one of the few characters in the movie who appears ill at ease with water, and she insists that "fish with faces" cause tsunamis. Her words will prove true.

Fujimoto recaptures Ponyo and brings her back to his watery dwelling, but by then Ponyo has not only fallen in love with Sōsuke but is also gaining the ability to turn human. Although Fujimoto attempts mightily to restore her to her original small, cute, and fishlike form and keep her trapped in a bubble, Ponyo's powers have begun to outstrip those of her father. Ponyo again escapes and invades her father's vault, where she drinks from the powerful elixirs stored there. These elixirs combine with Ponyo's own increasing powers to push her to the surface, in an exuberant scene in which she soars up from her father's house in dramatic upward spurts accompanied by golden lights and exhilarating music.

Intent on returning to Sōsuke, Ponyo conjures up gigantic tsunami-level waves. She runs along the tops of the leaping waves as crashing music, reminiscent of Wagner's "Ride of the Valkyries," resounds around her. Soon Ponyo spies Sōsuke and Lisa driving frenziedly home along the storm-lashed

Ponyo runs across the waves in *Ponyo*, Studio Ghibli, 2008.

coast and follows them, like some manic child stalker, her red hair and dress bobbing relentlessly along behind them as the winds and waves threaten to overwhelm their little car. Lisa stops the car at the entrance to their house, and a last giant wave brings Ponyo almost to their driveway. Ponyo races toward the startled Sōsuke and as she runs, she turns from human child to a creature evoking both a fish and a bird, until finally turning back into a human just in time to leap into Sōsuke's bewildered arms.

We see the action from Sōsuke's point of view—intimidating and ex-hilarating. The enormous waves offer a visual roller coaster ride, augmented by the crashing musical score. Ponyo's improbable mastery of the waves is something that children might well envy, yet to adult eyes, Ponyo's determined pursuit seems disturbingly intense. Her metamorphosis is also disturbing and, both to Sōsuke and his mother, bewildering.

Ponyo's transformations underline her magic powers, powers that in a previous scene she used to counteract her father's attempt to immobilize her by casting a spell on her. In the scene where she reunites with Sōsuke, Ponyo seems now to be aggressively in charge of her own metamorphosis, willing herself to be human so that Sōsuke will accept her. But the transformation itself is also suggestive of more primordial evolutionary changes since Ponyo goes from fish to birdlike creature to human in a way that mimics a hugely speeded up process of human evolution. This implicit reference to evolution foreshadows the remarkable scene later in the movie when the Earth itself regresses back to the Devonian period.

Before this all-encompassing event, however, Miyazaki offers a brief and charming interlude in which Lisa and Sōsuke introduce Ponyo to twenty-first-century Japan. Here we see the more quiet magic of Miyazaki—the ability to find enchantment in the ordinary. For unlike *The Tempest* or *The Little Mermaid*, the inspirations for *Ponyo*, Miyazaki's supernatural narrative is embedded squarely in a contemporary life familiar to its viewers.

Miyazaki has us perceive an ordinary household through the eyes of young children. We see Sōsuke proudly explaining human technology to his otherworldly guest as the two wait breathlessly for water to come out of a tap or marvel at the miraculous ability of dry ramen noodles to become soft and tasty. Privileging the prosaic, the scene expresses Miyazaki's understanding of a child's perception while sending an implicit message of the need to appreciate the wonder of the ordinary.

Abruptly the point of view shifts to Sōsuke's father, Kōichi, until then virtually a nonpresence, except for the scene where his work-related absence from home causes Lisa to have a tantrum. Like Fujimoto, Kōichi is connected with the sea; he is the captain of the *Koganeimaru*, presumably a fishing boat, although we do not see the crew catch anything. Instead, the ship itself is caught—by the towering tsunami wrought by Ponyo's enchantments. Lost and confused, the crew suddenly sees ahead of them what appears to be an unfamiliar but well-lighted shore. Wondering whether they have somehow reached America, they prepare to head toward it when the engine suddenly stops. At the same time, they realize that what they are viewing is not some solid coastline but a huge wall of water supporting an immense mass of becalmed ships piled on top of one another—a "ship's graveyard," says a crew member. While eerie music plays, the camera travels up above the "graveyard" to show us a gigantic and distorted moon hovering balefully over the trapped ships.

At this terrible moment a miraculous intervention arrives. An enormous brightly colored surging wave approaches and, resolving itself into the supine figure of a gigantic and beautiful woman, passes through the ship and somehow reactivates the engines. The figure continues through the waters, apparently restarting the other ships, before it ascends toward the moon, leaving a colorful vertical trace in the dark sky. The beautiful woman, we soon discover, is Ponyo's mother, Granmamare, the goddess of the sea, on her way to see Fujimoto. The image of her watery figure is Miyazaki's interpretation of Millais's Ophelia, but the crewmembers invoke a non-Western figure. They pray gratefully to Kannonsama, the salvific Bodhisattva of traditional Buddhism.

This traumatic yet beautiful scene is fascinating and troubling on many levels. It shows a genuinely apocalyptic scenario—the multiple "dead" ships and the near shipwreck of the *Koganeimaru* overlooked by the distorted and disturbing moon. Moreover, this is an apocalypse seen through the point of view of terrified adult men. Even more surprising for a Miyazaki film, the catastrophe resolves itself, not through human agency but through divine intervention by a Bodhisattva.

This scene suggests a newfound passivity in Miyazaki's characters and an unusual reliance on traditional religion. It also distinctly points to a vision of the collapse of patriarchal authority, already indicated by Ponyo's rebellion against her father. By this point Ponyo has outstripped her father in magic powers and flouted his authority. Miyazaki adds another scene in which we see her myriad fish sisters nibbling away at Fujimoto's perch as he stands on top of a pile of blobby henchmen, causing him to fall comically into the very ocean that had previously been his support. Not only Ponyo, therefore, but even her tiny sisters, not to mention her awe-inspiring mother, demonstrate that it is the power of the feminine that is the major dynamic in this film. On land, Lisa and the three old ladies also leave an indelible impression of female force in contrast to male impotence.

In an interview with Shibuya shortly after *Ponyo*'s release, Miyazaki spoke at length about the "weakening" of masculine authority in the modern world, stating that it was no longer possible to create boy heroes except very young ones like Sōsuke.[6] The director's concerns reflect a sense in Japanese society that younger male adults seemed increasingly feeble compared to those of previous generations. Miyazaki's anxieties may also reflect his own difficult relationship with his sons, particularly Goro, whose Ghibli-produced movie, the 2006 *Tales from Earthsea* (Gedo senki), had met with a savage reception from some Japanese critics.

It is possible that the director was also concerned about his own waning physical powers. He speaks in the same interview about his deteriorating eyesight and the frequent numbness in his fingers. Jokingly, he suggests that he and Suzuki should commit *shinjū,* the traditional term for a joint suicide by star-crossed lovers.[7] The darkness implied in this statement is under the surface in much of *Ponyo.*

Even in these dark passages, however, Miyazaki does not entirely give up hope. When pressed about his despair by Shibuya, he shifts gears and insists that he does not feel that way when he hears the voices of the children at the preschool next door, the school that he had worked to create. It is perhaps not surprising that in *Ponyo* the director painstakingly details Sōsuke's preschool and places it prominently next to an old-age home. In the director's eyes it is the oldest generation and the youngest who find hope in each other.

In *Ponyo* it is clear that it is the five-year-old Sōsuke who will come to the rescue, through his powers of love, resilience, and openness to the world of imagination. Sōsuke's toy boat will go on to play a major role in the movie's extraordinary second half, taking Sōsuke and Ponyo partly on a journey through history, evoking not only the prehistoric Devonian period and pre-twenty-first-century Japan, but also a metaphorical return to the womb, with Sōsuke in quest of his mother. In fact, there are several mother figures at the movie's end, including not only Lisa and Granmamare but also the fractious old lady Toki, who may well be another portrait of Miyazaki's own mother. Even Ponyo takes on maternal characteristics, at one point calming a peevish baby.

The journey begins the morning after the night of the tsunami. Sōsuke and Ponyo wake to discover that the sea has come all the way to the door-way of their house on the cliff. In distinct contrast to a genuine post-tsunami ocean, the sea surrounding them is a translucent green sea with small shin-ing waves lapping placidly up to their house. Even more fantastical, as the children soon find out, is that the sea has evolved backward into the Devo-nian era of millions of years before that Fujimoto had hoped to generate.

The two children get into the toy boat that Ponyo has magically en-larged and Sōsuke's mechanical expertise has helped to power. Together they skim across their newly flooded world. Appropriate to the era that they sail into, the children encounter scores of enormous prehistoric fish beneath them. But these fish are not swimming through a Devonian era seascape. Rather, they glide among the drowned detritus of twenty-first-century civ-ilization, floating over houses, roads, telegraph posts, and even bobbing, still-tethered boats, in a scene as exquisite as it is uncanny. To Sōsuke and Ponyo, the scene occasions only unmitigated joy—the sun sparkles on the water, their little boat putters along, and the two delight in identifying the bizarre sea creatures that swim alongside them.

In this joyous child's-eye vision of apocalypse the world is bright and pure, albeit (or perhaps because) bereft of humanity. The only shadow is the disappearance of both of Sōsuke's parents: Lisa has also vanished, dashing out the night before to help rescue the ladies at the old-age facility. The brave but headstrong Lisa apparently sees no problem in leaving the five-year-old Sōsuke to cope on his own, thus amplifying Miyazaki's message about childhood resilience but also setting up a potentially tragic situation.

Sōsuke calmly decides to go look for his mother. They set off on a rescue voyage, bringing a thermos of soup and Ponyo's favorite ham sandwiches. This journey, occupying most of the latter part of the movie, takes them into a world where festival, joy, and redemption compete with destruction, grief, and intimations of death.

Shortly after they embark, Ponyo and Sōsuke are unexpectedly hailed by another boat in the distance belonging to a small family— a mother, father, and baby—who, for reasons never explained, are drifting in the water outside the town. Neither parent seems particularly troubled by these strange circumstances, however. Their calmness is underscored by the old-fashioned but pretty dress that the mother wears, as if she were going to a prewar garden party. In this scene Miyazaki seems to be calling up recent Japanese history and even perhaps his own childhood: the mother's dress could easily have come from a period when his own mother was young and beautiful.

The scene gets even stranger as Ponyo and Sōsuke discuss with the parents the baby's need for breast milk (not explicitly translated in the English version) and end up donating their soup and sandwiches (minus the ham) to the family before continuing on their way. The only dark note in this bizarrely sunny encounter is the strikingly unattractive baby, who whines and cries and finally breaks into full-fledged howling. In a surprising display of maternal instinct for one so young, Ponyo manages to soothe the baby.

A flotilla of small ships floats into view to the strains of vaguely martial music and the sound of rowers' hearty shouts. These ships bear the people from the town who have somehow escaped the tsunami and are now heading towards a mountaintop that remains above the waterline. As with the family on the boat, the scene is suggestive of an older Japan.

Delighted to see them, Sōsuke describes the group as looking like a "festival." He uses the word *matsuri,* which originally referred to Shinto festivals. In contrast to Buddhism, which is often linked to funerals and death in Japan, Shinto rituals are usually seen as upbeat and life affirming. Boats are frequently included in Shinto festivals, and the word *matsuri* can also suggest a more generally carnivalesque occasion.

This festive scene stands in strong contrast to the dark vision of the "graveyard of ships" glimpsed previously by Sōsuke's father and, along with the feeding and comforting of the baby, suggests a potential turn toward "life and hope. At the same time, however, the entire post-tsunami sequence also gives off eerie emanations. Or, as Sugita puts it bluntly, "One can only see this sunken world as the world of death."[8] How could the townspeople possibly have survived this apocalyptic catastrophe, especially when Miyazaki takes pains to show visual evidence of the drowned world around them? Furthermore, while boats appear in Shinto festivals, in Buddhism they also serve as guides across the supernatural waters to the "other world" (*ano yo*) of death.

As the children continue on their way above the submerged town, their boat begins to lose power. Although Ponyo attempts to restart it, she too is "losing power," growing steadily sleepier while the boat begins to shrink beneath her. Finally, in a scene that resembles a child's fantasy version of *The African Queen*, Sōsuke is forced to get out and push the boat until it reverts to normal toy size, fortunately, just as they arrive on dry land.

The shrinking of the boat and Ponyo's sudden sleepiness are disconcerting in themselves, suggesting that neither magic nor boats can ultimately be relied upon and reminding the viewer that these are, after all, two children lost in a strange world. Miyazaki amplifies this feeling of insecurity even more in a subsequent poignant scene in which Sōsuke finds Lisa's abandoned car: Sōsuke rushes to open the car door, peering inside as if expecting his mother to somehow still be there, then runs frenziedly back and forth in tears calling for her heartbrokenly. For the first time the movie seems to be acknowledging the possibility of death, and death of the most traumatic kind, that of a young child's parent.

It is the sleepy Ponyo who provides a bit of parenting this time, taking Sōsuke by the hand and saying, "Let's look for Lisa." But their way is blocked by an ancient dark tunnel. Although Sōsuke feels that he has seen the tunnel before, Ponyo dislikes it and has to be dragged. By the time the children emerge from the tunnel, Ponyo has again transformed, first into a birdlike figure, then into fishlike form.

The walk through the tunnel echoes the passage of Chihiro and her parents through the tunnel between the human and the supernatural world in *Spirited Away*. In *Ponyo*'s case, however, the tunnel does not seem to divide human and magical. Rather, to build on Sugita's interpretation, it functions as a conduit to the land of the dead. This interpretation is strengthened when we find on the other side of the tunnel not only Lisa but also the members of the old-age home, all comfortably ensconced within a circular white structure that is apparently beneath the sea. Though their empty wheelchairs at the waterside evoke a sense of melancholy absence, the old women have actually been miraculously restored to youthful good health, so much so that they can race each other across their watery new home.

Again supporting the notion that this is a world after death, one of the women asks, "Is this the other world?" [*ano yo*], while another one exclaims, "I thought it was the palace of the sea dragon!" This reference is to the Urashima Taro legend, Japan's darker version of "Rip Van Winkle," in which a grateful turtle transports Urashima, a fisherman, to the palace of the sea dragon, where he lives happily until he decides to return home. Arriving back at his village, however, Urashima finds that three hundred years have passed, and he dies soon thereafter.

In *Ponyo*'s magical temporal structure, millions of years have come and gone. The Devonian Sea has returned to overwhelm the Earth, and Ponyo has evolved and regressed twice. This catastrophic situation seems almost unresolvable.

As was the case with his solution to the *Koganeimaru*'s incipient shipwreck, Miyazaki again returns to the supernatural and again to Ponyo's sea goddess mother, Granmamare, this time aided by Lisa. In the film's celebratory denouement, the two mothers, more or less supported by a rather ill-at-ease Fujimoto, decide that if Sōsuke agrees to accept Ponyo in all her forms—fish, half-fish, and human—then "the balance of nature will be restored." Accordingly, Granmamare asks Sōsuke whether he can love Ponyo in this way and he assures her that he can. Granmamare then asks Ponyo whether she is willing to give up her magic to be a human girl, and she eagerly assents.

With that the sea goddess announces, "The balance of nature is restored." The movie closes on a final vision of ascent as Ponyo in fish shape soars into the clouds and returns in human form to plant a kiss on Sōsuke's cheek.

*Ponyo* offers many pleasures. Roger Ebert, who had disliked Miyazaki's *Howl's Moving Castle,* called *Ponyo* a "poetic, visually breathtaking work."[9] The vividness and virtuosity of the hand-drawn animation (mostly done by Miyazaki himself) and the charm and dynamism of its characters appealed to viewers around the world. The upbeat ending song became a best seller, seeming to encapsulate the dynamism and vivacity of its heroine.

Despite being a fantasy, *Ponyo* includes strong real-world resonances that give the movie moral weight. Its highlighting of believable older characters in a home for the elderly continues *Howl's* exploration of the complexities of old age. The women's restoration to youth in the movie's final moments is touching, a wish-fulfilling fantasy that surely appealed to Japan's vast elderly population.

The movie also continues *Spirited Away*'s critique of middle-aged parents. Although Lisa and Kōichi are far from Chihiro's piglike materialistic parents, they are also distant from the sensitive and supportive mother and father in *Totoro* or *Kiki.* Lisa's behavior, including scenes of wild driving and drunkenness on hearing that her husband will not be home for dinner, is characterized in a way that few family movies would dare represent. While she clearly loves Sōsuke and is remarkably accepting of Ponyo's unexpected presence in their lives, she also comes across as immature. As previously noted, Kōichi, affable but largely absent, may also be a commentary on contemporary Japanese masculinity and on fatherhood in particular.

The movie's eerie forecast of the Fukushima disaster anticipates the darkness of reality. *Ponyo*'s scenes of wave and winds are aesthetically pleasing versions of the grim swirling torrents that overtook Fukushima. Even Ponyo's invasion of her magician father's undersea den—her breaking open his elixirs and her eruption out of the sea in a burst of colorful explosions— seems to uncannily foretell the spurting blasts of the nuclear power plant.

In a tragic irony, what had been fantasy turned out to be a forecast of reality. But Miyazaki's portrayal of two children pluckily dealing with disaster would turn out to be a beneficial tool to help real-world inhabitants process their own fears and horror, a textbook case of working through trauma. *Ponyo*'s vision of a restored natural order in which children will lead us to a purer, kinder world offers hope for a better future. Sōsuke's promise to love Ponyo "as a fish, as a half-fish, and as a human" also suggests an acceptance of difference, a strong message in a society where conformity is highly valued.[10] It also evokes *Princess Mononoke,* where beings of all forms are accepted as part of the larger order of an animistic world.

And yet the movie's overall impact is complicated. Even if we disagree with Sugita (and I do not) that the last part of the movie takes place in a postapocalyptic world of the dead, its forced upbeat ending of divine magic bringing about a cosmic resolution comes as a surprise. This happy ending, while echoing that of *Howl's Moving Castle,* seems out of character compared with the ambiguous and genuinely thought-provoking endings of many Miyazaki works. Despite its real-world references, the movie ultimately seems more of a fantasy than any previous Miyazaki film, even as it abruptly showcases an end to fantasy in Ponyo's agreeing to give up her magic and settle into an entirely human existence. This ending strongly contrasts with *Kiki* or *Howl,* in which the magical characters remain in full possession of their powers at movie's end.

Perhaps it is Miyazaki who is giving up on magic, implying that humans must deal with the world in all its painful reality with no more use for enchantment. This approach accords with a new direction in Miyazakiworld, the fact that his next and (so far) final film would be the historical work *The Wind Rises,* which has little trace of fantasy in it. The realistic *The Wind Rises* contrasts powerfully with *Ponyo,* a movie that until its climax is suffused in otherworldliness, from the supernatural powers of Fujimoto, Granmamare, and Ponyo to the fearsome natural forces of the wind and waves.

*Ponyo*'s intense highlighting of enchantment and sorcery may be seen as a kind of theatrical, operatic finale. Just as *The Tempest*'s Prospero mourns for the "insubstantial pageant" of "cloud-capped towers" and "gorgeous palaces," while declaiming "our revels now are ended," Miyazaki both celebrates and destroys the enchantment he has created. In the latter part of *Ponyo* he offers a vision of a serenely beautiful world in which the human actors have become merely spirits, pawns of the rushing waves of fate.

It is perhaps not surprising that in this late work Miyazaki crosses not only space but time itself, to early childhood and to the primordial sea. In this vision of temporal regression the movie resembles *The Drowned World*, J. G. Ballard's 1962 science fiction novel that was also predicated on an apocalyptic flood, in this case bringing the world back into the Triassic period, where monstrous fish and reptiles take over an oceanic Earth. Lost in an overpowering dreamlike daze, the last humans occasionally venture out on boats to survey their submerged civilization. Ballard has his main character self-consciously remark, "Perhaps these sunken lagoons simply remind me of the drowned world of my uterine childhood."[11]

Sugita mentions that the white membranelike structure protecting the characters under water at *Ponyo*'s end resembles the womb.[12] Indeed, the entire dreamlike second half of the film suggests a return to the womb, or at the very least to the unconscious. Miyazaki's work has always emphasized childhood, but *Ponyo*'s "childhood," linked not only to humans but to the Earth itself, suggests that the director is plumbing his own depths to ultimately offer a world that is truly "rich and strange"—sublime, powerful, and ultimately unknowable. The movie privileges a rich and intense past but ends with a surprisingly modest vision of the future into which, quite literally, a little child will lead us.

# 15
# "A Terrible Wind"
### The Wind Rises

The past is a foreign country. They do things differently there.

——L. P. HARTLEY

On July 20, 2013, Miyazaki announced that he had released his final film, *The Wind Rises*. He confessed in a long interview with Yōichi Shibuya that the experience had been "hellish.... I would spend all day drawing and at night I would think, 'Now I have to throw it all out.'" Such a lack of confidence seems unusual for a director with so many triumphs, but Miyazaki was feeling his age. He complained of failing eyesight and lower back pain. He felt alienated from the younger people at the studio, who seemed "lazy," "lacking ideals," and unable to draw without looking through a screen rather than basing their work on real life.[1]

It is also possible that the movie's subject matter weighed on him. For the first time in his career, Miyazaki had made a movie that was not technically a fantasy. He stated that after the 2011 earthquake and the financial crisis of 2008 he could "no longer do fantasy.... It would be a lie."[2]

Instead he turned to the past, specifically the most controversial time in Japan's history, the period leading up to the country's entry into the Second World War, and the development of Japan's greatest warplane, the Mitsubishi Zero. But *The Wind Rises* is not a conventional war movie—there are no scenes of fighting, and the movie's hero is a mild-mannered but brilliant engineer whose motivation for creating the Zero is not to serve his country but simply, as he states, "to make something beautiful," to design the most advanced, highest-performance aircraft of its time and in doing so to give himself over to a lifelong obsession with the science of flight and airplane design.

Indeed, *The Wind Rises* is a beautiful movie, conveying Miyazakiworld in its distillation of the director's own romantic yearnings, ideological anxieties, and core values more than it offers historical insight. Although there is no explicit fantasy, the film contains dream sequences and other evocative images that suggest an alternative to the rising militarism, extremes of poverty and wealth, and growing international tensions of 1930s Japan. *The Wind Rises* revels in luscious portrayals of Miyazaki's cherished Euroworld— the Italian countryside over which a handcrafted airplane swoops and swerves, a memorable view of a gargantuan German aircraft factory with the winter light shining through its high windows—but most stunning are the carefully rendered reimaginings of prewar Japan. A brother and sister take a boat across a river at sunset. An exquisite girl in a kimono stands gazing upon a classic Japanese garden. A young boy dreams of flying above the tiled roofs and willow-lined streets of a traditional Japanese town. And in one enormously poignant scene, Westerners and Japanese guests at a posh resort in the Japanese Alps gather around a piano to sing the bittersweet German song "Das Gibt's nur Einmal" (It Only Happens Once).

Perhaps the movie's most beautiful creation, at least in the eyes of Miyazaki and his protagonist, the young engineer Jirō Horikoshi, is the Mitsubishi Zero. Lightweight, powerful, and incredibly maneuverable, the Zero was a testament to Japanese engineering: its potency and efficiency a source of national pride. The film takes pains to emphasize that Japanese aircraft building was an area of expertise that had been dismissed by Western experts unable to believe that what many still saw as an inferior race could create such impressive technology.

Miyazaki was partly drawn to using the historical Horikoshi as protag-

Jirō lectures his engineering team in *The Wind Rises*, Studio Ghibli, 2013.

onist because he had read his autobiography as a teenager and been fascinated by Horikoshi's account of the Zero's creation. But *The Wind Rises* never
shows the Zero's deployment as a warplane, ending in 1937, just before the
planes were first used in the invasion of China. Instead, Miyazaki limits the
story to the brilliant but grinding, almost superhuman efforts that went into
its development, a paean to the remarkable achievement of the Zero and to
meticulous engineering, relentless work, hope, and dreams.

As such, it is also clearly a paean to the work that went into the movie
itself, and a summation of what the animation process has been to Miyazaki
over fifty years in the field, with Jirō and his story acting as a stand-in. Jirō, the
director suggests, was "in some ways a tragic figure" who "gave his all," and

his motivation to "make something beautiful" is a desire that accords with Miyazaki's own life work. While the director demurs when the critic Shibuya insists that Jirō is Miyazaki, saying, "I created the Jirō I wanted," it is evident that the effort depicted in the film is a proxy for Miyazaki's own lifelong toil.[3] Thus *The Wind Rises* becomes an expiation of Miyazaki's own superhuman commitment to work and a kind of bittersweet apology (or perhaps explanation) to his family and colleagues for the sacrifices he asked along the way. At the film's première, Miyazaki cried publicly for the first time in his career.

In the eyes of some viewers, both at home and abroad, however, *The Wind Rises,* with its celebration of the Zero, is a politically ugly film. To them, the movie brings up painful controversies involving evasion and obfuscation concerning the Zero's role and Japan's war responsibility. Most harshly, some critics suggest that the movie and its director are in outright denial of one of the darkest periods in Japan's twentieth-century history, the long buildup to a war that would end not only in the destruction of Japan but also in the devastation of the lands subject to Japanese militarism—Korea, China, and Southeast Asia. In their eyes, *The Wind Rises* is guilty of whitewashing the war and responsibility, choosing to ignore Japan's imperialist aggression and the hundreds of thousands of deaths it caused and instead highlighting the Zero's technological superiority. Indeed, the only actual death in the movie is a romantic one, when Jirō's beautiful young wife succumbs offscreen to tuberculosis.

Miyazaki acknowledged that his own staff and family had doubts about whether he should do the film, and perhaps he did as well. In the interview with Shibuya he mentions how he would put in and then take out a particular cut because of "cowardice." But Miyazaki is not a coward. He clearly wanted the film to be provocative, to stir up discussions of difficult matters his countrymen for decades wanted to sweep under the rug. As he said to Shibuya in a diatribe against the "stupidity" of his countrymen, "The Japanese always sit back and thereby end up choosing war . . . and we are doing exactly the same thing again," presumably a reference to the Japanese government's attempt to change the Constitution to allow for aggressive warfare.[4]

The film's provocation succeeded almost too well, setting off a critical storm that proved, if nothing else, that the seventy-two-year-old director could still command nationwide attention. To some critics, the film's very beauty is an issue in itself. To the filmmaker Fukasaku Kenta, in Jirō's desire to "make something beautiful" the director is using the term "beautiful" as a free pass: just as Jirō avoids the responsibility of having created a beautifully designed piece of technology responsible for immense destruction, so does Miyazaki deny responsibility for a movie that could be seen to glorify war. The outrage was extreme precisely because Japanese audiences over the years have relied on Miyazaki as an advocate for liberal causes. As Fukasaku says, "We live in uneasy times. . . . So we wanted to have [Miyazaki's animation] continue to attack present-day society with energy and a loud voice."[5]

Even more extreme was the response of the critic Minohiko Onozawa, who explicitly equated Miyazaki's vaunting of beauty with fascistic impulses. In an impassioned essay he explored how Miyazaki uses the ideology of the beautiful as "an abstract concept cut off from any relation to history or society," thereby allowing the director to duck any sense of moral responsibility for the violence and death wrought by the Zero. In Onozawa's eyes this is a form of fascist conformity that subverts what he calls "the essence of art, which is the role of looking at reality in a critical way."[6]

Onozawa seems to suggest that *The Wind Rises* abandoned Miyazaki's principle of looking at the world "with eyes unclouded," as *Princess Mononoke*'s Ashitaka famously advocated. This is a serious charge. As I have hoped to demonstrate, one of the fundamental building blocks of Miyazakiworld has been the way the director consistently presented his audiences with a nuanced and multilayered view of reality, made all the more memorable by his use of the fantasy and science fiction genres, combined with superb animation, to convey that reality. Is it reasonable to suggest that in *The Wind Rises* Miyazaki slanted history to make a piece of essentially fascist propaganda in which creating beauty becomes an excuse for humanity's darkest crimes?

The short answer is no. It would be grotesque to describe *The Wind Rises* as an apology for fascism, given the social and political critiques within the film itself, especially some of the disquisitions by Jirō's friend and colleague Hondo, whose unblinking view of work and politics is obviously meant to contrast with Jirō's myopic dreaminess. It is certainly true that the film is unique within Miyazaki's canon, not simply because of its lack of fantastic flourishes but because it is less subtle and more didactic. However, it still contains many intriguing layers, and its message is more complex and interesting than Onozawa gives it credit for.

We may even say that *The Wind Rises* is a unique version of Miyazaki's fantasy films. With a few dark exceptions, the film is a fantasy of the way history should have been, a world in which weapons of war are only beautiful and not lethal and where suffering occurs but is alleviated by joys, ranging from labor to love, that give meaning to human existence. While it implicitly references his own family's involvement in the war to show the compromises ordinary people had to make, it is not a defense of militarism. It allies with *Porco Rosso,* his fantasy film also set in the interwar period, to critique humanity's tendency to march toward disaster while offering more positive modes of being in the world.

Miyazaki's decision to place his film entirely within a genuine historical setting has many implications. On a personal level, it allows him to engage with issues important to his family's history. The film does a memorable job, for example, of re-creating the devastating Tokyo earthquake of 1923, an event that had a major impact on his grandfather's life. Far more obviously, the fact that his father and uncle had run a factory making conveyor belts for the Zeros suggests that the film is confronting his family's own responsibility in the war effort. Miyazaki refuses to condemn them, however. As Suzuki points out in an interview before the film's release, few people, especially with families to support, would have had the political courage to go against the increasing militarism of the Japanese state.[7]

The film's historical setting allows Miyazaki to use his artistry to re-create a "lost" prewar Japan. The film's visuals lovingly evoke prewar architecture and scenery, such as the stunning traditional house and garden of Jirō's boss Kurokawa, the quasi-European mansion belonging to Jirō's fiancée and her father, and the sumptuously realized pastoral setting of Karuizawa, the famous mountain resort in the Japanese Alps. Contrary to what Onozawa asserts, however, the film does not entirely neglect issues such as poverty and hunger. In one scene Jirō attempts to give cake to some starving children, only to be rebuffed, and in another he encounters desperate day laborers seeking jobs. The film's re-creation of the initial stages of the Great Kanto Earthquake is vivid and frightening, although, as Onozawa points out, the director does not touch on the dark aftermath of the earthquake, in which panicked urban mobs looking for scapegoats turned on and killed many Korean residents of Tokyo.[8]

Yet it must be acknowledged that the film suffuses even its darkest details with a literally golden, nostalgic light, allowing the past to seem not simply a "foreign country" but one that possesses a sensuous, deeply nostalgic appeal. While Miyazaki scrupulously re-creates the authentic details of a moment in history, the settings are so exquisite, the lighting so rich, and the music (as usual, by his favorite composer Joe Hisaishi) so evocative that the prewar period beckons invitingly. In a sense, Miyazaki has used history to create his ultimate fantasy country.

A fantasy quality suffuses the other distinctive element in the movie, which, truly unusually for Miyazaki, is an adult love story. In fact, the movie has two love stories: the romance of Jirō and Naoko, a young woman he meets under adventurous circumstances and will eventually court and marry, and the love affair between Jirō and his plane. A majority of the film is devoted to Jirō and his engineer colleagues as they imagine, invent, and rework the technology needed to develop the Zero.

The love story between Jirō and Naoko combines a fairy-tale quality with seriousness—in contrast, for example, to the adult romance in *Porco Rosso,* which is ultimately subsumed beneath the playful hijinks of the film's festive denouement. Adult love plays a more tragic role in *The Wind Rises.*

From the start, the romance suggests the mystery and excitement of an old-fashioned melodrama. Jirō meets the still very young Naoko on a train to Tokyo moments before the great earthquake derails the train and scatters the panic-stricken passengers. He gallantly rescues both Naoko and her maid, Okinu, even carrying the injured Okinu on his back and using his clean white shirt as a vessel to give the thirsty women some water. Earlier in the film, Jirō is seen taking on a group of bullies in defense of a weaker classmate. Unlike *Porco Rosso*'s world-weary and haunted protagonist, Jirō is shown as steadfast, pure, and kind.

While the popular-culture critic Toshio Okada has criticized Jirō's one-note personality as "inhuman," his kindness and simplicity are entirely appropriate to a romance or fairy-tale hero, and, as far as can be determined, his nature resembles the historical Jirō Horikoshi's.[9] Also appropriate to an old-fashioned romance is Naoko, whose personality differs notably from those of Miyazaki's typical heroines. Lovely, charming, and self-sacrificing, she also comes across as rather passive; tragically doomed, she suffers from tuberculosis that will eventually kill her. In fact, Naoko *is* a character straight out of a romance: she is inspired by the heroine of the novel *The Wind Rises*, by a favorite Miyazaki author, Tatsuo Hori. The novel chronicles a doomed love affair between a young man and a girl suffering from tuberculosis. But it is also likely that Naoko's tuberculosis in the film evokes Miyazaki's own mother, and his portrayal of her illness becomes another way for the director to process his personal loss.

Miyazaki essentially grafted Hori's love story onto the historical account of Jirō Horikoshi, no doubt to widen the movie's audience but also likely to deepen the emotional appeal of the film. The love affair leads to some of the most genuinely charming moments in the movie. As is typical of a melodramatic romance, the two are parted after their initial encounter on the day of the earthquake, only to meet again by chance one summer day years later at a hotel in the posh mountain resort of Karuizawa.

A picturesque town still popular with the elite and with Western expatriates, Karuizawa is also "The Magic Mountain," as Castorp, an enigmatic German guest at the same hotel, solemnly declares. Castorp is named for the protagonist of *The Magic Mountain* (1924), Thomas Mann's novel about a group of expatriates recuperating from tuberculosis in a sanatorium in the

Swiss Alps. Miyazaki acknowledges the book's influence, although the differences between his film and Mann's book are vast. However, the themes of disease and war course through both works. In both film and novel the image of a magic mountain suggests a world removed from the onrushing darkness of the war to come (World War I in Mann's novel, World War II in Miyazaki's film). Or as Miyazaki's Castorp says to Jirō, Naoko, and Naoko's father, "This summer is a good summer."

Castorp's implication is that such a summer will never come again, a foreboding underscored when Castorp, at the hotel's piano, leads a group of Japanese and Western guests, including Jirō and Naoko's father, through "Das Gibt's nur Einmal." The song's lyrics suggest that love, beauty, and life itself are precious but inevitably fleeting, a sentiment very much in tune with the Japanese aesthetic of *mono no aware*.

Indeed, the characters' lives soon darken as Jirō learns of Naoko's tuberculosis. Nevertheless, he vows to marry her, and the two wed in a sequence that in its own way might be considered a Japanese version of a "magic mountain," taking place in the elegant traditional Japanese home of Jirō's boss, Kurokawa, and his wife. Despite worries for Jirō and Naoko's future, Kurokawa's wife wholeheartedly supports the couple's decision to marry and helps to arrange a spur-of-the-moment wedding performed with grace and even humor as the four attempt to make up lines fitting the wedding service. Delicate and poised (and not looking the slightest bit ill), Naoko floats into Jirō's view wearing a gorgeous kimono and a flower in her hair. In front of her comes Mrs. Kurokawa carrying a lantern.

This appealing scene serves as a respite from the images of Jirō working in the Mitsubishi plane factory or occasional glimpses of future catastrophe that the movie also affords. Like Mann's magic mountain or the Karuizawa hotel, the Kurokawa mansion is a place that seems to exist outside of time and away from grief. In her flowing robes and long hair, Naoko looks less a traditional Japanese bride and more a fairy-tale heroine. But this scene also suggests a darker interpretation. Mrs. Kurokawa's appearance with the lantern raised and Naoko's ethereal presence have an almost ghostly aspect. In fact, the motif of a ghostly young girl following an older woman with a lantern is a popular trope in Japanese and Chinese supernatural fiction and art and perhaps a nod to *Panda and the White Serpent,* the ghost-story feature that inspired Miyazaki to become an animator.

Naoko's death has a spectral quality. The two celebrate their wedding night in perhaps the one genuinely sexy scene Miyazaki created, but Naoko soon grows weaker. It is up to Jirō's assertive younger sister to tell him that his wife secretly puts on makeup to look healthier. One day Naoko simply disappears, walking quietly out of Jirō's life in order not to burden him or take him away from his important work designing the Zero. We never see her die.

Toshio Okada has interpreted Naoko's decision as evidence of Jirō's fundamental selfishness. "Jirō loves Naoko because she is beautiful, like an airplane," he says. "Had she gotten old and lost her beauty, their love could not have continued."[10] Naoko's offscreen death, he argues, supports the unreal quality of the story. I agree, especially since the real Horikoshi's wife did not die young, and the couple had two children. The movie's ethereal Naoko—forever young and forever childless, romantically stained by the trauma of tuberculosis—supports the movie's otherworldly and fantastic quality, gesturing back to the vanishing-woman motif seen in *Castle of Cagliostro.*

Jirō seems to genuinely love Naoko, but there is no question that his major object of devotion is his passion for designing planes. This is made clear not only in the film itself but in the initial inspiration for the film, a manga series that Miyazaki drew in the early 2000s that appeared in the journal *Model Graphics,* a hobby magazine aimed at aficionados of plastic aircraft. Like the film, the series is entitled *The Wind Rises,* and it too contains a romance based on the Hori novel, although in much more attenuated form than in the movie. But the manga's main focus is on various kinds of military technology.

In striking contrast to Miyazaki's artwork, the story and characters in these manga, collected under the title of *Dream Notes,* are relatively unimportant. In page after page, carefully and intricately rendered images of war machines are front and center, occupying most of the manga. In general, rather than combat sequences, these manga seem to privilege military technology for its own sake—as complicated works of art that almost take on a life of their own.

We have seen this love of military technology in *Porco Rosso,* where the hero dotes on his striking red seaplane as if it were a beloved animal or even a part of himself, almost obsessively trying to disassociate it from its original purpose as a weapon of war. In *The Wind Rises* war is not forgotten so much as it is elided. Certainly, there are moments of foreboding. At one point Jirō and his colleague Hondo visit the monumental Junkers aircraft factory in Germany, and the steely behemoth they board seems to gleam with an evil predatory glint. Even more obvious are Jirō's occasional dark visions of broken tangled Zeros falling all around him.

Unlike Marco in *Porco Rosso,* Jirō in *The Wind Rises* does not exactly "dote" on the Zero, but his single-minded dedication to creating the perfect plane comes through in scene after scene. This dedication begins early on, with his fascination with a mackerel bone in his lunch whose shape he envisions as a model for the precisely curved surface of the Zero's wingspan. Late at night, he sits next to the sleeping Naoko, holding her hand and smoking a cigarette, while he intently draws aircraft designs with his free hand. As the Zero grows closer to reality, Miyazaki shows his protagonist's mounting excitement, along with that of his bosses and employees. In their eyes and, one suspects, in the eyes of the director as well, the plane becomes an object of pride, accomplishment, even awe.

In the movie far more than in the manga, however, the plane also becomes implicitly a thing of immense sadness, beauty distorted for evil and stupid purposes. At the end of the movie Miyazaki incorporates a dream sequence in which Jirō tells his imaginary mentor, the pioneering Italian aircraft maker Caproni, "Not a single one came back." Incredibly, Jirō is correct. The plane that had ruled the Pacific for a few brief years was ultimately eclipsed by more advanced aircraft that wrested control of the skies and helped to turn the tide of the war against Japan. The last part of the Zero's history was even more tragic. It became the vehicle ridden by the kamikaze fighters in the last months of the war, young men selected for suicide bombing missions against the American navy.

The movie makes no mention of the kamikaze. Nor, besides the occasional visions of destruction granted to Jirō and the occasional intonation of the word *hametsu* (destruction), does it ever come to grips with the terrible defeat that the Zero, by its early success, ironically helped create. By giving the Japanese an overinflated sense of confidence in their war effort, the Zeros helped to expand and prolong the war.

In movie after movie, Miyazakiworld has displayed the stupidity and horror of war, and Miyazaki has taken every opportunity to excoriate the military in interviews and speeches, so his final film's lack of confrontation with war and its aftermath seems especially problematic. It is hard to avoid the conclusion that Miyazaki is still working through guilt over his family factory's role in supporting the war and his family's relative comfort during the war. But I believe that more than guilt is operative. It is mixed in with the larger complex of emotions that have helped inspire some of Miyazaki's most interesting creations.

With a few exceptions in museums, the Zero no longer exists. Jirō's plane therefore was a safe fantasy to project dreams of perfection, flight, and power into the "foreign country" of the past, and the movie a silent wish to end the onrush of time at a golden moment before the reality of war set in. By dealing with military technology that is defunct, Miyazaki can engage with his personal and national past in a safely displaced form.

On one hand, Miyazaki loathes war and fiercely protests against it. On the other, he creates manga and films that celebrate the glories of military technology. Rather than explain the apparent contradiction, it is perhaps better to embrace it, as Miyazaki's producer, Toshio Suzuki, suggests. By his own account, it is Suzuki who, after reading the manga, persuaded Miyazaki to create the film version of *The Wind Rises*. The reason, according to the producer, was that he wanted to see how a supposed pacifist who loves to draw military technology would put these contradictory positions in a film. According to Suzuki, Miyazaki is not alone in his contradictions. The producer says, "Many Japanese people after the war felt this way," and goes on to suggest that *The Wind Rises* might serve as a "hint as to how to live in the times to come."[11]

In fact, across history and geography, humans have celebrated technological progress linked to suffering and death. Miyazaki deals directly with this troubling aspect of the human spirit when he has Caproni ask Jirō, "Which would you rather live in? A world with or without pyramids?" Caproni's implication is that the technological and aesthetic achievement of the pyramids was achieved only through hideous human suffering and sacrifice. Overall, the film seems to be arguing for the pyramids, no matter what cost, a thorny message that may be hard for some audiences to accept.

In *The Wind Rises* Miyazaki is attempting to confront a question that has engaged him in previous films, but to do so in a new and more challenging way. This is the question of whether technology can or should serve as an end in itself. In films such as *Nausicaä, Laputa,* and *Princess Mononoke,* science fiction and fantasy kept the issue at a safe remove. In this film, Miyazaki creates a new kind of fantasy—a history that stops just before the darker side of technological development appears. Yet this fantasy is historically grounded, and as such is no longer quite so arm's-length. That the Zeros were magnificent technological achievements that brought death to tens of thousands is more than an inconvenient truth. Miyazaki has talked about feeling "overtaken by history." More memorably and rather shockingly, he insists that his animation is also something to feel guilty about. "I have no pride or sense of accomplishment in this," he has said recently, noting once again that his young viewers ought to be outside rather than watching animation at home.[12]

The brash young animator who had long ago caused a sensation by making a robot girl come alive in 1962 had become a seventy-two-year-old man who at least at times seems to have relinquished the sense of mastery and control that made him a world builder of unparalleled accomplishments.

Now in 2013, after a lifetime of gargantuan effort and amazing triumphs, the director seemed to be painfully reacquainting himself with these feelings of powerlessness that united the Japanese at the end of the Second World War. He tells Shibuya, "The wind of *The Wind Rises* is the wind I felt roaring and shaking the trees while I lay in bed on the second floor after the [earthquake] and meltdown. . . . It's a terrible wind and it is roaring hard."[13]

Yet the movie does not end in tragedy, at least for its protagonist. In a coda set in the future after the war, Jirō sees Naoko appear before him, still young and beautiful, her white parasol whipping gaily in the wind. The movie's original ending had Naoko saying "Kite" (Come), but this was changed by Suzuki, apparently because "Come" suggested that Naoko was inviting Jirō to join her in the world of death. In the completed film that audiences see, she tells her husband, "Ikite"—Live—echoing Ashitaka's "Ikiro!" in *Princess Mononoke*. But in my view the world Naoko had asked Jirō to come to is not necessarily the world of death but the world of dreams, imagination, beauty, and hope. In other words, it is the animated universe that Miyazaki has conjured up over the past forty years, and one that his films will continue to invite us to for years to come.

# 16
# Conclusion

The *mononoke* set the princess on his shoulders and returned

to the mountain.

━ **PRINCESS MONONOKE**, The First Story

Miyazakiworld is a world of ambiguous and sometime open endings—the city that takes leave into the open sky at *Laputa*'s conclusion, Ashitaka's and San's uncertain future at the end of *Princess Mononoke,* even the ambiguous finale of *The Wind Rises*. A month and a half after the opening of *The Wind Rises* in 2013, Miyazaki announced his retirement, though as of 2018 that announcement may be premature. Still, the retirement press conference on September 1, 2013, is worth attention. Miyazaki opened with two succinct statements: "Through the years I have frequently talked about retiring, so many of you are perhaps wondering if this time I am really sincere." He paused a moment, looked hard at the crowd of reporters, and continued: "I am."

In the ensuing hour and a half, reporters asked about the state of his health, what he might have to say to his many fans in Korea about the controversial *The Wind Rises,* what part of his work had given him the most pleasure or the most difficulty. He was polite and forthcoming. With Suzuki at his side occasionally interjecting his own replies, Miyazaki explained that he was retiring not because of health problems but rather because he felt he had had enough of making full-length feature films: increasingly, more time and effort went into creating them. He spoke about focusing on the immensely popular Ghibli Museum, going for mountain walks, perhaps visiting Kyoto. He was gracious about the Ghibli Studio staff, some of whom had worked with him for the three decades of its existence, calling them a "team" and citing their many contributions. Admitting that the responsibilities of being a director had caused him "perplexity" and "confusion," he added a few lovely words on the beauty of animation, saying that it "allowed you to see the secrets of the world," such as "how the wind moves" or how "muscles work" or "where a glance falls." In response to the question about Korean reactions to *The Wind Rises,* he simply suggested that people should go and see the film and make up their own minds.

Twice Miyazaki pronounced himself "free." The reality, of course, is more complicated. With a career spanning five decades, an unparalleled work ethic that produced a string of masterpieces perhaps unsurpassed by any other auteur, and ongoing global popularity, it is hard to imagine the director being exactly "free" to spend the rest of his life walking in the mountains. In fact, he acknowledged that "as long as he could still drive," he planned to commute to his atelier every day. In the sole reference to his family, he said that he'd told his wife that he hoped she would continue to make daily bento box lunches for him.

The real question is whether Miyazaki can free his soul to relax and enjoy his final years. He is a man of immense contradictions and simple tastes (ramen rather than foie gras), who has spent his life constructing elaborate fantasy realms. He adores aircraft but doesn't enjoy flying and is deeply concerned about technology's pernicious effects. He loves children but becomes furious when they persist in watching a video rather than playing outside. He spends Sundays cleaning a river near his house but prefers not to be allied with ardent environmentalists. He emphasizes life but in the past decade or so has frequently talked of death.

A man who lives in his head and in his extraordinary imagination, Miyazaki is at the same time all too painfully aware of the darkness of the world around him. Throughout his life he has built utopian worlds, from the fantasy Euroworld of *Cagliostro* to the ethereal post-tsunami realm of *Ponyo.* As Karen Sands-O'Connor reminds us, however, "The search for utopia usually ends in two places, disillusionment or home."[1] It is easy to find disillusionment in many of Miyazaki's pronouncements. In the past decade in particular he at times has seemed to lose hope in a Japan that appears irredeemably shellshocked from two decades of recession and the triple horrors of earthquake, tsunami, and nuclear meltdown. The fact that the director had envisioned collapse in so many of his films only made things worse, as a statement he made after the March 2011 Fukushima nuclear disaster attests: "History has shown its face."[2]

Disillusionment also surfaces in his attitude toward Japanese animation, which he refuses to watch. Perhaps this is understandable, given his taste for a quiet life, but more disconcerting is the disappointment he sometimes shows toward Ghibli. The director's relationship with Takahata, so important early in his career, had severely attenuated, while the younger staff disappointed him. Miyazaki has lamented that his staff seems to care about him only for the paycheck he provides, and he has excoriated younger animators for their lack of talent. His torturous relationship with his son Goro, who had been taken on at Ghibli to direct a movie based on Ursula K. Le Guin's *Tales from Earthsea,* had become the stuff of tabloid fodder. By the time of the press conference Goro seemed to have redeemed himself with his successful direction of *Up on Poppy Hill* (Kokurikozaka kara, 2011). The young director Hiromasa Yonebayashi had also had a hit with *The Secret World of Arietty* (Karigurashi no Ariechi, 2010). Despite these relative successes, the director seemed to be "preparing himself for the worst," according to Yōichi Shibuya.[3]

But if Miyazaki were merely a misanthrope we would not be watching his films. He has moments of enthusiasm as well as moments of despair. In an earlier interview, he spoke of going for a Sunday walk along the river with his wife and feeling that "really Japan is a pretty good place."[4] In his movies the "pretty good" Japan still exists, in the rice paddies of *Totoro,* in the energy and community of *Spirited Away*'s bathhouse, in the spirit of renewal and hope in *Ponyo,* and in the ethereal gardens of *The Wind Rises.*

The many gardens that Miyazaki's films showcase may be his most beautiful representation of the "home" that O'Connor says is one side of utopian longing. Ranging from Gina's floral bower in *Porco Rosso* and Lady Eboshi's "secret garden" in *Princess Mononoke* to Howl's hideaway in *Howl's Moving Castle,* they offer peace, solitude, and tranquility, perhaps even a conduit to the beautiful garden of Miyazaki's childhood before the night of the air raids. As of this writing he is completing a short film he has wanted to make for decades about the life of a caterpillar, another nod to childhood and nature.

Miyazaki suffers because he loves the world and wants to be in it at the same time that he excoriates it and wants to give up. When I interviewed him in February 2014, he flitted back and forth between these two poles. He expressed delight in watching the children playing next door in the Ghibli nursery. He spoke of his pleasure in discovering *The Tales of Hoffman* stories during the New Year's break. He also stated that he "did not want to become another Kurosawa," the great live-action film director who, in some minds at least, continued creating films after he had lost his touch. Miyazaki's mention of Kurosawa suggested an active concern with maintaining his legacy.

Miyazaki's most striking remark, however, came at the end of our interview, when I asked him how he would like to be depicted if someone were to paint his portrait. What kinds of things would he like to include—books? Curios? He hesitated a minute, then sighed and shrugged his shoulders. "Nothing," he said. "They can just paint me walking into shadows."

This is the man who wrote, "Life is the light that shines in the darkness," and who has consistently provided the world with color and radiance. Nonetheless, there is a part of Miyazaki that just wants to retreat.

In 1980, long before he began work on *Princess Mononoke,* Miyazaki wrote and illustrated a children's book of the same name. Set in feudal Japan, it tells the story of a *mononoke,* a possessed spirit, who has taken the form of an enormous wildcat. Originally a prince, he has been turned into a beast due to his brutal and selfish behavior. The mononoke kidnaps a sturdy young princess, whom he attempts to marry, only to have her forcefully reject him. While clearly echoing *Beauty and the Beast,* the story ends with a delightful twist. After various adventures and enchantments, the mononoke and the princess return to his mountain hideout and live happily together, the possessed prince remaining in beast form. Among Miyazaki's illustrations for the book is one of the most enchanting he has ever made, a depiction of the furry striped beast lying contentedly near the fire, his boots up in a relaxed pose, the princess close by.

The story is adventurous and entertaining and a little dark. But its overall vision of acceptance is one that is at the heart of Miyazaki's work. I like to imagine the director, having completed his long professional journey, kicking back in a lovely fantasy world of his own devising, his manifold creations at hand to inspire and soothe him forever after.

# NOTES

### Prologue

1. Miyazaki, interviewed in Talbot, "The Auteur of Anime."
2. Miyazaki, *Turning Point*, 408.
3. Cavallaro, *The Anime Art of Hayao Miyazaki*, 16.
4. Kaoru, *Miyazaki Hayao no jidai*, 425.
5. Suzuki quoted in Kajiyama, *Jiburi majikku*, 210.
6. Oshii in conversation with Ueno, "Miyazaki no kōzai," 91.
7. Ibid., 101.
8. In retaliation for Oshii's "Stalinist" description, Miyazaki criticized him for his obsessive fondness for basset hounds. Miyazaki, *Kaze no kaeru basho*, 191–192.
9. Talbot, "The Auteur of Anime," 64.

### 1. *Hametsu*

1. Brigadier General Bonner Fellers, quoted in Dower, *War Without Mercy*, 41.
2. Miyazaki, "Kenpō kaeru nado no hoka," 4.
3. Louis, *Ends of British Imperialism*, 39.
4. Handō and Miyazaki, *Koshinukeaikokudangi*, 52.
5. Natsume Sōseki quoted in Yu, *Natsume Sōseki*, 120.
6. Isao Takahata, "Rokujū nen no heiwa no ōkisa," 21.
7. Nakagawa, "Sensō wa kowai," 19.
8. Miyazaki, "Jiyu ni nareru kūkan," 29.
9. Miyazaki quoted in Ōizumi, *Miyazaki Hayao no genten*, 174.
10. Ibid.
11. Hayao Miyazaki, *Sen to Chihiro no kamikakushi*, Program Guide, 2001, n.p.

12. See Napier, "Panic Sites."
13. Shimizu, "Sukoyaka naru bōsō," 93. Film scholar Peter Boss coined the term "intimate apocalypse" in relation to individual physical collapse. Boss, "Vile Bodies and Bad Medicine," 16. But I use the term in a wider sense to include familial or household collapse.
14. Handō and Miyazaki, *Koshinukeaikokudangi,* 112–116.
15. Ibid., 53–54.
16. Ōizumi, *Miyazaki Hayao no genten,* 35.
17. Ibid., 26.
18. Ibid., 27.
19. Ibid., 28.
20. Ibid., 32.
21. Ibid., 33.
22. Eng and Kazanjian, *Loss,* 2.


## 2. Constructing an Animator

1. Miyazaki, *Starting Point,* 97.
2. Ibid., 200.
3. See Takahata, *Juniseiki no animeeshon.*
4. Ōizumi, *Miyazaki Hayao no genten,* 58.
5. Cameron, "McLuhan, Youth, and Literature," 112.
6. Ōizumi, *Miyazaki Hayao no genten,* 57.
7. Miyazaki, "Kenpō o kaeru nado," 4.
8. Nathan, "Introduction," xiii.
9. Miyazaki, "Kenpō o kaeru nado," 5.
10. Ibid.
11. Miyazaki, *Turning Point,* 166.
12. Miyazaki, *Starting Point,* 45.
13. Ōizumi, *Miyazaki Hayao no genten,* 75.
14. Ibid., 68.
15. Ibid., 59–60.
16. Ibid., 61.
17. Miyazaki, *Starting Point,* 50.
18. Ōizumi, *Miyazaki Hayao no genten,* 79.
19. Miyazaki, quoted in Hikaru Hosoe, "Meisaku kansho Tonari no Totoro," 139.

20. Ibid., 90–91.
21. Miyazaki, *Starting Point,* 369, 372.
22. Miyazaki, *Shuppatsuten,* 82. The English version of *Shuppatsuten, Starting Point,* translates this key sentence as "Don't be stifled by your parents," but the original Japanese uses the word "kuikorosu," which translates as "devour" or "bite to death." As Shunsuke Sugita suggests, Miyazaki may also be referring to "A Madman's Diary," a famous story by the Chinese writer Lu Xun, in which the "madman" sees human history as a constant replay of "people eating people," and at the end cries out, "Save the children!" Sugita, *Miyazaki Hayaoron,* 10.
23. Handō and Miyazaki, *Koshinukeaikokudangi,* 52.
24. Ibid., 52.
25. Miyazaki, *Starting Point,* 208, 209.
26. Ōizumi, *Miyazaki Hayao no genten,* 80.
27. Miyazaki, *Starting Point,* 208.
28. Ibid., 209.
29. Ōizumi, *Miyazaki Hayao no genten,* 78.
30. Miyazaki, *Starting Point,* 130.
31. Ibid., 372.
32. Ōizumi, *Miyazaki Hayao no genten,* 38.
33. Miyazaki, *Starting Point,* 49.
34. Ibid.
35. Ibid., 70.
36. Ibid., 72.
37. Ibid., 91.

### 3. The Joy of Movement

1. Kotabe and Okuyama, "Kare wa kaze o kitte, hashite inai to ki ga sumanaindesu."
2. Ōtsuka, *Sakuga Asemamire,* 112, 105.
3. Ibid., 167, 25.
4. Ibid., 117.
5. Kotabe and Okuyama, "Kare wa kaze o kitte, hashite inai to ki ga sumanaindesu," 44.
6. Ōtsuka, *Sakuga Asemamire,* 117.
7. Shibaguchi, *Animeeshon no shikishokunin,* 62–63.
8. Miyazaki quoted in Kotabe and Okuyama, "Kare wa kaze o kitte, hashite inai to ki ga sumanaindesu," 46.

9. Ibid.

10. Yasuda quoted in Shibaguchi, *Animeeshon no shikishokunin*, 56.

11. It is also extremely likely that the plot of *Princess Mononoke* owes something to *Horus*. While Prince Ashitaka in *Mononoke* is a considerably more complex and interesting character than is Horus, both are young men forced into exile, both must journey to faraway villages, and both must deal with enigmatic young women.

12. Kotabe and Okuyama, "Kare wa kaze o kitte, hashite inai to ki ga sumanaindesu," 48, 45.

13. "Miyazaki Hayao, Staff Interview," 189.

14. Interview with Yasuo Ōtsuka, ibid., 182–183; Ōizumi, *Miyazaki Hayao no genten*, 122.

15. Ōtsuka, *Sakuga Asemamire*, 128; "Miyazaki Hayao, Staff Interview," 189; Miyazaki, *Starting Point*, 202.

16. Yasuda quoted in Shibaguchi, *Animeeshon no shikishokunin*, 61.

17. "Kaisha yori Horusu Sutafu ni haifu sareta chirashi," 142, 143.

18. Kotabe and Okuyama, "Kare wa kaze o kitte, hashite inai to ki ga sumanain-desu," 49.

19. Ibid.

20. Cooper-Chen, *Cartoon Culture*, 30.

21. Ōtsuka, *Sakuga Asemamire*, 184.

22. Ibid., 168, 180.

23. Takahata, "Afuren bakari no enerugi-to saiki," 182, 188–189.

24. Ōtsuka, *Sakuga Asemamire*, 169.

25. Ibid., 167.

26. Ōizumi, *Miyazaki Hayao no genten*, 127–128.

### 4. Ups and Downs

1. Boym, "Ruinophilia." Miyazaki, *Turning Point*, 397.

2. Miyazaki, *Starting Point*, 67.

3. Ōtsuka, *Sakuga Asemamire*, 186. Sugita, *Miyazaki Hayaoron*, 37.

4. Ōtsuka, *Asemamire*, 181. Miyazaki, "Miyazaki Hayao jisaku o kataru," 130.

5. Ōtsuka, *Asemamire*, 183. Kano, *Miyazaki Hayao Zensho*, 13.

6. "John Lasseter Pays Emotional Tribute to Hayao Miyazaki at Tokyo Film Festival," *Hollywood Reporter*, October 24, 2014. Ōtsuka, *Sakuga Asemamire*, 212.

7. Miyazaki quoted in Kano, *Miyazaki Hayao Zensho*, 11.
8. Sugita, *Miyazaki Hayaoron*, 37.
9. Sumikura, "Cagliostro," 100.
10. McCarthy, *Hayao Miyazaki*, 65. Kano, *Miyazaki Hayao Zensho*, 16.
11. Ōizumi, *Miyazaki Hayao no genten*, 125. Miyazaki's anecdote eerily echoes a reminiscence of one of Miyazaki's favorite writers, Natsume Sōseki, who spent two miserable years in London at the turn of the twentieth century and at one point confronted a "dwarfish fellow" walking toward him, who turned out to be his own reflection.
12. Miyazaki, *Starting Point*, 331.
13. Tateno, *Enpitsu senki*, 18.
14. Miyazaki, *Starting Point*, 204.
15. Katsukawa, "Miyazaki Hayao no ichinichi," 5. Miyazaki, *Starting Point*, 204.
16. Goro Miyazaki, quoted in Ōizumi, *Miyazaki Hayao no genten*, 177.
17. Miyazaki, *Starting Point*, 297.
18. Miyazaki, "Aru shiage kensa no josei," 155.
19. Miyazaki, *Starting Point*, 181.
20. Miyazaki, "Aru shiage kensa no josei," 135.
21. Miyazaki, *Starting Point*, 184.

## 5. *Nausicaä* and "the Feminine Principle"

1. Yōichi Shibuya interviewing Miyazaki in *Kaze no kaeru basho*, 261.
2. Kano, *Miyazaki Hayao Zensho*, 47.
3. Miyazaki, *Starting Point*, 392–393.
4. Miyazaki, *Kaze no kaeru basho*, 264.
5. Miyazaki, *Starting Point*, 336. Hisaishi's special contribution to *Nausicaä*, Kyoko Koizumi suggests, was to use the Dorian mode, developed in the early Byzantine church, to suggest "images of ancient Europe." Koizumi, "An Animated Partnership," 63. The association of the Dorian mode with the Christian liturgy is consistent with the impression of Nausicaä's character in the film as a Judeo-Christian messiah figure.
6. Katsukawa, "Miyazaki Hayao no ichinichi," 12, 13.
7. Miyazaki, *Starting Point*, 334.
8. Inoue, *Animeeshon Jienerēshon*, 217.
9. Quoted in Kano, *Miyazaki Hayao Zensho*, 70.

10. Miyazaki, *Starting Point*, 284.
11. Shaw, "Bug Love."
12. For an analysis of Japanese environmental issues in relation to citizen movements in the 1960s and 1970s, see McKean, *Environmental Protest and Citizen Politics in Japan*.
13. Miyazaki quoted in Kano, *Miyazaki Hayao Zensho*, 51–52.
14. Miyazaki, "Kenpo o kaeru mote no hoka," 4.
15. Miyazaki, quoted in Komatsu, "Mori no kamikoroshi to sono noroi," 49.
16. Miyazaki, *Starting Point*, 106.
17. Napier, *Anime from* Akira *to* Howl's Moving Castle, 166–167.
18. Robert Backus, *The Riverside Counselor's Stories* (Stanford: Stanford University Press, 1985), 43.
19. Tanaka, "Sanji ga munashiku hibiku Miyazki Hayao no taidō ga koko ni aru," 124.
20. Miyazaki, *Starting Point*, 393.
21. Ibid., 367.

## 6. Orphans of the Sky

1. Murase, *Miyazaki no fukami e*, 82.
2. Interview by Yōichi Shibuya, in Miyazaki, *Kaze no kaeru basho*, 291. Ibid., 290.
3. In 1971 Miyazaki had collaborated on an animated version of the Stevenson novel, called *Animal Treasure Island* (Dōbutsu Takarajima). For a comparison of Stevenson and Miyazaki, see Napier, "Where Shall We Adventure?"
4. Miyazaki quoted in Kano, *Miyazaki Hayao Zensho*, 86.
5. Ibid., 93.
6. Miyazaki quoted ibid., 83. Suzuki discusses the failure of this marketing strategy in Suzuki, *Jiburi no nakamatachi*, 22.
7. Miyazaki, *Starting Point*, 295, 296.
8. Ibid., 341.
9. Ibid., 50.
10. Miyzaki quoted in Kano, *Miyazaki Hayao Zensho*, 83.
11. Ibid., 107.
12. Lamarre, *The Anime Machine*, 95. Lioi, "The City Ascends."
13. While *Wall-E* was directed by Andrew Stanton, Pixar's head, John Lasseter, is an enormous fan of *Laputa*. In an interview in Japan in 2016 he describes how he was "spellbound" by the movie's "extraordinary appeal." Lasseter, "Interview," 30.

14. Lioi, "The City Ascends."
15. Moylan, *Demand the Impossible,* 34.
16. Muska's blindness is another hint that Miyazaki may still be working through parental issues in *Laputa.* Blindness is psychoanalytically linked to castration, as Freud suggests in his discussion of the Greek play *Oedipus Rex.* By blinding/castrating the male authority figure, Pazu (and Sheeta) assert their own potency in a parentless world.
17. According to Kano, the image of the tree in *Laputa* was inspired by a baobab tree in Antoine de Saint-Exupéry's *The Little Prince,* another fantasy work treasured by Miyazaki. Kano, *Miyazaki Hayao Zensho,* 100.
18. Lioi, "The City Ascends."
19. Ibid.

## 7. Umbrellas in the Haunted Forest

1. Hosoe, *Hyakukai "Tonari no Totoro" o mite mo akinai hito no tame ni.*
2. Boym, *The Future of Nostalgia,* 69, xiv.
3. Miyazaki, quoted in Hosoe, "Meisaku kansho Tonari no Totoro," 86.
4. Miyazaki, *Starting Point,* 355.
5. Brophy, *100 Anime,* 156. Ivy, *Discourses of the Vanishing,* 2.
6. For a discussion of the *satoyama*'s place in contemporary Japanese discourse, see Knight, "The Discourse of 'Encultured Nature' in Japan." Miyazaki, *Starting Point,* 402.
7. Ebert, *My Neighbor Totoro* review (1993).
8. This is basically Hosoe's theme throughout his article and subsequent book. But it becomes particularly clear in his article "Meisaku kansho Tonari no Totoro," 139–140.
9. Miyazaki quoted in Hirano, "Arakajime tsuihō sareta kodomotachi no supirito," 130.
10. Hosoe, "Meisaku kansho Tonari no Totoro," 139.
11. Ibid., 91. Kajiyama, *Jiburi majikku,* 51.
12. Tanaka, "Tonari no totoro to kodomo no fuantaji," 50.
13. Ibid.
14. See Hosoe, "Meisaku kansho Tonari no Totoro," 112.
15. Kajiyama, *Jiburi majikku,* 55.
16. Todorov, *The Fantastic.*

17. Tanaka goes even further in exploring Totoro's maternal potential, suggesting there may be an "ambivalence" in the depiction of his huge mouth (perhaps linking to Miyazaki's concern that children can be "devoured" by their parents) and of Totoro's supernatural companion the Catbus, which has a large mouth and teeth and a womblike interior. He also brings up intriguing parallels with Maurice Sendak's fantasy *Where the Wild Things Are*. Tanaka, "Tonari no totoro to kodomo no fuantaji," 51–56.

18. Hosoe, "Meisaku kansho Tonari no Totoro," 128.

19. Ibid., 133.

20. Kaplan and Wang, Introduction to *Trauma and Cinema*, 16.

21. Shimizu, *Miyazaki o yomu*, 213–242.

22. Ibid., 223.

23. Hiroshi Aoi has suggested some parallels between *Totoro* and the Spanish Civil War film *Spirit of the Beehive*, in which two sisters mingle fantasy with grim reality by hiding a fugitive soldier whom the younger one sees as a kindhearted monster figure. See Aoi, *Miyazaki anime no ango*, 30–33.

24. Hosoe, *Hyakukai "Tonari no Totoro" o mite mo akinai hito no tame ni*, 106.

## 8. The Witch and the City

1. Suzuki, *Jiburi no nakamatachi*, 32.

2. Ibid., 31.

3. Kawakami, *Kono eiga wa omoshiroi!* 22.

4. Sugita, *Miyazaki Hayaoron*, 141.

5. Kadono eventually acknowledged the significant differences between prose and visual art: "The sense of narrative in animation is completely different from storytelling in writing. In animation the viewer follows along with the story in front of their eyes, but in the case of writing, the story is supported by the read-er's anticipation and prediction each time you turn the page." Quoted in Kano, *Miyazaki Hayao Zensho*, 136.

6. Miyazaki, *Starting Point*, 262.

7. Murase, *Miyazaki Hayao no fukami*, 126–128.

8. Shunsuke Sugita, a male critic, remembers how much he adored Kiki as a young boy, precisely because she was more approachable and real than Nausicaä or Clarisse. Sugita, *Miyazaki Hayaoron*, 141.

9. Murakami, "Danseigenri o yume no ryōiki ni osameta shōjo no tabidachi," 135.

10. Sugita, *Miyazaki Hayaoron,* 140.
11. Miyazaki quoted in Suzuki, *Jiburi no nakamatachi,* 45.
12. Kano, *Miyazaki Hayao Zensho,* 148.
13. Ibid., 149.
14. Foster, "Haunting Modernity," 14.
15. Sugita, *Miyazaki Hayaoron,* 135.
16. Kano, *Miyazaki Hayao Zensho,* 151.

## 9. *Porco Rosso* Lands in Casablanca

1. Kōji Okuda discusses the relationship between *Casablanca* and *Porco Rosso* at some length, noting that, in Marco's character, Miyazaki has gone "beyond Rick." He also speculates that Marco's American bête noir, Curtis, is named for the director of *Casablanca,* Michael Curtiz, although it should be noted that Curtis is also the name of a company that manufactured some of the most important seaplanes of the period. See Okuda, "Kurenai no buta to 'hisen,'" 137–143.
2. Miyazaki, quoted in Kano, *Miyazaki Hayao Zensho,* 157.
3. Miyazaki, *Kaze no kaeru basho,* 84.
4. Kano, *Miyazaki Hayao Zensho,* 155.
5. Miyazaki, *Kaze no kaeru basho,* 85.
6. See Kano, *Miyazaki Hayao Zensho,* 170.
7. Miyazaki quoted in Miyazaki and Kato, *Toki ni wa mukashi no hanashi o,* 86.
8. Miyazaki, *Kaze no kaeru basho,* 92.
9. Okuda, "Kurenai no buta to 'hisen,'" 145.
10. Miyazaki, *Kaze no kaeru basho,* 80.
11. Ibid., 86.
12. Ibid.
13. Patrick Drazen also brings up the issue of survivor's guilt, specifically in relation to Marco's face changing into that of a pig after coming home from the war. Drazen, "Sex and the Single Pig," 198.
14. Miyazaki and Kato, *Toki ni wa mukashi no hanashi o,* 89.
15. Ibid.
16. Drazen, "Sex and the Single Pig," 198.
17. Dahl, "They Shall Not Grow Old," 66.
18. Kato in Miyazaki and Kato, *Toki ni wa mukashi no hanashi o,* 97.
19. Miyazaki, *Kaze no kaeru basho,* 81.

20. Patrick Drazen discusses what he sees as clearly sexual elements in *Porco Rosso* in Drazen, "Sex and the Single Pig."

## 10. From Messiah to Shaman

1. Miyazaki, *Nausicaä of the Valley of the Wind*, 7: 212.
2. Halifax, *Shamanic Voices*, 3.
3. Miyazaki, *Kaze no kaeru basho*, 222.
4. Brophy, *100 Anime*, 158.
5. Halifax, *Shamanic Voices*, 4.
6. Miyazaki, *Nausicaä of the Valley of the Wind*, 1: 129.
7. Koyama, *Miyazaki Hayao mangaron*, 168–169.
8. Miyazaki, *Nausicaä of the Valley of the Wind*, 1: 128.
9. Ibid., 3: 31.
10. Ibid., 4: 88.
11. Ibid., 5: 59.
12. Ibid., 5: 80.
13. Ibid., 5: 136, 141.
14. Halifax, *Shamanic Voices*, 21. Miyazaki, *Nausicaä of the Valley of the Wind*, 6: 29.
15. Miyazaki, *Nausicaä of the Valley of the Wind*, 6: 88.
16. Osmond, "*Nausicaä* and the Fantasy of Hayao Miyazaki," 72.
17. Miyazaki, *Nausicaä of the Valley of the Wind*, 7: 107.
18. Ibid., 7: 119.
19. Ibid., 7: 202.
20. Ibid., 7: 199.
21. Ibid., 7: 200, 201.
22. Ibid., 7: 208.
23. Ibid., 7: 208, 216.
24. Ibid., 7: 223.
25. Nagayama, "Sekusuresu purinsesu Naushika," 142. Koyama, *Naushika mangaron*, 6. Yoko Goi, "Jōka sareteyuku Miyazaki sekai no yami: Naushika no tadoritsuita basho," *Comics Box*, no. 1 (January 1995): 38. Sugita, *Miyazaki Hayaoron*, 302. Kano, *Miyazaki Hayao Zensho*, 47.
26. Ogihara-Schuck, "The Christianizing of Animism in Manga and Anime," 134.
27. Interview by Yōichi Shibuya in Miyazaki, *Kaze no kaeru basho*, 228, 225.
28. Miyazaki, *Nausicaä of the Valley of the Wind*, 7: 198.

## 11. The Faces of Others

1. Peter Paik sums up the conflict in *Princess Mononoke* as a "clash between two rights, pitting the defenders of the forest against a community of the oppressed and the outcast." Paik, *From Utopia to Apocalypse*, 94.

2. Karen Thornber in her book *Ecoambiguity* suggests that these questions are more typical of an East Asia worldview found in art and literature that goes beyond the romanticizing visions of East Asians as living in harmony with nature and presents a more intricate notion of how humans interact with the natural.

3. According to Mamoru Oshii, it was Miyazaki's longtime colorist, the formidable Michiyo Yasuda—a "tough lady" whom Miyazaki "would never go against"—who persuaded Miyazaki to use digital paint for *Princess Mononoke,* thus setting up the adoption of digital methods for the rest of the film. Oshii and Ueno, "Miyazaki no kōzai," 89.

4. Miyazaki, *Kaze no kaeru basho,* 152.

5. Suzuki, *Jiburi no nakamatachi,* 100, 105.

6. Kajiyama, *Jiburi majikku,* 49.

7. Suzuki, *Jiburi no nakamatachi,* 96.

8. Maslin, "Film Review: Waging a Mythic Battle to Preserve a Pristine Forest." Kajiyama, *Jiburi majikku,* 174.

9. In an interview shortly after the release of *Princess Mononoke,* Miyazaki specifically criticizes early Disney films as "simplistic" and goes on to praise such animated works as the Russian *Snow Queen* or the French *La Bergère et le Ramoneur.* Miyazaki, *Turning Point,* 92.

10. Not all critical reaction was laudatory. Kano mentions Emiko Okada's review in the Marxist newspaper *Akahata,* in which she appreciates the visuals but also states, "To put it plainly, the movie is hard to understand." Another prominent feminist critic, Minako Saito, dismissed the film as "the repulsiveness of having to watch some old guy's fantasies on the big screen." Quoted in Kano, *Miyazaki Hayao Zensho,* 217. The film critic Minoru Takahashi calls the movie a "failure." Takahashi, "Reo no kubi no yukue," 225.

11. In a discussion of *Princess Mononoke* with several scholars, Miyazaki mentions the "unfairness" of something like ectopic dermatitis afflicting a little girl and goes on to say, "In these times when such 'curses' will afflict them, our films need to feature boys and girls who must face those hardships." Miyazaki, *Turning Point,* 105. In the same discussion Miyazaki explains how he wanted to

situate Ashitaka as "being from a marginalized group" and acknowledges that the mark on Ashitaka's arm is a "mark of discrimination." Ibid., 114.

12. Suzuki felt that *Princess Mononoke* was a more intriguing title. He proudly recounts the story of his preemptive press release and Miyazaki's initial annoyance in *Jiburi no nakamatachi*, 171.

13. See Napier, "Confronting Master Narratives."

14. Miyazaki quoted in Kano, *Miyazaki Hayao Zensho*, 201.

15. Miyazaki, *Kaze no kaeru basho*, 181–182.

16. Takahata quoted in Kano, *Miyazaki Hayao Zensho*, 218.

17. Heise, *Sense of Place, Sense of Planet*, 304.

18. Whitley, *The Idea of Nature in Disney Animation*, 3.

## 12. The Intimate Apocalypse of *Spirited Away*

1. Miyazaki, *Kaze no kaeru basho*, 212–213.

2. Anno, "So shite densha wa iku," 125.

3. Miyazaki, *Turning Point*, 226.

4. Miyazaki, *Kaze no kaeru basho*, 223.

5. See Napier, *Anime from* Akira *to* Howl's Moving Castle, 156–157. Also see Shimizu, "Sukoyaka naru bōsō," 93.

6. Miyazaki, *Turning Point*, 235.

7. Miyazaki, "Jiyu ni nareru kūkan," 25.

8. Yoshioka, "Heart of Japaneseness," 272.

9. Miyazaki, "Jiyu ni nareru kūkan," 25.

10. Ibid.

11. Anno, "So shite densha wa iku," 124. For a detailed discussion of the film's imagistic hybridity see Yoshioka, "Heart of Japaneseness," 259–263.

12. Miyazaki, *Kaze no kaeru basho*, 210.

13. For further discussion of anorexia and bulimia as metaphors in *Spirited Away*, see Napier, "An Anorexic in Miyazaki's Land of Cockaigne." Also see Hansen, "Eating Disorders and Self-Harm in Japanese Culture and Cultural Expressions," 57–60.

14. Bordo, *Unbearable Weight*, 139, 141.

15. Ibid., 201.

16. Miyazaki, *Kaze no kaeru basho*, 208.

17. Kajiyama, *Jiburi majikku*, 196.

18. Miyazaki, *Kaze no kaeru basho,* 206.
19. Ibid., 214.
20. Ibid., 208.
21. Masashi Shimizu points to the many feminine and maternal aspects of the world of *Spirited Away,* such as the sea that surrounds the bathhouse and the womblike qualities of the bathhouse itself. Although it is hard to say how conscious Miyazaki was of all this in constructing his fantasy world, it is notable how relatively unimportant or weak the masculine presence appears, from Haku, who is indentured to Yubaba, to Kamaji the boiler man, who is never free to leave the building. Most interesting is No Face, who seems to be figured as masculine. His presence disrupts the bathhouse, but when forced out of it, he becomes a quiet, emaciated figure dependent on the maternal Zeniba. Shimizu, *Miyazaki o yomu,* 91–92.
22. Miyazaki, *Kaze no kaeru basho,* 216.

### 13. The Castle, the Curse, and the Collectivity

1. Kajiyama, *Jiburi majikku,* 201.
2. Miyazaki quoted in Kano, *Miyazaki Hayao Zensho,* 305.
3. Suzuki, *Jiburi no nakamatachi,* 190.
4. Ibid., 189.
5. Craig, "Interview with Diana Wynne Jones." Kano, *Miyazaki Hayao Zensho,* 278.
6. Miyazaki, *Kaze no kaeru basho,* 274.
7. Miyazaki, quoted in Kano, *Miyazaki Hayao Zensho,* 279.
8. Kano, *Miyazaki Hayao Zensho,* 303–304. Sugita, *Miyazaki Hayaoron,* 243.
9. Kano, *Miyazaki Hayao Zensho,* 306.
10. Kotani, "Mahōzukai wa dare da!?" 66. It is also possible to see the castle as exemplifying what Svetlana Boym calls the "off-modern," or "the architecture of adventure." See Boym, *Architecture of the Off-Modern.* Cassegard, *Shock and Naturalization in Contemporary Japanese Literature,* 5.
11. Chen, "Ugoku shiro no keifugaku," 88, 90–91.
12. Kotani, "Mahōzukai wa dare da!?" 66.
13. Ibid., 68. Conversely, E. Ann Kaplan suggests that aging itself can be a traumatic identity crisis, especially for women. Kaplan, *Trauma Culture,* 46.
14. Osmond, "Castles in the Sky."

15. Kano, *Miyazaki Hayao Zensho*, 304.
16. Sugita, *Miyazaki Hayaoron*, 234.
17. Chen, "Ugoku shiro no keifugaku," 91.

## 14. Rich and Strange

1. Sōseki had become entranced by this picture when he was living a lonely existence in London. Miyazaki went to London to see the picture and brought a poster back to hang on the wall of his atelier. The work inspired him to create a scene around Ponyo's sea goddess mother, Granmamare. Granmamare's supine position and long hair floating gently in the water evoke Ophelia's death pose in Millais's painting. For a discussion of the painting and other Sōseki inspirations on Miyazaki see Furuta, "Imēji no rensa."
2. Said, *On Late Style*. Hutcheon and Hutcheon. "Late Style(s)," 6.
3. Miyazaki, *Zoku Kaze no kaeru basho*, 138.
4. Ibid., 108, 103, 104.
5. Sugita, *Miyazaki Hayaoron*, 246.
6. Miyazaki, *Zoku Kaze no kaeru basho*, 116–117.
7. Ibid., 128, 108.
8. Sugita, *Miyazaki Hayaoron*, 148.
9. Ebert, *Ponyo* review.
10. Sōsuke's acceptance of Ponyo also contrasts with *The Little Mermaid* story. In both the original and the Disney version there is no sense of valuing the non-human world. The mermaid's transformation into human is clearly viewed as a step up.
11. Ballard, *The Drowned World*, 28.
12. Sugita, *Miyazaki Hayaoron*, 253.

## 15. "A Terrible Wind"

1. Miyazaki, *Zoku Kaze no kaeru basho*, 171, 179.
2. Ibid., 182.
3. Ibid., 163, 219.
4. Ibid., 174, 208.
5. Fukasaku, "Kaze wa mada fuite iru ka," 10.
6. Onozawa, "'Kaiken' to 'sensō,'" 13.

7. Suzuki, *Kaze ni fukarete*, 227.
8. Onozawa, "'Kaiken' to 'sensō,'" 15.
9. Okada, *Kaze tachinu o kataru*, 33.
10. Ibid., 36.
11. Suzuki, *Kaze ni fukarete*, 226.
12. Miyazaki, *Zoku kaze ni kaeru basho*, 209–210.
13. Ibid., 217.

## 16. Conclusion

1. Sands-O'Connor, "The Quest for the Perfect Planet," 181.
2. Miyazaki, *Zoku kaze no kaeru basho*, 183.
3. Yōichi Shibuya in Miyazaki, *Zoku kaze no kaeru basho*, 108.
4. Miyazaki, *Zoku kaze no kaeru basho*, 123.

# BIBLIOGRAPHY

Anno, Hideaki. "So shite densha wa iku." *Eureka* 33, no. 10 (2001): 124–127.

Aoi, Hiroshi. *Miyazaki anime no ango*. Tokyo: Shinchosha, 2004.

Ballard, J. G. *The Drowned World*. London: J. M. Dent, 1962.

Bettelheim, Bruno. *The Uses of Enchantment: The Meaning and Importance of Fairy Tales*. 1976; New York: Vintage, 2010.

Bordo, Susan. *Unbearable Weight: Feminism, Western Culture, and the Body*. Berkeley: University of California Press, 2003.

Boss, Peter. "Vile Bodies and Bad Medicine." *Screen* 27 (1986): 14–24.

Boym, Svetlana. *Architecture of the Off-Modern*. New York: Temple Hoyne Buell Center for the Study of American Architecture, 2008.

———. *The Future of Nostalgia*. New York: Basic, 2001.

———. "Ruinophilia." In *The Atlas of Transformation*, ed. Zybnek Baladran. Prague: J. R. P. Ringier, 2010.

Brayton, Dan. *Shakespeare's Ocean: An Ecocritical Exploration*. Charlottesville: University of Virginia Press, 2012.

Brophy, Phillip. *100 Anime*. London: British Film Institute, 2005.

Buscombe, Edward. "Ideas of Authorship." In *Theories of Authorship*, ed. John Caughie, 22–34. New York: Routledge, 1981.

Butler, David. *Fantasy Cinema: Impossible Worlds on Screen*. London: Wallflower, 2009.

Cameron, Eleanor. "McLuhan, Youth, and Literature." In *Crosscurrents of Criticism: Horn Book Essays, 1968–1977*, ed. Paul Heins, 98–120. Boston: Horn Book, 1997.

Caruth, Cathy. "Literature and the Enactment of Memory." In *Trauma and Visuality in Modernity*, ed. Lisa Saltzman and Eric Rosenberg, 189–221. Hanover, NH: Dartmouth College Press, 2006.

———. *Unclaimed Experience: Trauma, Narrative, and History*. Baltimore: Johns Hopkins University Press, 1996.

Cassegard, Carl. *Shock and Naturalization in Contemporary Japanese Literature.* Folkestone, UK: Global Oriental, 2007.

Cavallaro, Dani. *The Anime Art of Hayao Miyazaki.* Jefferson, NC: McFarland, 2006.

Chen, Dominick. "Ugoku shiro no keifugaku." *Eureka* 36, no. 13 (2004): 84–94.

Colson, Raphaël, and Gaël Régner. *Hayao Miyazaki: Cartographie d'un Univers.* Lyon: Moutons Électriques, 2010.

Cooper-Chen, A. *Cartoon Culture: Globalization of Japanese Popular Media.* New York: Peter Lang, 2010.

Craig, Amanda. "Interview with Diana Wynne Jones." *The Times* (London), March 2005.

Dahl, Roald. "They Shall Not Grow Old." In *Roald Dahl Collected Stories,* 59–75. New York: Knopf, 2006.

Darling-Wolf, Fabienne. "The 'Lost' Miyazaki: How a Swiss Girl Can Be Japanese and Why It Matters." *Communication, Culture and Critique* 9 (2016): 499–516.

Denison, Rayna. *Anime: A Critical Introduction.* London: Bloomsbury, 2015.

Dower, John. *War Without Mercy: Race and Power in the Pacific War.* New York: Random House, 1986.

Drazen, Patrick. "Sex and the Single Pig: Desire and Flight in *Porco Rosso.*" In *Mechademia 2,* ed. Frenchy Lunning, 189–199. Minneapolis: University of Minnesota Press, 2007.

Duncombe, Stephen. *Dream: Re-Imagining Progressive Politics in an Age of Fantasy.* New York: New Press, 2006.

Ebert, Roger. *My Neighbor Totoro* movie review. RogerEbert.com, www.rogerebert.com/reviews/great-movie-my-neighbor-totoro-1993.

———. *Ponyo* movie review. RogerEbert.com, www.rogerebert.com/reviews/ponyo-2009.

Eng, David, and David Kazanjian. *Loss: The Politics of Mourning.* Berkeley: University of California Press, 2003.

Foster, Michael Dylan. "Haunting Modernity." *Asian Ethnology* 71, no. 1 (2012): 3–29.

———. *Pandemonium and Parade: Japanese Monsters and the Culture of the Yōkai.* Berkeley: University of California Press, 2009.

Fukasaku, Kenta. "Kaze wa mada fuite iru ka." *Eiga geijutsu* 445 (2013): 10–12.

Furuta, Ryo. "Imēji no rensa: Sōseki kara Miyazaki Hayao e." *Geijutsu shinchō* (June 2013): 52–53.

Gerstner, David, and Janet Steiger, eds. *Authorship and Film.* New York: Routledge, 2003.

Halifax, Joan. *Shamanic Voices: A Survey of Visionary Narratives.* New York: Penguin, 1979.

Handō, Kazutoshi, and Hayao Miyazaki. *Koshinukeaikokudangi.* Tokyo: Bunko Jiburi, 2013.

Hansen, Gitte Marian. "Eating Disorders and Self-Harm in Japanese Culture and Cultural Expressions." *Contemporary Japan* 23 (2011): 49–69.

Hardacre, Helen. *Shinto: A History.* Oxford: Oxford University Press, 2017.

Harvey, David. *Spaces of Hope.* Berkeley: University of California Press, 2000.

Heise, Ursula. *Sense of Place, Sense of Planet: The Environmental Imagination of the Global.* Oxford: Oxford University Press, 2008.

Hirano, Katsumi. "Arakajime tsuihō sareta kodomotachi no supirito." *Kinema Muku* 6 (1999): 130–133.

Hori, Tatsuo. *Kaze Tachinu/Utsukushii mura.* Tokyo: Shinchosha, 2014.

Hosoe, Hikaru. *Hyakukai "Tonari no Totoro" o mite mo akinai hito no tame ni.* Osaka: Wasen Shoin, 2014.

———. "Meisaku kansho Tonari no Totoro: Haha Naru Shizen to Innosensu." *Konan Joshi Daigaku Kenkyū Kiyō Bungaku-Bunkahen* 42 (2006): 85–149.

Hutcheon, Linda, and Michael Hutcheon. "Late Style(s): The Ageism of the Singular." *Occasion: Interdisciplinary Studies in the Humanities* 4 (2012): 1–11.

Inoue, Shizuka. *Animeeshon Jienerēshon.* Tokyo: Shakai Hihyōsha, 2004.

Ivy, Marilyn. *Discourses of the Vanishing: Modernity, Phantasm, Japan.* Chicago: University of Chicago Press, 1995.

Jameson, Fredric. *Archaeologies of the Future: The Desire Called Utopia and Other Science Fictions.* London: Verso, 2005.

Kadono, Eiko. *Majo no takkyūbin.* Tokyo: Fukuinkan, 1985.

"Kaisha yori Horusu Sutafu ni haifu sareta chirashi." *Horusu no daibouken.* Tokyo: Tokuma Shoten, 1984.

Kajiyama, Sumiko. *Jiburi majikku: Suzuki Toshio no sōmōryoku.* Tokyo: Kodansha, 2004.

Kano, Seiji. *Miyazaki Hayao Zensho.* Tokyo: Film Art, 2007.

Kaoru, Kumi. *Miyazaki Hayao no jidai 1941–2008.* Tokyo: Chōeisha, 2008.

Kaplan, E. Ann. *Trauma Culture: The Politics of Terror and Loss in Media and Literature.* New Brunswick, NJ: Rutgers University Press, 2005.

Kaplan, E. Ann, and Ban Wang. "Introduction: From Traumatic Paralysis to the Force Field of Modernity." In *Trauma and Cinema: Cross Cultural Explorations,* ed. E. Ann Kaplan and Ban Wang, 1–22. Hong Kong: Hong Kong University Press, 2004.

Katsukawa, Katsushi. "Miyazaki Hayao no ichinichi: Donatte gomen ne." In *Kaze no tani no Nausicaä Guidebook*, 1–16. Tokyo: Tokuma Shoten, 1984.

Kawakami, Taiten. *Kono eiga wa omoshiroi!* Tokyo: Seikisha, 2015.

Key, Alexander. *The Incredible Tide*. Philadelphia: Westminster, 1970.

Kiridōshi, Risaku. *Miyazaki Hayao no "sekai."* Tokyo: Chikuma Shinsho, 2001.

Knight, Catherine. "The Discourse of 'Encultured Nature' in Japan: The Concept of *Satoyama* and Its Role in 21st-Century Nature Conservation." *Asian Studies Review* 34, no. 4 (2010): 421–441.

Koizumi, Kyoko. "An Animated Partnership: Joe Hisaishi's Musical Contributions to Hayao Miyazaki's Animated Films." In *Drawn to Sound: Animation Film Music and Sonicity*, ed. Rebecca Coyle, 60–74. London: Equinox, 2010.

Komatsu, Kazuhiko. "Mori no kamikoroshi to sono noroi." *Eureka* 29, no. 11 (1997): 48–53.

Kotabe, Yōichi, and Reiko Okuyama. "Kare wa kaze o kitte, hashite inai to ki ga suma-naindesu." In *Kinemamuku Filmmakers*, no. 6, *Miyazaki Hayao*, ed. Takeshi Yoro, 44–54. Tokyo: Kinemamukusha, 1999.

Kotani, Mari. "Mahōzukai wa dare da!?" *Eureka* 36, no. 13 (2004): 64–70.

Koyama, Masahiro. *Miyazaki Hayao mangaron*. Tokyo: Gendaishokan, 2009.

Lamarre, Thomas. *The Anime Machine: A Media Theory of Animation*. Minneapolis: University of Minnesota Press, 2009.

Lasseter, John. "Interview." *Kinema Muku*, July 2016.

Levinas, Emmanuel. "Enigma and Phenomenon." In *Basic Philosophical Writings*, ed. Adrian Peperzak, Simon Critchley, and Robert Bernasconi, 65–77. Bloomington: Indiana University Press, 1996.

Levitas, Ruth. *The Concept of Utopia*. Bern, Switzerland: Peter Lang, 2010.

Lioi, Anthony. "The City Ascends: *Laputa: Castle in the Sky* as Critical Ecotopia." *Image-TexT* 5, no. 2 (2010): http://www.english.ufl.edu/imagetext/archives/v5_2/lioi/.

Louis, Wm. Roger. *Ends of British Imperialism: The Scramble for Empire, Suez, and Decolonization*. London: Tauris, 2006.

Maslin, Janet. "Film Review: Waging a Mythic Battle to Preserve a Pristine Forest." *New York Times*, September 27, 1999.

McCarthy, Helen. *Hayao Miyazaki: Master of Japanese Animation: Films, Themes, Artistry*. Berkeley, CA: Stone Bridge, 1999.

McKean, Margaret A. *Environmental Protest and Citizen Politics in Japan*. Berkeley: University of California Press, 1981.

Miyazaki, Hayao. "Aru shiage kensa no josei 'Lupin Sansei to no kakawari' animeishon to mangaeiga jibun no genten." In *Kaze no tani no Naushika Guidebook*, 131–145. Tokyo: Tokuma Shoten, 1984.

———. *Hikōtei jidai*. Tokyo: DaiNihon kaiga, 2004.

———. "Jiyu ni nareru kūkan." *Eureka* 33, no. 10 (2001): 25–37.

———. *Kaze no kaeru basho: Nausicaä kara Chihiro made no kiseki*. Tokyo: rockin' on, 2002.

———. *Kaze tachinu*. Tokyo: DaiNihon kaiga, 2015.

———. "Kenpō kaeru no hoka." *Neppū*, July 2013, 21–25.

———. "Miyazaki Hayao jisaku o kataru." In *Kaze no tani no Naushika Guidebook*, 111–130. Tokyo: Tokuma Shoten, 1984.

———. *Nausicaä of the Valley of the Wind*. Vols. 1–7. San Francisco: VIZ Media, 2004.

———. *Orikaeshiten 1997–2008*. Tokyo: Iwanami, 2008.

———. *Shuppatsuten 1979–1996*. Tokyo: Tokuma Shoten, 1996.

———. *Starting Point, 1979–1996*. Trans. Beth Cary and Frederik L. Schodt. San Francisco: VIZ Media, 2009.

———. *Turning Point, 1997–2008*. Trans. Beth Cary and Frederik L. Schodt. San Francisco: VIZ Media, 2008.

———. *Zoku Kaze no kaeru basho: Nausicaä kara Chihiro made no kiseki*. Tokyo: rockin' on, 2013.

"Miyazaki Hayao, Staff Interview." *Horusu no daibouken*. Tokyo: Tokuma Shoten, 1984.

Miyazaki, Hayao, and Tokiko Kato. *Toki ni wa mukashi no hanashi o*. Tokyo: Tokuma Shoten, 1992.

Moylan, Tom. *Demand the Impossible: Science Fiction and the Utopian Imagination*. New York: Methuen, 1986.

Murakami, Tomohiko. "Danseigenri o yume no ryōiki ni osameta shōjo no tabidachi— Tezuka-teki femininizumu o koete." *Kinema Muku* 6 (1999): 134–137.

Murase, Manabu. *Miyazaki no fukami e*. Tokyo: Heibonsha, 2004.

Nagayama, Kaoru. "Sekusuresu purinsesu: manga *Kaze no tani no Nausicaä* no sei to furajiritē o megutte." In *Miyazaki Hayao no sekai* (Bamboo Mook), 142–150. Tokyo: Chikushobo, 2005.

Nakagawa, Rieko. "Sensō wa kowai." *Neppū*, July 2013, 16–19.

Napier, Susan. *Anime from* Akira *to* Howl's Moving Castle: *Experiencing Contemporary Japanese Animation*. New York: Palgrave, 2005.

———. "An Anorexic in Miyazaki's Land of Cockaigne." In *Devouring Japan,* ed. Nancy Stalker. Oxford: Oxford University Press, forthcoming.

———. "Confronting Master Narratives: History as Vision in Miyazaki Hayao's Cinema of De-Assurance." *positions: East Asian Cultures Critique* 9, no. 2 (2001): 467–493.

———. "Matter Out of Place: Carnival, Chaos, and Cultural Recovery in Miyazaki Hayao's *Spirited Away.*" *Journal of Japanese Studies,* Summer 2006.

———. "Panic Sites: The Japanese Imagination of Disaster from *Godzilla* to *Akira.*" In *Contemporary Japan and Popular Culture,* ed. John Treat, 235–262. Honolulu: University of Hawai'i Press, 1996.

———. "Where Shall We Adventure? Robert Louis Stevenson Meets Hayao Miyazaki." In *Effervescent Britannia,* ed. W. Roger Louis. London: Tauris, 2018.

Nathan, John. "Introduction." In Kenzaburō Ōe. *Teach Us to Outgrow Our Madness,* ix–xxv. New York: Grove, 1990.

Odell, Colin, and Michelle Le Blanc. *Studio Ghibli: The Films of Hayao Miyazaki and Isao Takahata.* Croydon, UK: Kamera, 2015.

Ogihara-Schuck, Eriko. "The Christianizing of Animism in Manga and Anime: American Translations of Hayao Miyazaki's *Nausicaä of the Valley of the Wind.*" In *Graven Images: Religion in Comic Books and Graphic Novels,* ed. A. David Lewis and Christine Hoff Kramer, 133–148. New York: Continuum, 2010.

———. *Miyazaki's Animism Abroad.* Jefferson, NC: McFarland, 2014.

Ōizumi, Mitsunari. *Miyazaki Hayao no genten.* Tokyo: Chode Hansha, 2002.

Okada, Toshio. *"Kaze tachinu" o kataru: Miyazaki Hayao to Sutajio Jiburi, son o kiseki to mirai.* Tokyo: Kobunsha, 2013.

Okuda, Kōji. "Kurenai no buta to 'hisen.'" In *Jiburi no mori e: Takahata Isao, Miyazaki Hayao o yomu,* ed. Miyuki Komemura, 118–151. Tokyo: Moribanashisha, 2003.

Okuhara, Rieko. "Walking Along with Nature: A Psychological Interpretation of *My Neighbor Totoro.*" *The Looking Glass: New Perspectives on Children's Literature* 10, no. 2 (2006): http://www.lib.latrobe.edu.au/ojs/index.php/tlg/article/view/104/100.

Okumiya, Masatake, and Jiro Horikoshi, with Martin Caidin. *Zero.* New York: i books, 2002.

Onozawa, Minohiko. "'Kaiken' to 'sensō' e to mukau jidai no ideorojii sōchi: Kaze Tachinu." *Eiga geijutsu* 445 (2013): 13–15.

Oshii, Mamoru, and Toshiya Ueno. "Miyazaki no kōzai." In *Miyazaki Hayao no sekai,* 87–106. Tokyo: Takeshobo, 2005.

Osmond, Andrew. "Castles in the Sky." *Sight and Sound,* October 2005, old.bfi.org.uk/sightandsound/issue/200510.

———. "*Nausicaä* and the Fantasy of Hayao Miyazaki." *Foundation: The International Review of Science Fiction* 72 (1998): 57–81.

Ōtsuka, Yasuo. *Sakuga Asemamire.* Tokyo: Tokuma Shoten, 2001.

Paik, Peter. *From Utopia to Apocalypse: Science Fiction and the Politics of Catastrophe.* Minneapolis: University of Minnesota Press, 2010.

Price, David. *The Pixar Touch: The Making of a Company.* New York: Knopf, 2008.

Rose, Gilbert J. *Trauma and Mastery in Life and Art.* Madison, CT: International Universities Press, 1996.

Said, Edward. *On Late Style: Music and Literature against the Grain.* New York: Vintage, 2007.

Sakai, Makoto. *Saigo no kokumin sakka: Miyazaki Hayao.* Tokyo: Bungei Shinsho, 2008.

Sands-O'Connor, Karen. "The Quest for the Perfect Planet: The British Secondary World as Utopia and Dystopia, 1945–1999." In *Utopian and Dystopian Writing for Children and Young Adults,* ed. Carrie Hints and Elaine Ostry, 179–195. New York: Routledge, 2003.

Shaw, Scott. "Bug Love." *New York Times,* August 23, 2014.

Shibaguchi, Yasuko. *Animeeshon no shishikishokunin.* Tokyo: Studio Ghibli, 1997.

Shimizu, Masashi. *Miyazaki o yomu: Bosei to kaosu no fuantaji.* Tokyo: Choeisha, 2001.

Shimizu, Yoshiyuki. "Sukoyaka naru bōsō: *Tonari no Totoro* no openu endingu o megutte." *Pop Culture Critique* 1 (1997): 92–101.

Sugita, Shunsuke. *Miyazaki Hayaoron: kamigami to kodomotachi no monogatari.* Tokyo: NHK, 2014.

Sumikura, Yoshiki. "Cagliostro: Shōjo no kokoro no nusumikata." *Eureka* 29, no. 11 (1997): 96–103.

Suzuki, Toshio. *Jiburi no nakamatachi.* Tokyo: Shinchosha, 2016.

———. *Kaze ni fukarete.* Tokyo: Chuo Koron-Shinsha, 2013.

Takahashi, Minoru. "Reo no kubi no yukue: Miyazaki wa kamikoroshi o kansei shitaka?" *Eureka* 29, no. 11 (1997): 223–229.

Takahata, Isao. "Afuren bakari no enerugi-to saiki." In *Kaze no tani no Naushika Guidebook,* 182–190. Tokyo: Tokuma Shoten: 1984.

———. *Juniseiki no animeishon-kokuhoemakimono ni miru eigateki, animeteki naru mono.* Tokyo: Tokuma Shoten, 1999.

———. "Rokujū nen no heiwa no ōkisa." *Neppū,* July 2013, 20–26.

Talbot, Margaret. "The Auteur of Anime." *New Yorker,* January 17, 2005, 64–75.

Tanaka, Eiji. "Sanji ga munashiku hibiku Miyazki Hayao no taidō ga koko ni aru." *Kinema Muku,* 6 (1999): 122–125.

Tanaka, Motoko. *Apocalypse in Contemporary Japanese Science Fiction*. New York: Palgrave, 2014.

Tanaka, Shinichi. "Tonari no totoro to kodomo no fuantaji." *Tokyo Kokusai Daigaku Rongi Ningen Shakai Gakubuhen* 1 (1995): 49–58.

Tateno, Hitomi. *Enpitsu senki: Dare mo shiranakatta sutajio Jiburi*. Tokyo: Chuokoron-sha, 2015.

Thornber, Karen. *Ecoambiguity: Environmental Crises and East Asian Literatures*. Ann Arbor: University of Michigan Press, 2012.

Todorov, Tzvetan. *The Fantastic: A Structural Approach to a Literary Genre*. Ithaca, NY: Cornell University Press, 1975.

Tolkien, J. R. R. "On Fairy Stories." In *The Monsters and the Critics,* ed. Christopher Tolkien, 109–161. London: George Allen and Unwin, 1983.

Warner, Marina. *Phantasmagoria*. Oxford: Oxford University Press, 2006.

Wells, Paul. *Understanding Animation*. London: Routledge, 1998.

Whitley, David. *The Idea of Nature in Disney Animation*. Farnham, UK: Ashgate, 2013.

Williams, Rosalind. *The Triumph of Human Empire: Verne, Morris, and Stevenson at the End of the World.* Chicago: University of Chicago Press, 2013.

Yoshioka, Shiro. "Heart of Japaneseness: History and Nostalgia in Hayao Miyazaki's *Spirited Away*." In *Japanese Visual Culture,* ed. Mark W. MacWilliams, 256–273. New York: M. E. Sharpe, 2008.

Yu, Beongcheon. *Natsume Soseki*. New York: Twayne, 1968.

# ACKNOWLEDGMENTS

Over the years of researching and writing I have received a great deal of help from a variety of individuals and institutions. Through a faculty research grant from Tufts I was able to spend a semester at the Tufts Center for the Humanities, presided over by Jonathan Wilson, but during my time there under the visiting director John Fyler. My then chairman Hosea Hirata supported my application, and I am very thankful. A grant from the Rockefeller Foundation allowed me to spend a precious six weeks at the Bellagio Center in Italy. Jennifer Robertson, Helen Hardacre, and Katherine Lasky all supported me in this effort. Both venues gave me the opportunity to try out my ideas in front of a wide and diverse audience. My current chairman, Gregory Carleton, arranged for me to have a reduced course load in my final year of writing, for which I cannot thank him enough. In the final stages of revisions I owe much thanks to the support of my friends Deb Weisgall, Katherine Lasky and Megan Marshall. Over the past six years I have offered a seminar on Miyazaki, and want to pay special tribute to my many wise and wonderful students who made the seminar the most enjoyable pedagogical experience of my life.

Among other individuals to whom I am grateful is Chao Chen, who, with endless patience, helped me explore a wide variety of reference materials. Eric Swanson and Ryoichi Kato assisted with some of the translation work. Janet Byrne was invaluable in aiding me with shaping the manuscript, and Branson Laszlo helped with technical matters. Steve Alpert advised me on some Studio Ghibli matters, and Mikiko Takeda assisted in arranging an interview with Hayao Miyazaki. I am, of course, beyond grateful to Mr. Miyazaki for spending time with me. Jonathan Nawrocki and Roland Kelts organized introductions for me to chat with former Ghibli staff members, including three whom I owe particular thanks: Atsuko Tanaka, Hiromasa Yonebayashi, and Eiko Tanaka. Michio Arimitsu was a wonderful sounding board in the early stages and provided me with important Japanese-language material. The two anonymous readers for Yale offered many excellent insights and suggestions.

I am very grateful to my editor at Yale University Press, Sarah Miller, for her consistent support, and to her assistant, Ash Lago. My copy editor at Yale, Dan Heaton, was inspiring to work with. My daughter Julia Napier, as always, provided useful feedback. Kathryn Hemmann and Roland Kelts read chapters and offered some useful revisions. Last and most important, my husband, Steve Coit, provided unstinting support, affection, and good humor during the eight long years of researching and writing. Steve and I met the year I started researching the book, so he has become an essential element of my own personal Miyazakiworld.

# INDEX

*The African Queen* (1951), 241

Aichi World Expo (2005), ix

*Akahata* (newspaper), 275n10

*Akira* (1988), 8, 85, 128

Akutagawa, Ryūnosuke, 6

*Alice in Wonderland* (Carroll), 109, 111, 198

*Animage* (magazine), 70

Animals: Miyazaki and, 49–50, 57, 77–78; *Nausicaä* and, xi, 73, 81–83; *Ponyo* and, 233–234, 244; *Porco Rosso* and, 149–153; *Princess Mononoke* and, 182–183, 186, 190, 193; *Spirited Away* and, 149, 198–199, 206, 231

*Animal Treasure Island* (1971), 270n3

Animation (anime): *Cagliostro* and, 64–65; culture and, 17; gender and, xi, 61, 74, 126; Ghibli and, 18, 45–46, 91, 177; history of, 17; Japan and, 17–18, 35–36, 61, 96; *Kiki* and, 123, 128; *Laputa* and, 89–90, 91; Miyazaki and, x, xiii, xviii, 16–19, 32–39, 43–44, 262, 275n9; *Nausicaä* and, 64, 76; *Ponyo* and, 231, 243; *Porco Rosso* and, 18, 146; *Princess Mononoke* and, 186; ruin and, xi; *Spirited Away* and, 196, 203–204;

Suzuki and, 233; Takahata and, 18, 35, 41–44, 102, 144, 215, 225; techniques of, 35–36, 42, 44; technology and, 96, 233; *Totoro* and, 18; *Wind Rises* and, 64, 248; work and, 135

Animism and, xii, 7, 75, 78, 84, 163, 173–176, 244

*Anne of Green Gables* (1979), 48–49

Anno, Hideaki, xvi–xvii, 197, 204

Aoi, Hiroshi, 272n23

Apocalypse. *See* Ruin and apocalypse

*Asahi Shimbun* (newspaper), 226

Aum Shinrikyo incident, 181

*Ballad of Tamlin* (song), 217

*Bambi* (1942), 187–188

*Beauty and the Beast* (1991), xiv, 264

Bodhisattvas, 84, 114, 237

Bordo, Susan, 207

Boss, Peter, 266n13 (ch. 1)

Boym, Svetlana, 56, 103, 277n10

Brophy, Philip, 104, 163

Buddhism, 6, 73, 80, 84, 114, 163, 237, 240–241

*Bungei Shunjū* (magazine), 26

*Cagliostro.* See *Castle of Cagliostro*

Cameron, Eleanor, 18

Carroll, Lewis, xii

*Casablanca* (1942), 140–157

Cassegard, Carl, 219

*Castle in the Sky.* See *Laputa: Castle in the Sky*

*Castle of Cagliostro* (1979), 55–69; animation and, 64–65; children and, 59; compared to *Conan,* 58, 67; compared to *Howl,* 59, 69, 218–219; compared to *Kiki,* 69; compared to *Laputa,* 87, 94; compared to *Nausicaä,* 64, 69; compared to *Porco Rosso,* 59, 67; compared to *Princess Mononoke,* 177; compared to *Spirited Away,* 69; compared to *Wind Rises,* 64, 255; curses and, 6; families and, 59; gender and, 56–57, 59, 63, 67; humanity and, 55, 59–60; inspiration for, xvi, 56–57, 62; Kano on, 60; love and, 67–68; making of, 58; manga and, 57, 59; Miyazaki on, 58; morals and, 59, 64; nature and, 56; politics and, 29, 58; reception of, 73–74; ruin and, xii, 55, 58, 66; setting of, 60; sexuality and, 25, 57, 67; symbolism and, 59–60; technology and, 64–66; tropes and, 66

Castles, Miyazaki's love of, 56, 218–219

Cavallaro, Dani, xiii

Chagall, Marc, 96

Chaplin, Charlie, 64

*Charlie and the Chocolate Factory* (Dahl), 152

Chen, Dominick, 219, 227

Children: *Cagliostro* and, 59; *Conan* and, 54; *Kiki* and, 125, 127; *Laputa* and, 13–14, 92–93, 97–98; Miyazaki and, 4, 13–14, 22, 93, 106, 261, 263; *Nausicaä* and, 83–84; *Nausicaä* manga and, 173; *Ponyo* and, 14, 47, 84, 231–232, 236, 239, 244, 245; *Princess Mononoke* and, 14; *Spirited Away* and, 84, 196, 211; *Totoro* and, xiii, 13–14, 22, 103, 105–106, 111–113, 121. *See also* Families; Mothers

Christianity, 7, 84, 158, 160, 163, 173, 175

Chuang Tze, 110, 115–116

*Conan.* See *Future Boy Conan*

Culture: animation and, 17; East Asian, 78, 110, 134, 173–175, 275n2; *Howl* and, 212, 216, 219, 226–227; *Kiki* and, 125, 127; *Nausicaä* manga and, 160; *Ponyo* and, 243; *Spirited Away* and, 197, 200–201, 203–204, 207; Western, 110, 160, 173–175; *Wind Rises* and, 3, 250–251. *See also* Tropes

Curses: *Cagliostro* and, 6; *Howl* and, 6, 216–217, 220–225; *Kiki* and, 220; *Laputa* and, 220; *Ponyo* and, 6, 220; *Porco Rosso* and, 6, 220; *Princess Mononoke* and, 6, 177, 182, 186, 194, 220; *Spirited Away* and, 26, 198, 220. *See also* Illness; Spirits

Dahl, Roald, 152–154

"Das Gibt's nur Einmal" (Heymann and Gilbert), 247, 254

Disasters. *See* Ruin and apocalypse

*Discourses of the Vanishing* (Ivy), 104

Disney, Walt, xii

Disney Studios, 21, 32, 36–37, 58, 176, 179–180, 187, 213

Dower, John, 1–2

*Dragon Ball Z* (1989), 33, 154

Drazen, Patrick, 152, 273n13, 274n20 (ch. 9)

*Dream Notes* (Miyazaki), 255–256

*The Drowned World* (Ballard), 245

*Dune* (Herbert), 73, 78

Earthquakes: Kantō (1923), 2, 10, 181, 251–252; Kobe (1995), 181; Tōhoku (2011), xiii, 232, 246, 262

East Asian world view, 78, 110, 134, 173–175, 275n2

Ebert, Roger, 105, 243

Emotions: *Howl* and, 223; *Kiki* and, 124–125, 139; *Nausicaä* manga and, 161; *Princess Mononoke* and, 183, 190, 192–193; *Spirited Away* and, 196–197; *Totoro* and, 102

Eng, David L., 14

Environmentalism, 77–78, 185–186, 261. *See also* Nature

Evslin, Bernard, 75

Fairy tales, 34, 67, 126–128, 132, 196–198, 217–218, 252–254

Families: *Cagliostro* and, 59; *Howl* and, 227–228; *Laputa* and, 271n16 (ch. 6); Miyazaki and, 2–4, 9–11, 16–32, 61–62, 238; *Ponyo* and, 23, 230; *Totoro* and, 16–32; *Wind Rises* and, 23–24, 251, 257. *See also* Children; Mothers

*The Fantastic* (Todorov), 110

Female protagonists. *See* Gender

Feminine principle, 51, 70–85, 131

Feminism, 126–128, 156

Folklore, 125–126, 217, 242–243

*For Those Who Have Watched Totoro a Hundred Times and Are Still Not Tired of It* (Hosoe), 102

Freud, Sigmund, 210, 271n16

Fu Fu, 1

*Fushigi* ("mysterious and wonderful"), 197–198

*Future Boy Conan* (1978), 49–54; children and, 54; compared to *Cagliostro*, 58, 67; compared to *Laputa*, 86–88, 93; compared to *Ponyo*, 230; compared to *Princess Mononoke*, 177; gender and, 32, 51–52, 67, 79; humanity and, 54; making of, 51–52; politics and, 29, 31, 53; ruin and, 53–54, 56; Takahata and, 51, 53; trauma and, 54; utopia and, 99

Gaiman, Neil, 179

Gardens, Japanese, 11, 185, 263

*The Gate* (Sōseki), 234

*Gekiga* (manga), 30–32

Gender: animation and, xi, 61, 74, 126; *Cagliostro* and, 56–57, 59, 63, 67; *Conan* and, 32, 51–52, 67, 79; feminine principle and, 51, 70–85, 131; feminism and, 126–128, 156; Ghibli and, 125–127, 129, 156; *Howl* and, 27, 69, 219–220; Japan and, 61, 67, 74, 126, 129, 238; *Kiki* and, 69, 122, 124–133; *Laputa* and, 87–88; Miyazaki and, xi–xii, 27–28, 34, 46, 49, 68–69; *Nausicaä* and, 79, 158; *Ponyo* and, 27, 238, 243;

Gender (*continued*)

    *Porco Rosso* and, 32, 67, 146, 154–156;
*Princess Mononoke* and, 27, 183–184;
*shōjo* and, 27, 52, 67–68, 87, 126, 130,
143, 222; *Spirited Away* and, 69

Ghibli, Studio: animation and, 18, 45–46,
91, 177; design of, 144; development
of, xiii, 34, 91, 210–211, 214; gender
and, 125–127, 129, 156; *Howl* and,
212–214, 227; Kano on, 139; mission
of, 111; Miyazaki and, 135, 184, 195, 201,
214, 233, 262; museum of, xv, 214, 261;
nature and, 144; politics and, xvii, 99;
reception of, 120, 122–123, 139, 148,
158, 179–180, 215, 233; *Spirited Away*
and, xviii, 196, 201, 213, 227; Suzuki
and, xiv, xvii, 15, 61, 90–91, 135, 144,
179; Takahata and, xiii, 34, 90–91, 215;
trauma and, 3; utopia and, xvii; work
and, 135

*Ghost in the Shell* (1995), xvi

Giardina, Domnico, 86

Goi, Yoko, 173

Good versus evil, 175, 180

*Grave of Fireflies* (1988), 102, 123, 226

*The Great Adventure of Horus: Prince of
the Sun* (1968), 35, 41–45, 49–50, 207

Guilt. *See* Trauma

*Gulliver's Travels* (Swift), 21, 36, 88

*Gulliver's Voyage beyond the Moon*
(1965), 21, 35–38, 49

*Gundam* (1979), 74

Halifax, Joan, 160, 164

*Harry Potter* (Rowling), 5, 92

Hartley, L. P., 246

*Heidi* (1974), 21, 48, 50, 60, 68

*Heidi* (Spyri), 21, 48

Heise, Ursula, 186

Heroines. *See* Gender

*Hikkikomori* phenomenon, 226–227

Hisaishi, Joe, 71–72, 113, 252, 269n5

*Hōjōki* (13th century classic), 180–181

*Hōjōkiden* (Hotta), 180–181

*Home Alone* (1990), 46

Hori, Tatsuo, xvi, 9, 253

Horikoshi, Jirō, 247–248, 253, 255

Hosoda, Mamoru, 214–215

Hosoe, Hikaru, 22, 101, 106, 115, 117, 121

*Howl's Moving Castle* (2004), 212–228;
compared to *Cagliostro,* 59, 69,
218–219; compared to *Kiki,* 214–215,
221; compared to *Laputa,* 219–220,
228; compared to *Nausicaä,* 216;
compared to *Ponyo,* 216, 244;
compared to *Princess Mononoke,*
219, 220, 224; compared to *Spirited
Away,* 212, 219–221; compared to
*Wind Rises,* 216; culture and, 212, 216,
219, 226–227; curses and, 6, 216–217,
220–225; emotions and, 223; family
and, 227–228; gender and, 27, 69,
219–220; Ghibli and, 212–214, 227;
humanity and, 216, 224; inspiration
for, 31, 213–217, 223; Japan and, 216,
219; Kano on, 214–215; making of,
213–214; Miyazaki on, 215; mothers
and, 220; reception of, 215–219,
226–227; ruin and, 8, 227; setting of,
216–218; symbolism and, 212; trauma
and, 215–216; utopia and, 212, 228;
war and, 213, 215, 217, 223, 225

Humanity: *Cagliostro* and, 55, 59–60; *Conan* and, 54; *Howl* and, 216, 224; *Laputa* and, 94–96; Miyazaki and, 77–78, 262; *Nausicaä* and, xi, 76–77, 79–81, 83; *Nausicaä* manga and, 159–161, 163–166, 169, 171, 174; *Ponyo* and, 231, 242, 244; *Princess Mononoke* and, xiii, 177, 181–185, 188–189, 191; *Totoro* and, 105, 109, 114–115

*The Hunger Games* (Collins), 80

Hutcheon, Michael and Linda, 231

Ikari, Gendou, xvii

Illness: *Laputa* and, 271n16 (ch. 6); Miyazaki and, 9, 17, 22; *Princess Mononoke* and, 184; *Spirited Away* and, 206–208; *Totoro* and, 105, 116, 121; *Wind Rises* and, 9, 254

*The Incredible Tide* (Key), 50–51

Inoue, Shizuka, 74

*The Interpretation of Dreams* (Freud), 210

Ivy, Marilyn, 104

James Bond, 56–57

*Jane Eyre* (Brontë), 92

Japan: animation and, 17–18, 35–36, 61, 96; constitution of, xiii, 3, 148, 249; families and, 23, 226–227; gender and, 61, 67, 74, 126, 129, 238; *Howl* and, 216, 219; *Kiki* and, 122, 128–129; Miyazaki and, xiii, 16–17, 19, 103–104, 262–263; nature and, 7, 77, 103–105, 181, 200; occupation of, 3–4, 18–19, 28–29; politics and, 3, 40–41, 157, 200; *Ponyo* and, 239–240, 263; *Princess Mononoke* and, 183–184; religion and, 240; ruin and, 7–8, 14, 77, 181, 232; *Spirited Away* and, 201, 263; technology and, 96; *Totoro* and, 102–104, 120–121, 263; trauma and, 10, 108–109, 181, 232; war and, 1–4, 14, 148; *Wind Rises* and, xii, 258, 263; work and, 61, 127

*Japan Sinks* (Komatsu), 7–8

*Jidaigeki* (historical samurai drama), 34, 176–177, 181, 183–184

Jones, Diana Wynne, 214, 216

*Journey to the West* (Chinese story), 31, 154

Kadono, Eiko, 124–127, 136, 272n5

*Kamikaze,* 8, 154, 257

Kamo no Chōmei, 6, 134, 155, 180–181, 194, 196, 224

Kano, Seiji: on *Cagliostro*, 60; on Ghibli, 139; on *Howl*, 214–215; on *Laputa*, 94, 271n17; on Miyazaki, xv, 58, 90, 145, 147, 184; on *Nausicaä*, 70–71, 173

Kantō earthquake (1923), 2, 10, 181, 251–252

Kaoru, Kumi, xiv

Kaplan, E. Ann, 119, 277n13

Kato, Kazuhiko, 57, 59

Kato, Tokiko, 147, 149–150, 153

Kawakami, Taiten, 124

Kazanjian, David, 14–15

Kazutoshi, Handō, 24

Kenta, Fukasaku, 250

*Kidnapped* (Stevenson), 92

*Kiki's Delivery Service* (1989), 122–139; animation and, 123, 128; children and, 125, 127; compared to *Cagliostro*, 69; compared to *Howl*, 214–215, 221; compared to *Laputa*, 124, 129–130; compared to *Nausicaä*, 124, 130; compared to *Ponyo*, 232, 243–244; compared to *Porco Rosso*, 148; compared to *Spirited Away*, 199; compared to *Totoro*, 127, 129–130, 138–139; culture and, 125, 127; curses and, 220; emotions and, 124–125, 139; gender and, 69, 122, 124–133; inspiration for, xvi, 45, 124–126, 131, 134–136; Japan and, 122, 128–129; making of, 123, 125, 129, 135; Miyazaki on, 125, 126–127, 137; mothers and, 130–131; nature and, 123, 127, 131, 133; reception of, 122–123, 129, 132, 135, 137–139; setting of, 123, 127–128; Suzuki and, 123, 129; symbolism and, 130–131, 133–135; Takahata and, 125; technology and, 130, 138; tropes and, 126–128, 138; work and, 128–132, 136–137

Kobe earthquake (1995), 181

Kondo, Yoshifumi, 195, 215

Kotabe, Yōichi, 33, 38, 41, 45, 48

Kotani, Mari, 218–221

Koyama, Masahiro, 165, 173

Kurosawa, Akira, xvi, 181, 183, 263

"The Lady Who Loved Insects" (court tale), 80

Lamarre, Thomas, 96, 174

*Laputa: Castle in the Sky* (1987), 86–100; animation and, 89–90, 91; children and, 13–14, 92–93, 97–98; compared to *Cagliostro*, 87, 94; compared to *Conan*, 86–88, 93; compared to *Howl*, 219–220, 228; compared to *Kiki*, 124, 129–130; compared to *Nausicaä*, 91, 94; compared to *Porco Rosso*, 148; curses and, 220; families and, 271n16 (ch. 6); gender and, 87–88; humanity and, 94–96; illness and, 271n16 (ch. 6); inspiration for, 27, 88–90, 94, 271n17; Kano on, 94, 271n17; love and, 88; making of, 86, 90–91; Miyazaki on, 91–92; morals and, 52; mothers and, 14, 94; nature and, 96; politics and, 29, 91, 98–99; reception of, 86, 91–94, 123; ruin and, 98–99; setting of, 86–88; sexuality and, 86; symbolism and, 97–99; Takahata and, 91; technology and, 87–90, 95–99; trauma and, 99; tropes and, 88, 92, 94–97; utopia and, 86, 94, 96, 98–99; war and, 97–99

Lasseter, John, 58, 63, 213, 270n13

Leblanc, Maurice, 57

Levinas, Emmanuel, 188

Lewis, C. S., 4

Lindgren, Astrid, 45–46

Lioi, Anthony, 96, 98

*The Little Mermaid* (Andersen), 236, 278n10

*The Little Prince* (Saint-Exupéry), 271n17

*Lolita* (Nabokov), 67

*The Long Afternoon of Earth* (Aldiss), 78

Louis, Roger, 2

Love: *Cagliostro* and, 67–68; *Laputa* and, 88; *Nausicaä* and, 73; *Ponyo* and, 230,

232, 238; *Porco Rosso* and, 148, 156;
  *Wind Rises* and, 9, 247
*Lupin III* (1971), 57, 125

"A Madman's Diary" (Xun), 267n22
*The Magic Mountain* (Mann), 9, 253–254
Manga: *Cagliostro and*, 57, 59; Miyazaki
  and, 17, 21–22, 30–31, 33, 70, 145; *Nausicaä* and, 70–73; *Porco Rosso* and,
  149; *Wind Rises* and, 255–257. *See also*
  *specific titles*
Mann, Thomas, 9, 253–254
Marxism, 29, 53, 160
Maslin, Janet, 179
Materialism, 91, 104, 125, 129, 145, 181,
  200, 216
Matsukawa incident, 28
*Matsuri* (Shinto rituals), 240
*Mazacon* (mother complex), 72–73
McCarthy, Helen, xiv, 60
Meguro Gajoen, 201
Millais, John Everett, 229, 237
Minamata Bay, chemical poisoning of,
  77, 82
Mishima, Yukio, 29
Miyazaki, Arata (brother), 11, 13, 18,
  20–22, 25, 27–30
Miyazaki, Goro (son), xv, 62, 214, 238, 262
Miyazaki, Hayao: on *Castle of Cagliostro*,
  58; compared to literary figures,
  xii, 21, 31; early career of, 33–51;
  education of, 17–21, 29–30; Ghibli
  and, 135, 184, 195, 201, 214, 233, 262;
  on *Howl*, 215; identity of, 39, 51–52,
  60, 84, 103; illness and, 9, 17, 22;
  influences on, xiv–xvi, 5–6, 31–32, 78,

96, 271n17; Kano on, xv, 58, 90, 145,
  147, 184; on *Kiki*, 125, 126–127, 137; on
  *Laputa*, 91–92; on *Nausicaä*, 71, 85;
  on *Nausicaä* manga, 160–161, 174;
  on *Ponyo*, 232–233, 238; on *Porco
  Rosso*, 149; on *Princess Mononoke*,
  184–185, 275–276n10; reception of,
  xiv, 123, 177–178; retirement of, ix,
  xv, 260–261, 264; Shibuya on, xv,
  238, 262; *shōjo* and, 27, 52, 67–68, 87,
  126, 130, 143, 222; on *Spirited Away*,
  196–197, 204–205, 209–210; Suzuki
  and, xv, 15, 30, 135, 238, 260–262;
  Takahata and, xvi, 15, 21, 30, 34–35,
  44–49, 262; on *Totoro*, 106; on *Wind
  Rises*, 246, 249, 258–259
Miyazaki, Katsuji (father), 2–4, 10, 19,
  23–26, 59
Miyazaki, Shirō (brother), 72, 94
Miyazaki, Yoshiko (mother), 9, 23, 26–27,
  72–73, 80, 85, 94
Miyazawa, Kenji, 119, 210
*Modern Times* (1936), 64–65
*Momotaro's Divine Sea Eagles* (1943), 34
*Momotaro's Divine Sea Warriors* (1945), 34
*Mono no aware* ("sadness of things")
  aesthetic, 8, 99, 254
Morals: *Cagliostro* and, 59, 64; good
  versus evil, 175, 180; *Laputa* and,
  52; *Nausicaä* and, xi, 79; *Nausicaä*
  manga and, 161, 164, 172, 175; *Ponyo*
  and, 243; *Porco Rosso* and, 146;
  *Princess Mononoke* and, 175, 177, 182,
  183–187, 190–191; *Spirited Away* and,
  200–202, 211; *Totoro* and, 121; *Wind
  Rises* and, 175, 250

*Mōsō Nōtō* (Miyazaki), 145

Mothers: *Howl* and, 220; *Kiki* and, 130–131; *Laputa* and, 14, 94; Miyazaki and, xiv, 13, 17–18, 26–29, 72–73, 85, 106, 147; *Nausicaä* and, 73, 75; *Nausicaä* manga and, 161, 165; *Ponyo* and, 14, 231, 239; *Spirited Away* and, 277n21; *Totoro* and, 13–14, 101, 105, 111, 116, 121, 272n17. *See also* Children; Families

Moylan, Tom, 96

Murakami, Haruki, 128

Murakami, Tomohiko, 128, 132

Murase, Manabu, 86, 127

*My Neighbor Totoro* (1988), 101–121; animation and, 18; children and, xiii, 13–14, 22, 103, 105–106, 111–113, 121; compared to *Kiki,* 127, 129–130, 138–139; compared to *Nausicaä,* 84; compared to *Ponyo,* 111, 243; compared to *Porco Rosso,* 148; compared to *Princess Mononoke,* 111; compared to *Spirited Away,* 107, 196, 198–199, 201; emotions and, 102; families and, 16–32; humanity and, 105, 109, 114–115; illness and, 105, 116, 121; inspiration for, 22, 47, 106–107, 113–114, 119–120, 272n17; Japan and, 102–104, 120–121, 263; making of, 101, 106–107, 113; Miyazaki on, 106; morals and, 121; mothers and, 13–14, 101, 105, 111, 116, 121, 272n17; nature and, 11, 78, 105–109, 111, 113–115, 117–118; otherness and, 111–112, 119; reception of, xiii, 101–102, 105–106, 108, 119–120, 123; religion and, 109–110; setting of, 102, 105, 107; spirits and, 7, 107–108, 113, 119; Suzuki and, 107, 110; symbolism and, 22–23, 111, 114–115, 119–121; trauma and, 105–109, 116, 118; tropes and, 101–102, 119; utopia and, 102–103, 106, 120–121; war and, 272n23

"My Point of Origin" (Miyazaki), 93

Nagayama, Kaoru, 173

Nakagawa, Rieko, xiv, 4

Nakao, Sasuke, 104

Nature: *Cagliostro* and, 56; Ghibli and, 144; Japan and, 7, 77, 103–105, 181, 200; *Kiki* and, 123, 127, 131, 133; *Laputa* and, 96; Miyazaki and, 2, 6–7, 11, 49, 77–78, 261; *Nausicaä* and, xi, 74, 76, 78–80, 181; *Nausicaä* manga and, 160, 163–168, 170, 174; *Ponyo* and, 232, 242–244; *Princess Mononoke* and, xiii, 78, 176–177, 181–194; ruin and, 6–7; *Spirited Away* and, 7, 26, 200–201; Takahata and, 78; *Totoro* and, 11, 78, 105–109, 111, 113–115, 117–118; *Wind Rises* and, 2, 11

*Nausicaä of the Valley of the Wind* (anime) (1984), 70–85; animals and, xi, 73, 81–83; animation and, 64, 76; children and, 83–84; compared to *Cagliostro,* 64, 69; compared to *Howl,* 216; compared to *Kiki,* 124, 130; compared to *Laputa,* 91, 94; compared to *Ponyo,* 84, 232, 244; compared to *Princess Mononoke,* 193; compared to *Spirited Away,* 84; compared to *Totoro,* 84; gender and,

70–85, 158; humanity and, xi, 76–77, 79–81, 83; inspiration for, xv–xvi, 75, 80; Kano on, 70–71, 173; love and, 73; making of, 70–71; manga and, 70–73; Miyazaki on, 71, 85; morals and, xi, 79; mothers and, 73, 75; nature and, xi, 74, 76, 78–80, 181; politics and, 181; *Princess Mononoke* and, 177, 181; reception of, 74, 84–85, 158; religion and, 71, 79–80, 84, 269n5; ruin and, 74, 75, 77; setting of, 75; Shibuya on, 174; spirits and, 85; Suzuki and, 70, 91; symbolism and, 71, 75, 79–80, 84–85, 158–175; Takahata and, 71–72; technology and, xi, 76; tropes and, 81; utopia and, 82, 99–100; war and, 76

*Nausicaä of the Valley of the Wind* (manga) (1994), 158–175; children and, 173; culture and, 160; emotions and, 161; humanity and, 159–161, 163–166, 169, 171, 174; inspiration for, 160–161; making of, 158–159; Miyazaki on, 160–161, 174; morals and, 161, 164, 172, 175; mothers and, 161, 165; nature and, 160, 163–168, 170, 174; politics and, 160, 175; reception of, 161–163, 165; religion and, 163–164, 166, 170, 173–175; ruin and, 159, 162, 168, 170; shamanism and, 160, 164–168, 173; spirits and, 160, 173; symbolism and, 159–175; technology and, 162, 174–175; trauma and, 173; tropes and, 172; utopia and, 167, 171–172, 175; war and, 163

*Neon Genesis Evangelion* (Anno), xvi–xvii

*Neppū* (journal), xiii–xiv, 3–4, 24

*Night on the Galactic Railroad* (1934), 210

*Night Train to the Stars* (Miyazawa), 31, 119

*Norwegian Wood* (Murakami), 148

Occupation of Japan, 3–4, 18–19, 28–29

*The Odyssey* (Homer), xi, 75

Ōe Kenzaburō, 7, 19, 126, 128

Ōizumi, Mitsunari, xiv, 5, 12–13, 20, 26, 28, 54

Okada, Emiko, 275n10

Okada, Toshio, xv, 253, 255

Okawa, Hiroshi, 34

Okuda, Kōji, 148, 273n1

Okuyama, Reiko, 33, 38, 43

Onozawa, Minohiko, 250–252

Ophelia (Millais), 229, 237

*The Origins of Cultivated Plants and Agriculture* (Nakao), 78

Osamu, Tezuka, 21, 33

Oshii, Mamoru, xvi, xvii, 265n8, 275n3

Osmond, Andrew, 169, 226

Ota, Akemi (wife of Miyazaki), 61–62

Otherness: *Ponyo* and, 111, 244; *Porco Rosso* and, 153; *Princess Mononoke* and, 111, 187–191; *Totoro* and, 111–112, 119

Ōtomo, Katsuhiro, 8, 85

Ōtsuka, Yasuo, xv, 34–37, 39, 43–44, 51–52, 57–58, 68, 72

Ozu, Yasujirō, 24

Paik, Peter, 275n1

*Panda and the Magic Serpent* (1958), 27, 31–35

*Panda and the White Serpent* (1961), 93, 182, 255

*Panda Go Panda* (1972), 31, 46–47, 50, 67
*Panda Go Panda! Rainy Day Circus* (1973), 1–2, 34, 46–47
Pearl Harbor attack, 1–2, 34
*A Personal Matter* (Ōe), 128
*Pippi Longstocking* (unreleased), 45–46
*The Pippi Longstocking That Never Was* (Ghibli), 46
Politics: *Cagliostro* and, 29, 58; *Conan* and, 29, 31, 53; Ghibli and, xvii, 99; Japan and, 3, 40–41, 157, 200; *Laputa* and, 29, 91, 98–99; Marxism and, 29, 53, 160; Miyazaki and, xiii–xiv, 14–17, 26–29, 40–41, 49, 53, 90–91, 160; *Nausicaä* and, 181; *Nausicaä* manga and, 160, 175; *Porco Rosso* and, 29, 142–143, 146–149, 152–153, 181; *Princess Mononoke* and, 31; *Spirited Away* and, 200, 213; Takahata and, xiv, 53, 78; *Wind Rises* and, 249–251
*Pom Poko* (1994), 215
*Ponyo* (2008), 229–245; animals and, 233–234, 244; animation and, 231, 243; children and, 14, 47, 84, 231–232, 236, 239, 244, 245; compared to *Conan*, 230; compared to *Howl*, 216, 244; compared to *Kiki*, 232, 243–244; compared to *Nausicaä*, 84, 232, 244; compared to *Spirited Away*, 242–243; compared to *Totoro*, 111, 243; compared to *Wind Rises*, 244; culture and, 243; curses and, 6, 220; families and, 23, 230; gender and, 27, 238, 243; humanity and, 231, 242, 244; inspiration for, 229–231, 234, 236–237; Japan and, 239–240, 263; love and, 230, 232,
238; magic and, 231, 233, 236, 244; Miyazaki on, 232–233, 238; morals and, 243; mothers and, 231, 239; nature and, 232, 242–244; otherness and, 111, 244; reception of, 233, 243; religion and, 237, 240–242; ruin and, 8, 230–232, 237, 239, 243; setting of, 232, 242; Shibuya on, 232–233; symbolism and, 239, 245; technology and, 236; trauma and, 237, 244; tropes and, 244
*Porco Rosso* (1992), 140–157; animals and, 149–153; animation and, 18, 146; *Casablanca* and, 140–157; compared to *Cagliostro*, 59, 67; compared to *Kiki*, 148; compared to *Laputa*, 148; compared to *Princess Mononoke*, 81; compared to *Spirited Away*, 149; compared to *Totoro*, 148; compared to *Wind Rises*, 251–253, 256; curses and, 6, 220; gender and, 32, 67, 146, 154–156; inspiration for, 141–142, 146–147, 152–153, 161, 273n1; love and, 148, 156; making of, 144–146; manga and, 149; Miyazaki on, 149; morals and, 146; otherness and, 153; politics and, 29, 142–143, 146–149, 152–153, 181; reception of, 148; setting of, 140–142; sexuality and, 25, 154, 272n20; Shibuya on, 148–149, 154; Suzuki and, 145; symbolism and, 149, 154–155; technology and, 146; trauma and, 146, 149–150, 153; utopia and, 156–157; war and, 18, 143, 148, 154
*Princess Mononoke* (1997), 176–194; animals and, 182–183, 186, 190, 193; animation and, 186; children and,

14; compared to *Cagliostro*, 177; compared to *Conan*, 177; compared to *Howl*, 219, 220, 224; compared to *Nausicaä*, 177, 181, 193; compared to *Porco Rosso*, 81; compared to *Spirited Away*, 195–196, 200, 207; compared to *Totoro*, 111; compared to *Wind Rises*, 250; curses and, 6, 177, 182, 186, 194, 220; emotions and, 183, 190, 192–193; gender and, 27, 183–184; humanity and, xiii, 177, 181–185, 188–189, 191; illness and, 184; inspiration for, xv, xvi, 180, 182–184, 187, 189; Japan and, 183–184; making of, 178–179, 182–183, 210, 275n3; Miyazaki on, 184–185, 275–276n10; morals and, 175, 177, 182, 183–187, 190–191; nature and, xiii, 78, 176–177, 181–194; otherness and, 111, 187–191; politics and, 31; reception of, xiii, 177, 179–180, 275n1, 275nn10–11; ruin and, xiii, 176, 181–182, 186, 193–194, 230; setting of, 177–178; spirits and, 43, 187; Suzuki and, 178–180, 183, 275n12; symbolism and, 182–183, 188–190, 194; Takahata and, 185; technology and, 182; trauma and, 6; tropes and, 183–185, 192; utopia and, 100; war and, 176–177, 182

*Princess Mononoke: The First Story* (Miyazaki), 260, 263–264

*Puella Magi Madoka Magica* (2011), 8

"A Record of the Battle to Make *Nausicaä*" (Katsukawa), 72

Religion: animism and, xii, 7, 75, 78, 84, 163, 173–176, 244; Buddhism, 6, 73, 80, 84, 114, 163, 237, 240–241; Christianity, 7, 84, 158, 160, 163, 173, 175; Japan and, 240; *Nausicaä* and, 71, 79–80, 84, 269n5; *Nausicaä* manga and, 163–164, 166, 170, 173–175; *Ponyo* and, 237, 240–242; Shamanism, 160, 164–168, 173; Shintoism, 7, 84, 90, 109, 118, 240–241; Taoism, 110, 163; *Totoro* and, 109–110; Zoroastrianism, 7. *See also* Spirits

"Ride of the Valkyries" (Wagner), 234

Romance. *See* Love

Rowling, J. K., xii, 5

Ruin and apocalypse: animation and, xi; *Cagliostro* and, xii, 55, 58, 66; *Conan* and, 53–54, 56; *Howl* and, 8, 227; Japan and, 7–8, 14, 77, 181, 232; *Laputa* and, 98–99; Miyazaki and, xiii, 7–9, 14–15, 49, 77–78, 262; nature and, 6–7; *Nausicaä* and, 74, 75, 77; *Nausicaä* manga and, 159, 162, 168, 170; *Ponyo* and, 8, 230–232, 237, 239, 243; *Princess Mononoke* and, xiii, 176, 181–182, 186, 193–194, 230; *Spirited Away* and, 200; *Wind Rises* and, 1, 257

Said, Edward, 231

*Sailor Moon* (1992), 33–34

Saito, Minako, 275n10

*Sally the Witch* (1966), 126

Sands-O'Connor, Karen, 262–263

*Sanshiro* (Sōseki), 128

Satō (Miyazaki's teacher), 29–30

Sayama incident, 120

*The Secret World of Arietty* (2010), 262

*Seven Samurai* (Kurosawa), xvi

Sexuality: *Cagliostro* and, 25, 57, 67; *Laputa* and, 86; Miyazaki and, 25; *Porco Rosso* and, 25, 154, 272n20; *Spirited Away* and, 208; *Wind Rises* and, 255

Shamanism, 160, 164–168, 173

Shaw, Scott, 70, 77

Shibuya, Yōichi: on Miyazaki, xv, 232–233, 238, 262; on *Nausicaä*, 174; on *Ponyo*, 232–233; on *Porco Rosso*, 148–149, 154; on *Spirited Away*, 209, 211; on *Wind Rises*, 246, 249, 259

Shimamoto, Sumi, 71

Shimizu, Masashi, 119–120, 277n21

*Shinkokinshū* (13th-century poetry collection), 99

Shintoism, 7, 84, 90, 109, 118, 240–241

*Shōjo* (young girls), 27, 52, 67–68, 87, 126, 130, 143, 222

*Snow Queen* (1957), 32, 275n9

Sōseki, Natsume, xvi, 3, 5–6, 229, 269n11, 278n1, 278n10

*Space Battleship Yamato* (1974), 8, 74

Spells. *See* Curses

*Spirited Away* (2001), 195–211; animals and, 149, 198–199, 206, 231; animation and, 196, 203–204; childhood and, 196, 211; children and, 84; compared to *Cagliostro*, 69; compared to *Howl*, 212, 219–221; compared to *Kiki*, 199; compared to *Nausicaä*, 84; compared to *Ponyo*, 242–243; compared to *Porco Rosso*, 149; compared to *Princess Mononoke*, 195–196, 200, 207; compared to *Totoro*, 107, 196, 198–199, 201; culture and, 197, 200–201, 203–204, 207; curses and, 26, 198, 220; emotion and, 196–197; gender and, 69; Ghibli and, xviii, 196, 201, 213, 227; illness and, 206–208; inspiration for, 7, 196–197, 201, 210–211, 230; Japan and, 201, 263; making of, 195, 197, 204–205, 209–210, 213; Miyazaki on, 196–197, 204–205, 209–210; morals and, 200–202, 211; mothers and, 277n21; nature and, 7, 26, 200–201; politics and, 200, 213; reception of, 180, 196, 201, 212–213; ruin and, 200; sexuality and, 208; Shibuya on, 209, 211; spirits and, 6, 107, 196, 198; Suzuki and, xviii, 196, 204, 208, 213–214; symbolism and, 149, 199–200, 207–208, 212; trauma and, 198–199, 209

Spirits: Miyazaki and, 7, 32, 85; *Nausicaä* and, 85; *Nausicaä* manga and, 160, 173; *Princess Mononoke* and, 43, 187; *Spirited Away* and, 6, 107, 196, 198; *Totoro* and, 7, 107–108, 113, 119. *See also* Religion

Spyri, Johanna, 48

*Starting Point* (Miyazaki), xv

Steampunk, 89

Sugita, Shunsuke, xv, 57, 173, 226, 233, 244–245, 267n22, 272n8

Sumikura, Yoshiki, 59–60

Suzuki, Toshio: animation and, 233; Ghibli and, xiv, xvii, 15, 61, 90–91, 135, 144, 179; *Kiki* and, 123, 129; Miyazaki and, xv, 15, 30, 135, 238, 260; *Nausicaä*

and, 70, 91; *Porco Rosso* and, 145; *Princess Mononoke* and, 178–180, 183, 275n12; *Spirited Away* and, xviii, 196, 204, 208, 213–214; *Totoro* and, 107, 110; *Wind Rises* and, 251, 257–259
Sweden, Miyazaki's travels to, 45–46
Swift, Jonathan, 36, 88
Symbolism: *Cagliostro* and, 59–60; *Howl* and, 212; *Kiki* and, 130–131, 133–135; *Laputa* and, 97–99; Miyazaki and, xiii; *Nausicaä* and, 71, 75, 79–80, 84–85, 158–175; *Nausicaä* manga and, 159–175; *Ponyo* and, 239, 245; *Porco Rosso* and, 149, 154–155; *Princess Mononoke* and, 182–183, 188–190, 194; *Spirited Away* and, 149, 199–200, 207–208, 212; *Totoro* and, 22–23, 111, 114–115, 119–121; *Wind Rises* and, 259. *See also* Tropes

Takahashi, Minoru, 275n10
Takahata, Isao: animation and, 18, 35, 41–44, 102, 144, 215, 225; *Conan* and, 51, 53; Ghibli and, xiii, 34, 90–91, 215; *Kiki* and, 125; *Laputa* and, 91; Miyazaki and, xvi, 15, 21, 30, 34–35, 44–49, 262; nature and, 78; *Nausicaä* and, 71–72; politics and, xiv, 53, 78; *Princess Mononoke* and, 185; war and, 3
Talbot, Margaret, xviii
Tale of Kasa Jizō, 113–114
*Tales from Earthsea* (2006), 238, 262
*The Tales of Hoffman* (Offenbach), 263
Tama Zenshōen, 184

Tanaka, Shinichi, 107–108, 272n17
Taoism, 110, 163
Tarkovsky, Andrei, xvi
Tateno, Hitomi, 61
Technology: animation and, 96, 233; *Cagliostro* and, 64–66; Japan and, 96; *Kiki* and, 130, 138; *Laputa* and, 87–90, 95–99; Miyazaki and, 2, 16, 18–19, 37–39, 49, 261; *Nausicaä* and, xi, 76; *Nausicaä* manga and, 162, 174–175; *Ponyo* and, 236; *Porco Rosso* and, 146; *Princess Mononoke* and, 182; *Wind Rises* and, xii, 20, 247, 256, 257–258
*The Tempest* (Shakespeare), 229, 231, 236, 244–245
Tennyson, Alfred, 212
Thornber, Karen, 275n2
Todorov, Tzvetan, 110, 117
Tōei Animation, 33–40, 44–45, 61, 68, 90, 126
Tōhoku earthquake (2011), xiii, 232, 246, 262
Tokuma, Yasuyoshi, 179
Tokuma Shoten (company), 179
Tolkien, J. R. R., xii, 4–5
*Tom's Midnight Garden* (Pearce), 11, 31
Topcraft (company), 71, 91, 123
*Totoro.* See *My Neighbor Totoro*
Totoro's Forest, 105
Trauma: *Conan* and, 54; Ghibli and, 3; *Howl* and, 215–216; Japan and, 10, 108–109, 181, 232; *Laputa* and, 99; Miyazaki and, 3–5, 8, 12–13, 54, 149–150; *Nausicaä* manga and, 173; *Ponyo* and, 237, 244;

Trauma (*continued*)
  *Porco Rosso* and, 146, 149–150, 153; *Princess Mononoke* and, 6; *Spirited Away* and, 198–199, 209; *Totoro* and, 105–109, 116, 118; *Wind Rises* and, 5, 255
*Treasure Island* (Stevenson), 89
Tropes: *Cagliostro* and, 66–67; fairy tales and, 34, 67, 126–128, 132, 196–198, 217–218, 252–254; folklore and, 125–126, 217, 242–243; *Kiki* and, 126–128, 138; *Laputa* and, 88, 92, 94–97; *Nausicaä* and, 81; *Nausicaä* manga and, 172; *Ponyo* and, 244; *Princess Mononoke* and, 183–185, 192; *Totoro* and, 101–102, 119; *Wind Rises* and, 251–252, 255. *See also* Symbolism
*Turning Point* (Miyazaki), xv

Ueno, Toshiya, xvii
*Up on Poppy Hill* (2011), 262
Urashima Taro legend, 242
Utopia: *Conan* and, 99; Ghibli and, xvii; *Howl* and, 212, 228; *Laputa* and, 86, 94, 96, 98–99; Miyazaki and, xvii, 14, 100, 262, 263; *Nausicaä* and, 82, 99–100; *Nausicaä* manga and, 167, 171–172, 175; *Porco Rosso* and, 156–157; *Princess Mononoke* and, 100; *Totoro* and, 102–103, 106, 120–121

Verne, Jules, xii, 89

Wales, Miyazaki's travels to, 90–91
*WALL-E* (2008), 96
Wang, Ban, 119
War: *Howl* and, 213, 215, 217, 223, 225; Japan and, 1–4, 14, 148; *Laputa* and, 97–99; Miyazaki and, xiii–xiv, 1–4, 10–14, 16, 19–20, 146–148; *Nausicaä* and, 76; *Nausicaä* manga and, 163; *Porco Rosso* and, 18, 143, 148, 154; *Princess Mononoke* and, 176–177, 182; Takahata and, 3; *Totoro* and, 272n23; trauma and, 3–4; *Wind Rises* and, 1–2, 20, 246–251, 254, 256
*War Without Mercy* (Dower), 1–2
Western worldview, 110, 160, 173–175
*Where Now Are the Dreams of Youth?* (Ozu), 24
*Where the Wild Things Are* (Sendak), 272n17
*Whisper of the Heart* (1995), 215
Whitley, David, 188
*The Wind Rises* (2013), 246–259; animation and, 64, 248; compared to *Cagliostro,* 64, 255; compared to *Howl,* 216; compared to *Ponyo,* 244; compared to *Porco Rosso,* 251–253, 256; compared to *Princess Mononoke,* 250; culture and, 3, 250–251; families and, 23–24, 251, 257; illness and, 9, 254; inspiration for, xvi, 3, 70, 246–248, 251–253, 255; Japan and, xii, 258, 263; love and, 9, 247; making of, 246–249; manga and, 255–257; Miyazaki on, 246, 249, 258–259; morals and, 175, 250; nature and, 2,

11; politics and, 249–251; reception of, 249–250, 252–253, 255; ruin and, 1, 257; setting of, 24, 246–247, 251–252; sexuality and, 255; Shibuya on, 246, 249, 259; Suzuki and, 251, 257–259; symbolism and, 259; technology and, xii, 20, 247, 256, 257–258; trauma and, 5, 255; tropes and, 251–252, 255; war and, 1–2, 20, 246–251, 254, 256

*The Wind Rises* (Hori), xvi, 9, 253

*Winnie-the-Pooh* (1972), 31, 46

*The Wizard of Oz* (1939), 136, 209

Yakushima (island), xv, 189, 230

Yasuda, Michiyo, 41, 45, 275n3

Yoshioka, Shiro, 201

Zero (plane), 2, 8, 247–252, 255–258

Zoroastrianism, 7

Zuiyo Eizō Studios, 48